First World War
and Army of Occupation
War Diary
France, Belgium and Germany

15 DIVISION
46 Infantry Brigade
Highland Light Infantry
10/11th Battalion
1 May 1916 - 31 May 1918

WO95/1952/1

The Naval & Military Press Ltd
www.nmarchive.com
Published in association with The National Archives

Published by

The Naval & Military Press Ltd

Unit 10 Ridgewood Industrial Park,

Uckfield, East Sussex,

TN22 5QE England

Tel: +44 (0) 1825 749494

www.naval-military-press.com

www.nmarchive.com

This diary has been reprinted in facsimile from the original. Any imperfections are inevitably reproduced and the quality may fall short of modern type and cartographic standards.

© Crown Copyright
Images reproduced by permission of The National Archives, London, England, 2015.

Contents

Document type	Place/Title	Date From	Date To
Heading	1952/1 10/11 Battalion Highland Light Infantry		
Heading	15th Division 46th Infy Bde 10/11th Bn High'd Lt Infy. May 1916-May 1918 from 10 Bn 9 Div 28 Bde. To 14 Div. 43 Bde As 10 Battalion		
War Diary	Le Bizet	01/05/1916	03/05/1916
War Diary	Le Touquet	04/05/1916	08/05/1916
War Diary	Le Bizet	09/05/1916	13/05/1916
War Diary	Le Bizet	14/05/1916	14/05/1916
War Diary	Bethune	14/05/1916	14/05/1916
War Diary	Fouquereuil	14/05/1916	16/05/1916
War Diary	Brigade Reserve	17/05/1916	17/05/1916
War Diary	Hulluch Section	18/05/1916	18/05/1916
War Diary	Quarries Subsection	18/05/1916	25/05/1916
War Diary	Brigade Reserve	26/05/1916	27/05/1916
War Diary	Sailly Labourse	28/05/1916	31/05/1916
Heading	War Diary Of 10/11 B (S) Bn Highland L. Infantry From 1st June/16 To 30 June/16		
War Diary	Sailly Labourse	01/06/1916	04/06/1916
War Diary	Hohenzollern Sector	05/06/1916	20/06/1916
War Diary	Bethune	20/06/1916	27/06/1916
War Diary	Brigade Reserve	28/06/1916	29/06/1916
War Diary	Right Subsector	30/06/1916	30/06/1916
Heading	War Diary 10th/11th Highland Light Infantry From 1st July 1916 To 31st July 1916		
War Diary	Right Subsection	01/07/1916	01/07/1916
War Diary	Hulluch Section	02/07/1916	06/07/1916
War Diary	Bde Reserve	07/07/1916	07/07/1916
War Diary	Hulluch Section	08/07/1916	08/07/1916
War Diary	Centre Sub-Section	09/07/1916	09/07/1916
War Diary	Hulluch Section	10/07/1916	13/07/1916
War Diary	Centre Sub Section Hulluch Section	14/07/1916	14/07/1916
War Diary	Labourse	15/07/1916	21/07/1916
War Diary	Lapugnoy	22/07/1916	22/07/1916
War Diary	Hestrus	23/07/1916	26/07/1916
War Diary	Blangerval	27/07/1916	27/07/1916
War Diary	Villers L'Hopital	28/07/1916	31/07/1916
Miscellaneous	Account Of Minor Operations By 10/11th Bn. Highland Light Infantry, On Night Of 4/5th July 1916 Appendix A	05/07/1916	05/07/1916
Heading	46th Brigade. 15th Division. 10/11th Battalion Highland Light Infantry August 1916 Appendices attached Reports on Operations 14th 17th/18th Aug.		
War Diary	Montonvillers	01/08/1916	04/08/1916
War Diary	Molliens Au Bois	05/08/1916	05/08/1916
War Diary	Franvillers	06/08/1916	07/08/1916
War Diary	Bde Reserve	08/08/1916	08/08/1916
War Diary	Martinpuich Area	09/08/1916	13/08/1916
War Diary	Left Sub-Section Martinpuich Area	14/08/1916	18/08/1916
War Diary	Reserve In Shelter Wood	19/08/1916	19/08/1916
War Diary	Albert	20/08/1916	27/08/1916

Type	Description	Start	End
War Diary	Bde. Support Bazentin Area	28/08/1916	29/08/1916
War Diary	In Left: Sub Section Bazentin Area	30/08/1916	30/08/1916
War Diary	Left. Sub-Section	31/08/1916	31/08/1916
Miscellaneous	Report On Bombing Attack By 10/11th High. L.I. on Switch Linn on 14.8.16	14/08/1916	14/08/1916
Miscellaneous	Evidence of R.E. Who Accompanied 10/11th High. L.I. In Attack on Morning of 14th Aug.	14/08/1916	14/08/1916
Miscellaneous	Headquarters, 15th Division	18/08/1916	18/08/1916
Miscellaneous	Preliminary Report on Operations carried out against German Switch Line 17th-18th August.	18/08/1916	18/08/1916
Miscellaneous	10/11th (S) Bn Highland Light Infantry Report On Operations Against The German Switch Line 17/18 Aug. 1916	21/08/1916	21/08/1916
Heading	War Diary for September 1916 10/11th Bn. Highland L.I.		
War Diary	Bde. Reserve Lear Bazentin Le Petit	01/09/1916	02/09/1916
War Diary	Left Sub Section	03/09/1916	04/09/1916
War Diary	Bde Reserve	05/09/1916	05/09/1916
War Diary	Albert	06/09/1916	12/09/1916
War Diary	Gourlay Tr.	13/09/1916	14/09/1916
War Diary	In Action Martinpuich area	15/09/1916	15/09/1916
War Diary	Gourlay Trench.	16/09/1916	16/09/1916
War Diary	Martinpuich	17/09/1916	17/09/1916
War Diary	Scotts Redoubt	18/09/1916	18/09/1916
War Diary	Lavieville	19/09/1916	19/09/1916
War Diary	Behencourt	20/09/1916	30/09/1916
Miscellaneous	Appendix "A" 10/11th (S) B'n. Highland Light Infantry. Report on The Recent Operations 13th to 17th September. 1916	17/09/1916	17/09/1916
Miscellaneous	10/11th. (S). Bn. Highland Light Infantry. Report On Recent Operations 13th-15th. September, 1916	13/09/1916	13/09/1916
Miscellaneous	A Form. Messages And Signals		
Heading	War Diary for October 1916 10/11th H.L.I.		
War Diary	Albert	01/10/1916	09/10/1916
War Diary	Lozenge Wood	10/10/1916	14/10/1916
War Diary	26th Ave Bde. Support	15/10/1916	16/10/1916
War Diary	In Support Le Sars Area	17/10/1916	17/10/1916
War Diary	In front line Le Sars Area	18/10/1916	19/10/1916
War Diary	Lozenge Wood Camp	20/10/1916	24/10/1916
War Diary	St. Front line Le Sars Area	25/10/1916	26/10/1916
War Diary	Martinpuich	27/10/1916	31/10/1916
Heading	War Diary November 1916 10/11th H.L.I.		
War Diary	Scott's Redoubt near Contalmaison	01/11/1916	01/11/1916
War Diary	Millencourt	02/11/1916	05/11/1916
War Diary	Henencourt	06/11/1916	06/11/1916
War Diary	Baizieux	07/11/1916	15/11/1916
War Diary	Naours	16/11/1916	27/11/1916
War Diary	Warloy	28/11/1916	30/11/1916
Heading	War Diary 10th/11th H.L.I. From 1st December 1916 to 31st December 1916		
War Diary	Warloy	01/12/1916	01/12/1916
War Diary	Becourt	02/12/1916	14/12/1916
War Diary	Shelter Wood North	14/12/1916	14/12/1916
War Diary	Sevenelms M.28.d.3.6	15/12/1916	15/12/1916
War Diary	Seven Elms	16/12/1916	17/12/1916
War Diary	M-22 of 6/1/2, a.	18/12/1916	19/12/1916

War Diary	Pioneer Camp	20/12/1916	21/12/1916
War Diary	M. 22. d. 6/1/2. O.	22/12/1916	23/12/1916
War Diary	Scots Redoubt South	24/12/1916	30/12/1916
War Diary	26th Avenue	31/12/1916	31/12/1916
Heading	10/11th Battn The Highland Light Infy January. 1917		
War Diary	Acid Drops	01/01/1917	02/01/1917
War Diary	26th Avenue	02/01/1917	03/01/1917
War Diary	Scots Redoubt South	04/01/1917	08/01/1917
War Diary	Seven Elms M. 28d. 3.6. Quevaucourt 1/10000	09/01/1917	10/01/1917
War Diary	Rt. Bn. Support area (Seven Elms)	10/01/1917	10/01/1917
War Diary	Pioneer Camp	11/01/1917	12/01/1917
War Diary	Bde. Rt. Sub Section.	12/01/1917	13/01/1917
War Diary	Bde Rt. Sub Section of Divl front	13/01/1917	16/01/1917
War Diary	Cinque Ports. Camp	17/01/1917	20/01/1917
War Diary	Villa. Camp	20/01/1917	22/01/1917
War Diary	Acid Drop Camp	22/01/1917	24/01/1917
War Diary	26th Avenue	25/01/1917	28/01/1917
War Diary	Cinque Ports. Camp.	29/01/1917	30/01/1917
War Diary	Albert	31/01/1917	31/01/1917
Heading	10/11th Batt'n The Highland Light Infy February, 1917		
War Diary	Albert	01/02/1917	04/02/1917
War Diary	Warloy	05/02/1917	13/02/1917
War Diary	Beauval	14/02/1917	14/02/1917
War Diary	Outrebois	15/02/1917	15/02/1917
War Diary	Fortel	16/02/1917	16/02/1917
War Diary	Ambrines	17/02/1917	23/02/1917
War Diary	Duisans	24/02/1917	26/02/1917
War Diary	Arras	27/02/1917	28/02/1917
Heading	War Diary for 10/11th Highland Light Inf From 1st March 1917 to 31st March 1917		
War Diary	Arras	01/03/1917	03/03/1917
War Diary	Habarcq	04/03/1917	10/03/1917
War Diary	Izel-Lez-Hameau	11/03/1917	19/03/1917
War Diary	Arras	20/03/1917	30/03/1917
War Diary	Noyellette	31/03/1917	31/03/1917
Heading	10/11th (S) Bn. High. L.I. War Diary April 1917 Vol 2		
War Diary	Noyellette	01/04/1917	04/04/1917
War Diary	Arras	05/04/1917	09/04/1917
War Diary	Feuchy	10/04/1917	10/04/1917
War Diary	Monchy	11/04/1917	12/04/1917
War Diary	Arras	13/04/1917	14/04/1917
War Diary	Duisans	15/04/1917	21/04/1917
War Diary	Arras	22/04/1917	22/04/1917
War Diary	Tilloy	23/04/1917	24/04/1917
War Diary	Brown Line	25/04/1917	27/04/1917
War Diary	Arras	28/04/1917	28/04/1917
War Diary	Duisans	29/04/1917	30/04/1917
Operation(al) Order(s)	10/11th (S) B'n. Highland Light Infantry. Operation Order No. 78	03/04/1917	03/04/1917
Operation(al) Order(s)	10/11th. (S) Battalion Highland Light Infantry Correction and Addenda to Operation Order No. 78	07/04/1917	07/04/1917
Operation(al) Order(s)	10/11th. (S). Bn. Highland Light Infantry. Operation Order No. 78. Appendix A.	03/04/1917	03/04/1917
Miscellaneous	46th Infantry Brigade. Appendix B	14/04/1917	14/04/1917
Operation(al) Order(s)	10/11th. (S). Bn. Highland Light Infantry. Operation Order No. 81 Appendix C.	22/04/1917	22/04/1917

Type	Description	From	To
Miscellaneous	Operations 1917. 2nd. Phase. Report On Operations (23-4-1917-26-4-1917) Appendix. D.	23/04/1917	23/04/1917
Heading	10/11th (S) Bn. High L.I. War Diary May 1917		
War Diary	Duisans	01/05/1917	07/05/1917
War Diary	Barly	08/05/1917	21/05/1917
War Diary	Sus-St-Leger	22/05/1917	22/05/1917
War Diary	Fortel	23/05/1917	23/05/1917
War Diary	Le Ponchel	24/05/1917	31/05/1917
Heading	Cover for Documents. Nature of Enclosures. 10/11th (S) Bn. High L.I. War Diary for June 1917		
War Diary	Le Ponchel	01/06/1917	30/06/1917
Heading	Cover for Documents. Nature of Enclosures. 10/11th (S). Bn. High L.I. War Diary July 1917		
War Diary	Ecole Ypres	01/07/1917	01/07/1917
War Diary	Toronto Camp.	02/07/1917	02/07/1917
War Diary	Watou	03/07/1917	08/07/1917
War Diary	Point Du Jour	09/07/1917	21/07/1917
War Diary	Winnezeele	22/07/1917	22/07/1917
War Diary	Watou	23/07/1917	23/07/1917
War Diary	H 16 C. 2.2	24/07/1917	31/07/1917
Operation(al) Order(s)	10/11th. (S). Bn. Highland Light Infantry. Operation Order No. 94 Appendix A	15/07/1917	15/07/1917
Miscellaneous	10/11th. (S). Bn. Highland Light Infantry. Report On Operations 31st July-1st. August. 1917 Appendix B	05/08/1917	05/08/1917
Miscellaneous	Appendix II. Dumps. Carrying Parties and Equipment.		
Miscellaneous	Appendix III. Personnel Left Out of Action		
Operation(al) Order(s)	10/11th (S). B'n. Highland Light Infantry. Addenda to Operation Order No. 94. of 15.7.1917	24/07/1917	24/07/1917
Miscellaneous	Appendix VI.		
Miscellaneous	Appendix V. Prisoners of War.		
Miscellaneous	Appendix I. Medical Arrangements.		
Map	15th Division. Map No. 2. Scale-1: 10,000-		
Map	15th-Division. Map No. 02. Scale. 1:10,000		
Heading	10/11 (S) Bn. High L.I. War Diary For August 1917 Vol 26		
War Diary	In Action	01/08/1917	02/08/1917
War Diary	Winnezeele	03/08/1917	16/08/1917
War Diary	Ypres	17/08/1917	17/08/1917
War Diary	Square Farm	18/08/1917	21/08/1917
War Diary	Ypres	22/08/1917	22/08/1917
War Diary	Ecole Ypres	23/08/1917	23/08/1917
War Diary	H17a.0.9	24/08/1917	24/08/1917
War Diary	H. 18. C. 0.8	25/08/1917	25/08/1917
War Diary	O.G. Area	26/08/1917	26/08/1917
War Diary	Pommern Castle	27/08/1917	29/08/1917
War Diary	O.G. Area	30/08/1917	30/08/1917
War Diary	Camp at H17 Q.O.G.	31/08/1917	31/08/1917
Heading	War Diary For Sept 1917 10/11 High L.I.		
War Diary	Wemaers Cappel	01/09/1917	01/09/1917
War Diary	Agnez Les Duisans	02/09/1917	06/09/1917
War Diary	Blangy	07/09/1917	07/09/1917
War Diary	Pelves Section	08/09/1917	15/09/1917
War Diary	Scots Valley	16/09/1917	23/09/1917
War Diary	Blangy Park	24/09/1917	30/09/1917
Heading	10/11 High L.I. War Diary for October 1917		
War Diary	Blangy Park.	01/10/1917	01/10/1917

War Diary	Rt. Bn. Roeux Sector	02/10/1917	09/10/1917
War Diary	Stirling Camp H. 13 d. 8.7	10/10/1917	15/10/1917
War Diary	Stirling Camp	16/10/1917	17/10/1917
War Diary	Arras	18/10/1917	25/10/1917
War Diary	Left Bn. Pelves Sector	26/10/1917	31/10/1917
Heading	10/11 (S) Bn. High. L.I. War. Diary. Nov. 1917		
War Diary	Left. Bn. Pelves Sector	01/11/1917	02/11/1917
War Diary	Wilderness Camp	03/11/1917	10/11/1917
War Diary	Arras	11/11/1917	18/11/1917
War Diary	Right Battalion Roeux Sector	19/11/1917	26/11/1917
War Diary	H 23 C.	27/11/1917	29/11/1917
War Diary	Brigade Reserve H.16 b.	30/11/1917	30/11/1917
Miscellaneous	Warning Order.	15/11/1917	15/11/1917
Miscellaneous	10/11th (S) Battn. Highland Light Infantry. 10/11th High. L.A. Addendum no. 1 to A/334 of 16.11.17	15/11/1917	15/11/1917
Heading	War Diary 10/11th High L.I. December 1917		
War Diary	Reserve Right Sub-Sector. H 16 8.7.6	01/12/1917	03/12/1917
War Diary	Left Division Right Area Sector H 24 d 8.8	04/12/1917	08/12/1917
War Diary	In Reserve Billets Bn. H.Q. at 18 Rue Baudimont Arras	09/12/1917	17/12/1917
War Diary	Left Subsector Left. Sector XVII Corps. Bn. H.Q. H. 6.6.3.3	18/12/1917	23/12/1917
War Diary	In Support H 11 C.	24/12/1917	25/12/1917
War Diary	Centre Sub-Sector	26/12/1917	27/12/1917
War Diary	Left Subsector Bn. H.Q. H 6 d. O.O.	28/12/1917	29/12/1917
War Diary	Reserve H 6 to 16	30/12/1917	31/12/1917
Heading	10/11th (S) Bn. High. L.I. War Diary For January 1918 to 120th Bde 1-2-18		
War Diary	Left Support Bn. Left Bde Left Div XVII Corps. Gavrelle Switch	01/01/1918	01/01/1918
War Diary	Arras	02/01/1918	02/01/1918
War Diary	Berneville	03/01/1918	01/02/1918
War Diary	Mory	02/02/1918	06/02/1918
War Diary	Right Subsection Left Brigade 40th ?Division Bn. ?H.U. Sheet 516 S U 25.6.8.1	06/02/1918	11/02/1918
War Diary	Ervillers	12/02/1918	16/02/1918
War Diary	Blairville	16/02/1918	21/02/1918
War Diary	York Line Mercatel	21/02/1918	28/02/1918
Heading	40th Division. 120th Infantry Brigade War Diary 10th/11th. Battalion Highland Light Infantry March 1918		
War Diary	Berles-au-Bois	01/03/1918	12/03/1918
War Diary	Ervillers	13/03/1918	26/03/1918
War Diary	Adinfer	27/03/1918	27/03/1918
War Diary	Warluzel	28/03/1918	29/03/1918
War Diary	Magnicourt En. Comte	30/03/1918	30/03/1918
War Diary	Nouveau Monde	31/03/1918	31/03/1918
Miscellaneous	10/11th (S) Battn. Highland Light Infantry. Report On Operations Appendix A	21/03/1918	21/03/1918
Heading	40th Division. 120th Infantry Brigade 10th/11th Battalion The Highland Light Infantry April 1918		
War Diary	Rouge De Bout H 31 a. 75.80 36 N.W.	01/04/1918	04/04/1918
War Diary	Killay Hall N2 d.30.30	05/04/1918	06/04/1918
War Diary	Estaires Camp at L. 23.b	07/04/1918	08/04/1918
War Diary	In Action.	09/04/1918	11/04/1918
War Diary	Strazeele	12/04/1918	12/04/1918
War Diary	Pradelles	13/04/1918	13/04/1918

Type	Description	From	To
War Diary	Zuytpeene	14/04/1918	14/04/1918
War Diary	Tatinghem	14/04/1918	21/04/1918
War Diary	Val D'Acquin	21/04/1918	30/04/1918
Miscellaneous	10/11th (S) Bn. Highland Light Infantry. Report on Operations Appendix "A"	09/04/1918	09/04/1918
Miscellaneous	List of Officer Casualties. Operations 9th to 13th April 1918	09/04/1918	09/04/1918
Heading	Letter from Major P.W. Jupe 10/11 H.L.I. (40 Div) See also diary 6/7 R. Sc. Fus. (Pi) (59 Div)		
Miscellaneous	Sheet 51.b. S.W. 1/20,000. 57. d. 1/40,000. to Lt.-Col. Forbes, D.S.O. 10/11th Battn. H.L.I.	02/04/1918	02/04/1918
Miscellaneous	Windwhistle, Freshfield, Lancashire. 8th November, 1926, The Secretary, Historical Section (Military Branch), London, E.C.4	08/11/1926	08/11/1926
Miscellaneous	Ref. 1918/M/33. Major P.W. Jupe, D.S.O., Windwhistle, Freshfield, Lancs.	18/01/1926	18/01/1926
Map	Sheet 57c		
Miscellaneous	Windwhistle, Freshfield, Lancashire. 15th April 1926	15/04/1926	15/04/1926
Heading	10/11th Highland Light Infantry War Diary For May 1918 Vol 36		
War Diary	Seninghem	01/05/1918	03/05/1918
War Diary	Watten	04/05/1918	09/05/1918
War Diary	Esquelbecq	10/05/1918	31/05/1918

1952/1
10/11 Battalion Highland
Light Infantry.

15T. DIVISION
46TH INFY BDE

10/11TH BN HIGH'D LT INFY.
MAY 1916 - MAY 1918

10 BN
From 9 DIV 28 BDE

To 14 DIV 43 BDE
AS 10 BATTALION

WAR DIARY
INTELLIGENCE SUMMARY.
(Erase heading not required.)

Army Form C. 2118.

Instructions regarding War Diaries and Intelligence Summaries are contained in F. S. Regs., Part II. and the Staff Manual respectively. Title pages will be prepared in manuscript.

Place	Date	Hour	Summary of Events and Information	Remarks and references to Appendices
	MAY			
LE BIZET	1/5/16		In rest billets	P.A.
"	2.5.16		In rest billets	P.A.
"	3.5.16	7.45p	Commenced relieving 6th K.O.S.B. in trenches at LE TOUQUET	P.A.
		9.30p	Relief complete	P.A.
LE TOUQUET	4.5.16		Situation Quiet	P.A.
	5.5.16		Situation Quiet	P.A.
	6.5.16		Situation Quiet	P.A.
	7.5.16		Situation Quiet	P.A.
	8.5.16	7.45p	Relief by 2nd Batt. 1st South African Infantry Bgde commenced	P.A.
		10 pm	Relief complete	P.A.
	9.5.16		In rest billets	P.A.
F BIZET	10.5.16		In Rest billets	P.A.
	11.5.16		In Rest billets	P.A.
	12.5.16		In Rest billets	P.A.
	13.5.16		In Rest billets. Received orders to move on 14th inst to BETHUNE to amalgamate with 10th H.L.I. & join 46 Bgde. 15th Division	P.A.

Army Form C. 2118.

WAR DIARY
or
INTELLIGENCE SUMMARY.
(Erase heading not required.)

Instructions regarding War Diaries and Intelligence Summaries are contained in F. S. Regs., Part II. and the Staff Manual respectively. Title pages will be prepared in manuscript.

Place	Date	Hour	Summary of Events and Information	Remarks and references to Appendices
LEBIZET	14.5.16	11 a.m.	Batth marched out of LEBIZET for STEENWERCK and entrained for BETHUNE, the Transport having left by road.	P.A.
BETHUNE		6 pm	Arrived BETHUNE and received orders to march to FOUQUEREUIL and billet there.	P.A.
FOUQUEREUIL		7.30 pm	Arrived in billets.	
	15.5.16	7 pm	Received Orders to Amalgamate with 10" Bttn. in yellow's dg	P.A.
	16.5.16	8.45 pm	to proceed to Trenches. Amalgamation commenced.	
		9.30 am	Fifty two Coy marched off for Trenches.	10/11 H.L.I.
		1.30 pm	Second two Coys 10/11 Bttn Marched off for Trenches.	
		5.30 pm	Relief complete Battalion was in Brigade Reserve in HULLUCH Section.	
Brigade Reserve	17.5.16		10/11 H.L.I. Major H. T. Col. R. H. Forbes took over command of 10/11 H.L.I. on amalgamation. In Brigade Reserve finding numerous working parties	P.A. P.A.
HULLUCH SECTION	18.5.16	9 am	Commenced relieving 5" HOSP of QUARRIES Subsection.	

Army Form C. 2118.

WAR DIARY
or
INTELLIGENCE SUMMARY.
(Erase heading not required.)

Instructions regarding War Diaries and Intelligence Summaries are contained in F. S. Regs. Part II. and the Staff Manual respectively. Title pages will be prepared in manuscript.

Place	Date	Hour	Summary of Events and Information	Remarks and references to Appendices
QUARRIES Subsector	18.5.16	11am	Relief complete. 10th Scottish Rifles on our right. 6th Camerons on our left.	
	19.5.16		Situation Normal. Enemy very quiet. Trench Mortars Active. Trenches in bad condition & mining on hill side very active.	
	20.5.16		Situation Normal. 2/Lt. M. Hutcheson & Lt. C.C. Rent killed.	
	21.5.16		Situation Normal.	
	22.5.16		Situation Normal.	
	23.5.16		Situation Normal.	
	24.5.16		Mining officer reported that enemy might be expected to blow a mine at any time in our front. All precaution were taken.	
	25.5.16		Relieved by 10th Scottish Rifles and proceeded such to Brigade Reserve Trench.	
Brigade Reserve	26.5.16		In Brigade Reserve	
	27.5.16		Relieved by 7th Camerons & proceeded to Rest billets in SAILLY LABOURSE.	
SAILLY LABOURSE	28.5.16		In Rest billets	

Army Form C. 2118

WAR DIARY
or
INTELLIGENCE SUMMARY

(Erase heading not required.)

Instructions regarding War Diaries and Intelligence Summaries are contained in F. S. Regs., Part II. and the Staff Manual respectively. Title Pages will be prepared in manuscript.

Place	Date	Hour	Summary of Events and Information	Remarks and references to Appendices
SAILLY LABOURSE	28.5.16	11pm	Received orders to be prepared to move at a few minutes notice	RA.
	29.5.16		In Rest billets. Finding working parties at night.	RA.
	30.5.16		In Rest billets	RA.
	31.5.16		In Rest billets.	RA.

R. Starke Lt. Col.
Cmdg 10/11 H.L.I.

Confidential

War Diary
of
10/11ᵗʰ (S) Bn Highland L. Infantry
from 1ˢᵗ June/16 to 30ᵗʰ June/16

WAR DIARY
or
INTELLIGENCE SUMMARY

Army Form C. 2118.

(Erase heading not required.)

Place	Date	Hour	Summary of Events and Information	Remarks and references to Appendices
SAILLY LA BOURSE	1st		In billets. Finding various working parties at night.	P.2.
	2nd		In billets.	P.2.
	3rd		In billets.	P.2.
	4th	9am	Battalion left billets for the Trenches to take over from 8th Seaforth in left Subsector of HOHENZOLLERN Sector	We also received various things in return of 7 S.M.M. gunners in attendance, 2 machine gun models, all the usual Very lights, alarm rockets, telephones & lines.
HOHENZOLLERN SECTOR		11am	Relief complete.	
	5th		Situation normal.	P.2.
	6th		Situation normal.	P.2.
	7th		Situation normal.	P.2.
	8th		Situation normal.	P.2.
	9th		Situation normal.	P.2.
	10th	9 a.m.	Relief by 7/8th A.&S.H. O.S.B. commenced	P.2.
		12 noon	Relief complete and Battalion went back to Brigade Reserve in Tarabs Rd. Numerous working & fatigue parties found.	
	11th		In Brigade Reserve.	
	12th	7.30 a.m.	Relief of 10th Scots Rifles in Centre Subsection commenced	
		10 a.m.	Relief complete.	
	13th		Situation normal. This sector was subjected to considerable shelling by enemy Minenwerfer.	P.2.
	14th		Situation normal.	P.2.
	15th		Situation normal.	P.2.
	16th		Situation normal.	P.2.
	17th		Situation normal. Finding carrying parties to take Gas Cylinders up to Trenches. Fatigue & carrying parties to take Gas Cylinders up to Trenches.	P.2.

WAR DIARY
or
INTELLIGENCE SUMMARY

Army Form C. 2118.

Place	Date	Hour	Summary of Events and Information	Remarks and references to Appendices
	18th	9am	Relief by 7/8 H.L.I. commenced	
		11am	Relief complete. Battalion moved into Brigade Reserve in Trenches. Finding carrying parties to take gun officers up to trenches.	P.S.
	19th		In Brigade Reserve	P.S.
	20th	12 noon	Relief by 13th Royal Scots commenced	
BETHUNE		1.45 pm	Relief complete. Battalion proceeded to billets in Ouplunque	
	21st		In billets	P.S.
	22nd		In billets. Finding various working parties	P.S.
	23rd		In billets	P.S.
	24th		In billets	P.S.
	25th		In billets. Two Coys moved to VERQUIGNEUL	P.S.
	26th		In billets	P.S.
	27th		In billets. Lewis Gun Section proceeded to trenches. 2/Lt N NEWMAN was killed while performing duties of Lewis Gun Officer	P.S.
Brigade Reserve	28th	8.30 am	Battalion left billets to relieve 9th Black Watch in Brigade Reserve to HULLUCH Sector	P.S.
		1pm	Relief complete	
	29th		In Brigade Reserve	P.S.
Right Subsector	30th	9pm	Commenced relief of 10 Sco. Rifles in Right Subsector	P.S.

J Combe Lt Col
Comdg 10/11 H.L.I.

C10/11 H.L.I.
Vol. 12

15/ Infantry

3 'L'
Sheets

CONFIDENTIAL

WAR DIARY

10th/11th HIGHLAND LIGHT INFANTRY

FROM
1st July 1916
TO
31st July 1916

Army Form C. 2118

WAR DIARY
or
INTELLIGENCE SUMMARY
(Erase heading not required.)

Instructions regarding War Diaries and Intelligence Summaries are contained in F.S. Regs., Part II. and the Staff Manual respectively. Title Pages will be prepared in manuscript.

Place	Date	Hour	Summary of Events and Information	Remarks and references to Appendices
Right Sub-Section HULLUCH Section	1.7.16		Situation quiet. Making arrangements and reconnoitering ground for proposed minor enterprise.	Apx.
	2.7.16		Situation normal. Our artillery cutting gaps in wire.	Apx.
	3.7.16		Situation normal. Final orders received from Brigade re minor enterprise to be carried out on night of 4/5th	Apx.
	4.7.16	11.55 pm	Raiding party left trenches. For details and result of raid please see Appendix A.	See Appendix A
	5.7.16		Situation normal	Apx.
		11 pm	The wires being personally cut off from along our front, at the same time bombarding enemy trenches. Enemy's retaliation was considerable.	Apx.
	6.7.16	9 am	Relief by 7/8th K.O.S.B. commenced	Apx.
		11.30 am	Relief completed. Battalion moved back to Bde. Reserve	
Bde Reserve HULLUCH Section	7.7.16		In Bde. Reserve. Finding working parties.	Apx.
	8.7.16	9 am	Relief of 10th Scottish Rifles in Centre Sub-section commenced.	Apx.
		11.15 am	Relief completed	
		8.30 pm	Enemy commenced heavy bombardment of left Company front.	
		9 pm	Bombardment became intense	
		9.30 pm	Enemy attempted to break our trenches but only succeeded in gaining an entrance in two places and was quickly ejected.	Apx.
Centre Sub-Section HULLUCH Section	9.7.16		Situation normal. Repairing our trenches which had been considerably damaged by enemy bombardment of previous evening	Apx.
	10.7.16		Situation normal. Our artillery carried out prepared short bombardments of enemy front.	Apx.
	11.7.16		Situation normal. Short bombardments continued.	Apx.
	12.7.16		Situation normal	Apx.
	13.7.16		Situation normal	Apx.

Army Form C. 2118

WAR DIARY
or
INTELLIGENCE SUMMARY
(Erase heading not required.)

Instructions regarding War Diaries and Intelligence summaries are contained in F. S. Regs., Part II. and the Staff Manual respectively. Title Pages will be prepared in manuscript.

Place	Date	Hour	Summary of Events and Information	Remarks and references to Appendices
Cambrin Sub Sector	14.7.16	12 noon	Relief by 6/7th R.S.F. commenced	9am
HULLUCH Sector		2.15 pm	Relief complete. Batt. moved to that billets in LABOURSE	9am
LABOURSE	15.7.16		In Hut billets	9am
	16.7.16		In Hut billets	9am
	17.7.16		In Hut billets	9am
	18.7.16		In Hut billets	9am
	19.7.16		In Hut billets	9am
	20.7.16		In Hut billets. Warned to be in readiness to move on morning of 21st	9am
	21.7.16	12.30 am	Received orders to proceed to billets in LAPUGNOY	9am
		10.30 am	Batt. marched out from LABOURSE	
		3.30 pm	Arrived at LAPUGNOY	
		6 pm	Received orders to continue march on following morning to HESTRUS	9am
LAPUGNOY	22.7.16	7.15 am	Marched out of billets. Received orders at MARLES LES MINES to proceed to HESTRUS	9am
		3 pm	Arrived HESTRUS	
HESTRUS	23.7.16		In billets	9am
	24.7.16		In billets	
	25.7.16		In billets. Received orders to continue march to BLANGERVAL	9am
	26.7.16	8.50 am	Marched out of billets	
		1.30 pm	Arrived at BLANGERVAL	
		8 pm	Received orders to continue to VILLERS L'HÔPITAL	
BLANGERVAL	27.7.16	7.30 am	Marched out of billets	9am
		12 noon	Arrived at VILLERS L'HÔPITAL	
		10.30 pm	Received orders to continue march to FIENVILLERS	

Army Form C. 2118

WAR DIARY
or
INTELLIGENCE SUMMARY
(Erase heading not required.)

Instructions regarding War Diaries and Intelligence Summaries are contained in F.S. Regs., Part II. and the Staff Manual respectively. Title Pages will be prepared in manuscript.

Place	Date	Hour	Summary of Events and Information	Remarks and references to Appendices
VILLERS L'HÔPITAL	28.7.16	7.30 am	Marched out 9 hours.	pm.
		12.30 pm	Arrived at FIENVILLERS. Two companies proceeded to billets at CANDAS.	
	29.7.16		In billets.	pm.
	30.7.16		In billets.	
		4.15 pm	Received orders to continued march to MONTONVILLERS	pm.
	31.7.16	6.10 am	Marched out 9 hours: 4.10 am	
			Arrived MONTONVILLERS 9.45 am	M.1.

A.J. Ingles
Lt. Col.
Cmdg 10/11 Nth'd

1875 Wt. W593/826 1,000,000 4/15 J.B.C. & A. A.D.S.S./Forms/C. 2118.

Appendix A

ACCOUNT OF MINOR OPERATIONS BY 10/11th Bn.
HIGHLAND LIGHT INFANTRY, ON NIGHT OF 4/5th
JULY 1916.

Strength of Parties.
"A" Party. 1 Officer, 2 N.C.Os., & 22 Men.
"B" Party. 1 Officer, 2 N.C.Os., & 22 Men.
"C" Party. 1 Officer, 3 N.C.Os., & 30 Men.
"D" Party. 1 Officer, 2 N.C.Os., & 16 Men.

"A" Party.

"A" Party left our Trenches at 5 Minutes before Zero time and getting successfully through our own wire, reorganized beyond. They then commenced crawling across towards Saphead at H.13.c.4½.1. Enemy were throwing up "Very" Lights on the left and firing Machine Gun from Saphead which delayed Party as they had to lie flat for a short time. Party then carried on in perfect formation and Artillery Barrage opened when they were about 15 yards from wire immediately in front of Enemy's Sap. The Enemy then put up two Red Lights. 2/Lieut. A.Fraser, who was in charge of the Party, ordered his men to rush forward, which they did, but found themselves up against a tremendous maze of wire which they could not get through. He then moved his Party to the right and found a Gap in the Wire which they got through with great difficulty owing to the loose pieces. On entering Sap, two of the three Squads (of which Party was composed) proceeded at once towards Enemy's Front Line. 2/Lieut. Fraser walked along the Parapet of Sap towards the Head, while the Third Squad followed him from inside the Sap. He jumped in on reaching Saphead, nearly falling down a deep Dug-out, which had only one Entrance. He shone his Torch down the Entrance and saw one of the Enemy at whom he fired at with his Revolver, the Squad with him also throwing a Bomb down. 2/Lieut. Fraser, leaving the Third Squad guarding the Entrance of Dugout and the Machine Gun Emplacement alongside, went down Sap to look for R.E. Party. When R.E. arrived they blew up both Dug-out and Emplacement. There seems to be no doubt that the Machine Gun was in the Dug-out as it had been heard firing from the Emplacement as the Party was coming across and could not possibly have got down the Sap to Front Line. Squads 1 and 2, working along Sap to the Front Line, met with stubborn resistance, but succeeded in driving the Enemy back to behind their Bombing Block, quite close to the Base of the Sap. Finding that they could get no further at that place, as "C" Party (Centre Party) had so far not succeeded in working Northwards along Front Line to Base of Sap, 2/Lieut. Fraser withdrew all except 6 Men, (who were left to hold Enemy at Bombing Block) back to about half way down Sap. From this point he ordered these Men to throw Bombs in Enemy's Front Line North of Sap, as our Party at Bombing Block

was being bombed from there. The idea of holding
the Enemy thus was to enable the R.E. to carry out
demolitions at Saphead.

L./Cpl. Wilson and one Man then entered Enemy
Front Line Trench, just North of Sap, there capturing
two Prisoners of the 5th Bavarian Regiment, 2nd
Bavarian Corps, who were at once handed over to some
men of "C" Party, who had become separated from
their Party, and happened to be outside the Trench
at that point. L./Cpl. Wilson and man then proceeded
to bomb down Sap, taking the Enemy in the rear.
They fought their way through and rejoined Party,
at the same time throwing a "P" Bomb back at
junction of Sap and Fire Trench to cover return
of Party. The Party then withdrew to our Trenches
without any difficulty.

"C" Party.

"C" Party left our Front Line Trench at
6 Minutes before Zero time. They were delayed a bit
at getting through our Wire, as there were loose
Strands which caught on the Men's clothing. Most
of this Party was about half-way across when the
Barrage started. At this time some of the Men on
the left lost direction and joined "A" Party. The
remainder went forward to Gap in Enemy's Wire, but
found same had been filled in with made up Wire,
evidently thrown out and picketed to the ground.
2/Lieut C.H.Graham, finding that Party was unable
to get through at this point, proceeded along the
Wire to the South, at the same time throwing Bombs
into the Trench, and found a Gap, near junction
of Southern Sap and Front Line at H.13.c.5¾.¼.
Party entered the Trench here, one Squad proceeding
Northwards to junction of Communication Trench and
Front Line, down which they threw Bombs at the
retreating Enemy. They were unable to penetrate down
Communication Trench, as, owing to delay in getting
through Wire, it was practically time to return
to our Trenches. Another Squad of this Party bombed
a Dug-out which was undoubtedly occupied at the
time, at junction of Southern Sap and the Front
Line. Party returned unmolested to our Trenches.

"B" Party.

"B" Party left our Trench at 5 minutes before
Zero time and got outside our own Wire without any
trouble. Party then headed for Saphead at H.13.c.4¾.
0, and were more than half-way across when our
Artillery Barrage commenced. On reaching Gap in the
Enemy's Wire, 2/Lieut A.Craig (who was in Command
of the Party) found that Gap had been filled in with
made up Wire. At this time Party was evidently
seen as Enemy started firing Rifle Grenades at them
from his Support Line and throwing Bombs at them
from Saphead. The Party at once bombed back at the
Saphead and endeavoured to get through the wire, but
found it was impossible, so continued bombing Sap
until just before time to return, when they succeeded
in silencing Enemy Bombers at Saphead. The Party

the Party returned unmolested to our Trenches.

"D" Party.

"D" Party left our Trench at 5 Minutes before Zero time, but was held up by part of "C" Party being delayed in getting through Gap in our Wire. When our Barrage started this Party was still inside our own Wire, so 2/Lieut. Pratt (who was in command of the Party) at once got his Party through the Gap and formed them up outside, sending forward as arranged, 4 Men to each "A", "B" and "C" Parties. These Men carried Ladders which they placed in position in German Front Line Trench and Saps, to facilitate the return of the other three Parties. Men of this Party also followed "A", "B" and "C" Parties paying out white Tape to the Gaps in the German Wire, also to facilitate the return of the Parties. This Party also assisted in evacuating wounded and directing men back to our own Lines.

R.E. Party.

This Party went across with "C" Party. They succeeded in blowing up a Machine Gun Emplacement and Machine Gun Dug-out at head of Northern Sap. They also destroyed both Entrances of another Dug-out in the Front Line and an Open M.G. Emplacement in Sap. From their point of view the Raid was entirely successful as they had only 6 or 7 minutes in the German Trenches on account of delay in getting through German Wire. A more detailed report of this Party will be forwarded later.

Total number of German Prisoners taken -2, and 1 Officer and about 20 men were accounted for. Our total Casualties were 14 wounded, of which 3 were stretcher cases.

To sum up, I feel confident that surprise effect was accomplished. More time might have been allowed for the Infantry to get over, before the Barrage commenced. Owing to the difficulty at first in getting through the German Wire, more time was lost, thus still further curtailing the time allowed for in the German Trenches. If these delays had not occurred I feel sure more damage could have been done.

(Signed) R.P. Forbes.
Lieut. Colonel
Commanding 10/11th H.L.I.

5/7/16.

46th Brigade.
15th Division.

10/11th BATTALION

HIGHLAND LIGHT INFANTRY

AUGUST 1 9 1 6

Appendices attached:-

Reports on Operations 14th:17th/18th Aug.

Army Form C. 2118

WAR DIARY
or
INTELLIGENCE SUMMARY

(Erase heading not required.)

Instructions regarding War Diaries and Intelligence Summaries are contained in F.S. Regs., Part II. and the Staff Manual respectively. Title Pages will be prepared in manuscript.

Place	Date	Hour	Summary of Events and Information	Remarks and references to Appendices
MONTONVILLERS	1.8.16		In Rest.	am
"	2.8.16		In Rest.	pm
"	3.8.16		In Rest.	pm
	4.8.16	6.30am	Received orders to continue march on following day to MOLLIENS AU BOIS	
			Marched out of MONTONVILLERS	
		9 am	Arrived at MOLLIENS AU BOIS	
MOLLIENS AU BOIS	5.8.16	5 am	Received orders to continue the march on following day to FRANVILLERS	pm
			Marched out of MOLLIENS AU BOIS	
		8.30 am	Arrived at FRANVILLERS	
			In Rest	
FRANVILLERS	6.8.16		Received orders to march on following day to the trenches and relieve 8th K.O.Y.L.I in Bde Reserve near FRICOURT	pm
	7.8.16	6.30 am	Marched out of FRANVILLERS	pm
		9.45 am	Arrived at halting-place between ALBERT and BECOURT	am
		2 pm	Continued march to Bde. Reserve area on FRICOURT – CONTALMAISON ROAD	
		6 pm	Relief of 8th K.O.Y.L.I. Completed. In Reserve to Right Brigade in Left Division of III Corps	pm
Bde Reserve MARTINPUICH AREA	8.8.16		In Brigade Reserve.	pm
	9.8.16		In Brigade Reserve.	pm
	10.8.16		In Brigade Reserve.	am
"	11.8.16		In Brigade Reserve. Received orders to relieve 12th H.L.I. on following day in Left Sub section.	pm
"	12.8.16	7 pm	Two Companies moved up to Support R.W.H.L.I. in Left Sub-section during their attack on SWITCH	pm
"	13.8.16	6 am	Relief of 12th H.L.I. begun	pm
"		8 am	Relief Completed. In Left Sub section from "Scottish Ryde" on our right, 45th Bde on our left.	pm

Army Form C.2118

WAR DIARY
or
INTELLIGENCE SUMMARY
(Erase heading not required.)

Instructions regarding War Diaries and Intelligence Summaries are contained in F. S. Regs., Part II. and the Staff Manual respectively. Title Pages will be prepared in manuscript.

Place	Date	Hour	Summary of Events and Information	Remarks and references to Appendices
Aft. Std. Section MARTINPUICH AREA	14·8·16	10 a.m.	On scrutinous all orders received made a bombing attack on enemy SWITCH LINE from the position opp. Parity from right sap reached its objective but was forced to retire from lack of support from parity working from left. sap. The parity had been held up by M.G. fire.	JMM
		12.30 p.m.	Situation normal. 4th Bde on our left.	JMM
"	15·8·16		Situation normal. Digging H.L.I. trench from our front line to SWITCH ELBOW 7/8th K.O.S.B.s on our right.	JMM
"	16·8·16		Situation normal. Digging H.L.I. trench.	JMM
"	17·8·16	10 a.m.	7th Cameron High[rs]. on our left attack SWITCH ELBOW for an operation on this day against the SWITCH and work of consolidation during the night See Appendix A	See Appendix A
			Situation Normal.	JMM
"	18·8·16	3 p.m.	Enemy arto. heavy barrage behind our front system.	
		4 p.m.	Orders received to hand over to 12th H.L.I. and proceed to Reserve position held H.Q. at SHELTER WOOD	
		7·30 p.m.	Relief complete.	
		8·30 p.m.	Orders received for leaving on a following day to 7th R.S.F. and proceeding to bivouacs between ALBERT and BECOURT	JMM
Reserve in SHELTER WOOD	19·8·16	8 a.m.	Relief begun.	
		9·30 a.m.	Relief complete.	
		12 noon	On Divisional Reserve to bivouacs.	
ALBERT	20·8·16		On Divisional Reserve finding working parties.	JMM
"	21·8·16		On Divisional Reserve	JMM
"	22·8·16		On Divisional Reserve	JMM

WAR DIARY or INTELLIGENCE SUMMARY

(Erase heading not required.)

Army Form C. 2118

Instructions regarding War Diaries and Intelligence Summaries are contained in F.S. Regs., Part II. and the Staff Manual respectively. Title Pages will be prepared in manuscript.

Place	Date	Hour	Summary of Events and Information	Remarks and references to Appendices
ALBERT	23.8.16		In Divisional Reserve	
"	24.8.16		In Divisional Reserve	
"	25.8.16		In Divisional Reserve. Receive orders to relieve 2nd Munsters in Bde. Support BAZENTIN area on 27th	
"	26.8.16		In Divisional Reserve	
"	27.8.16	10 a.m.	Marches out of Bivouacs	
		11 a.m.	Relief of 2nd Munsters in Bde. Support BAZENTIN LE PETIT and HIGH WOOD areas begins	
		2 p.m.	Relief complete	
Bde. Support BAZENTIN area	28.8.16		In Brigade Support. Warn received to relieve 12th H.L.I. in left sub-section on following day	
"	29.8.16	3.15 a.m.	Relief begins	
		6.30 a.m.	Relief complete. 10th Scottish Rifles on our right, 11th Royal Scots on our left. Engaged in digging strong points with a view to containing SWANSEA TRENCH to form up with which dug by 45th Bde. from SANDERSON TRENCH (the German SWITCH) and to cut off German see reports. INTERMEDIATE TRENCH between us and the 45th Bde. Then strong points constructed and lines marked out.	
			Work of strengthening the enemy by digging continues. 7/8th KOSBs on our right. 8/7 R.S.F. on our left.	
Left Sub-sector BAZENTIN area	30.8.16	5 p.m.	Considerable numbers of the enemy in the INTERMEDIATE TRENCH give themselves up to the R.S.F. Then attempting to make their escape through our line of strong points are shot down.	
		6 p.m.	2 Lt. Band led a patrol down our block in the INTERMEDIATE TRENCH to reconnoitre the line. They took 2 N.C.O.s and 13 men prisoner and brought back a machine gun. Sending down the prisoner "Lt. Band" again took out his party and entirely bombing succeeded in establishing communication with the 45th Bde. on our left. Lewin & Second machine gun was taken, and two other prisoners to find of SWANSEA TRENCH	

Army Form C. 2118

INTELLIGENCE SUMMARY
or
WAR DIARY

(Erase heading not required.)

Instructions regarding War Diaries and Intelligence Summaries are contained in F. S. Regs., Part II. and the Staff Manual respectively. Title Pages will be prepared in manuscript.

Place	Date	Hour	Summary of Events and Information	Remarks and references to Appendices
	30.9.16 (cont)		Orders received to hand over to following morning to 12th H.L.I. and return to Bde. Support	
Hyde Park huts	31.9.16	4 a.m. 10 a.m.	Relief begun. Relief completed. In Bde. Support as OC ?	R. S. Jabez Lieut-Colonel Comdg 10th H L I

1875 Wt. W593/826 1,000,000 4/15 J.B.C. & A. A.D.S.S./Forms/C. 2118.

REPORT ON BOMBING ATTACK BY 10/11th
HIGH.L.I. on SWITCH LINE on 14.8.16.

By 10 a.m. all parties were in position.
Right Sap Y.K.L.
No 1 Party left the North end of Sap at zero time reaching German line with very few casualties and Nos XXX 1 and 2 parties bombed their ways East and West. No 1 party which was bombing East reached its objective very quickly and the R.E. party which was following closely then created their block. At this juncture bombs gave out and as the men had been throwing them unnecessarily. The Lewis Gun Team had few casualties before reaching enemy's parados, the remaining two men fired the gun at the enemy who were retiring over the open, until they were both knocked out.

No 2 party bombed their way along the Trench to the West but owing to the lack of Support from the left Sap party which they were to meet and bombs giving out as they threw them unnecessarily and also because they met with strong opposition they were unable to carry on and were eventually forced to retire.

As far as I can gather some one in No 1 party shouted the word "Retire" and the party came back to our Sap.

Left Sap W.V. Parties were in position at zero hour. Nos 1 and 2 parties left Sap as arranged in good order. No 1 Party was met by heavy rifle or Machine Gun fire and failed to effect an entry.

No 2 party got fairly close up and found they could not get in. The remaining parties never left the Sap owing to Machine Gun fire. Enemy opened shell fire on SWITCH LINE and Sap Head two minutes after commencement accompanied by brisk rifle or Machine Gun fire. The O.C. Coy. finding it impossible to get any men over the left Sap sent as many men as he could collect to right Sap, but on their arrival there the attack on the right had failed.

From the above collaborated report from O.C., Coys. and what I have personally heard since I deduce that on the right the attack was entirely successful and the position might have been maintained if the two officers who were responsible for this attack had not been knocked out at an early stage in the proceedings. I understand that the right bombing party was in the enemy's trench about one hour and this party which was met by heavy opposition inflicted severe losses on the enemy as did also the Lewis Gun before the last two men were knocked out. I consider the failure of this party to be due to the indiscriminate throwing of bombs and the Officer leading this party being knocked out, and the Officer what was directing the supply of men and bombs from the Sap, also being knocked out.

A number of the enemy were seen to retire from their Trench over the open and were accounted for by Lewis and Machine Gun Fire.

Enemy trenches appear to be strongly held.

(Sgd) R. FORBES, Lt. Col.
Commanding, 10/11th High.L.I.

EVIDENCE OF R.E. WHO ACCOMPANIED 10/11th HIGH.L.I. IN ATTACK ON MORNING OF 14th Aug.

Cpl. TWEEDIE was in charge of a party of three sappers who went with the infantry attacking up the Right sap (i.e. continuation of WELCH ALLEY)

The R.E. followed "B" party ("A" and "B" parties being bombing parties). We formed up in the sap and the attack started at 10a.m. All the parties, "A", "B", and "C" went across hard on each other's heels. It was a run of quite 50 yards from head of sap to enemy's trench. I found the Infantry in front of me all in a cluster. the officer and his party had gone to the left. The others didn't appear to be going to move. They didn't appear to know what they were to do, so I called out to them "Get along, get along the bombers, to the right". They went to the right and the R.E. after them. We went along about 50 yards, when an Officer of the H.L.I. appeared on top of the parapet and took command of the bombers. We all went on to the right still further. past the light railway and about 20 yards beyond it. The officer then disappeared.

The trench had been well manned with Germans all of whom were killed as far as we went. These germans were all caught in little shelters scooped out in the front parapet and sides of traverses. I didn't see a single German in the trench itself. they were all in the shelters. I cannot state the number of dead Germans that I passed.

The trench was quite six feet below ground level, too much knocked about for me to state the width. no revetments, but the shelters were supported by semi-circular corrugated. I cannot say how deep into the sides of the trench the shelters went.

When the Officer disappeared, as already stated, the bombers continued throwing bombs, and bombs were being thrown at them. I told them to hold on where they were, and we would form a block. They hung on and the R.E. formed a temporary block in the trench. I told the bombers to hold on there while I could get the wire to form the obstacle in the trench, and the second block, I couldn't find the wire, so I started the second (rearmost) block. The bombers at this time began to shout for more bombs, so I sent three of my working party to find bombs. A few minutes afterwards they passed up some bombs, but only in ones and twos - about half a dozen in all. By this time I had the block built up sufficiently for the inserting of my loophole frame. I passed the word along for this, but it couldn't be found (it was to have come up with the carrying party that was to have followed the attack later on) By this time we had run out of bombs and I called upon the Lewis gunner to get behind my block and cover the trench as the bombers were forced to come back. I then started to utilise sandbags to make a sandbag loophole, and having started my sappers on that I went off to the left to see the officer in charge of the left party of the right attack about bombs. I met him and asked him what he was going to do, so he went along to the right and I called for a volunteer to go back to fetch bombs: two men volunteered and set out. (Since the attack I have seen one of these two men. he had twisted his knee coming across and has now been sent to hospital; the other, when we returned later, I saw lying in the sap breathing his last).

2.

I went along to the right then to where my party were at work. I found the Officer there and in command. A few seconds afterwards a bomb came and wounded the Lewis Gunner and I think it must have killed or knocked out the Officer (Lt. LEWIN) for I never saw him again. Then having no bombs and no Lewis gunner I told my party of R.E. to stop work and come along to see if we could find any bombs. When we got back to the point where we had originally entered the trench, we saw the H.L.I. all on top rushing for the sap, so I ordered my party to come along quick too, and Sapper Jackson was the last man to leave the German trench. When retiring the rifle and machine gun fire was very hot, but there were very few shells.

On return to our trenches I reported to a Captain of H.L.I. who told me to make my party "stand by", which we did from about 11.20 a.m. to 3 p.m.

If we had had the bombs we would never have had to retire, but the carrying party never came over after us.

(Sgd) H.M.P. PALMER, Captain, R.E.

73rd Fd Coy RE

Headquarters,
   15th Division.

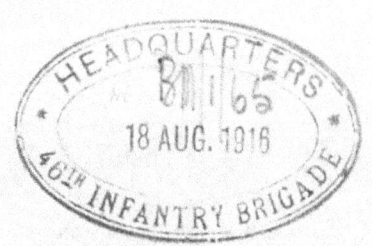

    The attached report by O.C. 10/11th High.L.I. (Left Battalion) on operations against SWITCH LINE is forwarded.

                    Sgd   T. G. MATHESON
                              Brig. General.
Brigade H.Q.   Commanding.
   18th Aug. 1916.   46th Inf.Bde.

Preliminary Report on Operations carried out against
      German SWITCH LINE 17th - 18th August.

           About 6 p.m. last night the Seaforths attacked
     the German SWITCH LINE W. of the SWITCH ELBOW and
     bombed their way eastwards along it . One company
     of the 10/11th High.L.I. taking advantage of the
     opportunity joined them in small parties from
     H.L.I. trench and the enemy was driven along towards
     the railway and a block was established about 120 yards
     E. of the SWITCH ELBOW. The enemy meanwhile established
     created a barrage right down and across our communications
     behind, which continued for an hour. The 10/11th High.L.I.
     dug H.L.I. Trench through to the SWITCH and carried up
     S.A.A. bombs , R.E. material, Very lights, etc. About
     8.15 p.m., O.C., 10/11th High.L.I. from information
     received, arranged for the barrage to lift 75 yards for
     150 yds. E. of the ELBOW. Report later from the front
     line show that this was the opportune moment, for the enemy
     by this time disorganised, had taken to the open only to
     find themselves in the midst of the lifted barrage.
     The work of consolidation continued commenced. The
     SWITCH LINE proved to be wide and rather shallow. Also it
     had been , in parts, almost obliterated by our
     bombardments. Sandbags were filled and every effort was
     made to construct a serviceable trench out of the wreck.
     A strong bombing block was established on the right and
     four Lewis Guns taken forward to help hold the line, the
     Vickers remaining for defensive purposes in our old
     fire-trench. The work of carrying and digging was much
     interrupted and impeded by shell fire , but good progress
     was made and by daylight H.L.I. trench had been made into
     a useful communication and the left pusher sap was dug
     through although very shallow in most places. During the
     night the Seaforths sent out patrol covering the whole front
     of the SWITCH LINE. Patrol came upon isolated parties of
     Germans taking refuge in shell holes , but these fled at
     their approach. They reported the whole area incredibly
     broken up by shell fire .
           During the night also a company of 10th Sco. Rif.
     occupied KOYLI TRENCH vacated by our company when it moved
     up. Early this morning reconnoitring of the SWITCH LINE
     beyond our block commenced and 10 of the enemy gave
     themselves up. It was arranged that a party of one officer
     and 25 men from the 10th Sco.Rif. should, if no opposition
     were encountered , create a strong point about 50 yards
     west of the Railway. A party consisting of
     one N.C.O. and 2 men preceeded them and again reconnoitred
     the trench where three more prisoners were taken. All these
     belonged to the 179th (Saxon (Regt. of Infantry.

     18th August, 1916.   (Sgd) R.F. FORBES, Lt.Col.
                            Commanding, 10/11th High.L.I.

10/11th (S) Bn Highland Light Infantry

REPORT ON OPERATIONS AGAINST THE GERMAN SWITCH LINE 17/18 Aug. 1916

During the forenoon of the 17th the 7th Cameron Highlanders succeeded in forcing their way along the SWITCH LINE to a point a short distance East of the SWITCH ELBOW. At this point their bombs appeared to run short, as they were observed retiring Westwards and were throwing picks and shovels at the enemy. They were forced back to a position West of the SWITCH ELBOW where they created a block. Bombs were supplied by the 10/11th H.L.I. which were passed along LANCS TRENCH to the Camerons. It appeared to officers on the spot that but for the timely supply of bombs the Camerons would have been bombed still further back.

About 6 p.m. a party of the 8th Seaforth Highlanders made a bombing attack on the SWITCH LINE by forcing their way along the trench from the block already established by the Camerons. When they reached a point a short distance East of the junction of H.L.I. TRENCH and the SWITCH they were seen from H.L.I. TRENCH which was manned by the 10/11th H.L.I. and about a dozen men of that Battalion under 2nd Lieut. D.A. Anderson, rushed over the open from H.L.I. TRENCH and attacked the enemy in the SWITCH with bombs. About 20 yards East of the junction of the SWITCH and H.L.I. TRENCH they came upon the survivors of a machine gun team endeavouring to get their gun into action. The first to arrive was Pte McGarva of "D" Coy. and he having no bombs, succeeded in knocking out the first German by throwing his rifle at him, and the remainder were scattered with bombs, as the rest of the H.L.I. party came up. The gun was captured and sent back to our front line. After that, little opposition was encountered and a bombing block was established about 120 yards East of the SWITCH ELBOW, and about 20 to 30 yards East of the left pusher sap. This block was held during the night by the 10/11th H.L.I.

During the attack the enemy had created a heavy barrage behind our front system right across the valley between BAZENTIN LE PETIT WOOD and WELCH ALLEY and this barrage did not lift for well over an hour and was continued intermittently throughout the night. Meanwhile the work of consolidation had begun, Chiefly through the efforts of 2nd Lieut. Anderson a party was immediately set to dig H.L.I. TRENCH through to join the SWITCH and a considerable quantity of R.E. material, S.A.A., bombs, very lights, etc, together with 3 Lewis Guns from the 10/11th H.L.I. were carried across to the captured trench. By 7.30 p.m. everything was organized in practical fashion and the new trench was manned by a combined party of Seaforths and H.L.I., but only up to a point because our barrage was still on the Eastern postion of the SWITCH. At 8.15 p.m. O.C., 10/11th H.L.I. from information received from the front line caused the artillery to lift their barrage 75 yards from the SWITCH as far along as the railway. Later reports from the firing line go to show that this was done at the most opportune moment because the enemy, pressed on their flank, and now thoroughly disorganized had taken to the open and were caught in the lifted barrage. The SWITCH was then partially cleared as far as our block, and rough fire steps prepared. H.L.I. TRENCH was completed and by daybreak the left pusher sap was almost dug through. During the night one of the enemy came to the bombing block and gave himself up and no attempt was made by them to attack our new position, instead they sent up red and green lights at intervals and occasionally blew whistles. The Seaforths sent out a patrol which covered our whole front and found nothing unusual. They saw several small parties of the enemy crouching in shell holes but these invariably fled at their approach. The patrol reported that the ground had been almost incredibly broken up by our shell fire. During the night KOYLI TRENCH vacated by our men who had

About 6 a.m. L/C Blackburn "B" Coy. crossed the Block and proceeded to reconnoitre the SWITCH LINE. The Trench was littered with dead and dying Germans, there was no water and the bread of which there was a quantity was covered with blue mould. He met with little opposition as he went along and one little group of the enemy which ventured near our block was driven off with bombs.

Shortly afterwards 10 Germans approached the block, threw down their Arms and were taken prisoners.

It was arranged that if little opposition were met with a strong point should be constructed about 50 yards West of the Railway in, or near the SWITCH LINE and almost opposite the Right Pusher Sap. This was to be done by a party of 1 Officer and 25 men from the 10th Scottish Rifles sent to assist us. Lance Corporal Blackburn again reconnoitred the Trench and killed one German Officer.

Three of the enemy gave themselves up and a Stretcher Bearer was afterwards taken.

At about 12 noon the Brigade Major ordered Corporal McDonald who was in charge of the right bombing block to go along the SWITCH LINE and create another block further on to protect working party on strong post. He reconnoitred the trench for 250 yards beyond the Railway where his party (consisting of 4 men and himself) encountered a German Officer and 4 men. The German privates ran away and the Officer was bayoneted as he attempted to fight.

The party then came back and created a block near the Railway. Under cover of this block a strong point was constructed immediately in rear of the old German Trench at a distance of about 50 yards from the Railway.

Altogether 16 prisoners were taken and it is believed that many more, who had taken to the open, would have given themselves up had it not been impos impossible to do so because of the continuous sniping which came from our left.

21-8-1916

(Sgd) R.F. FORBES, Lt.Col.
Commanding, 10/11th High.L.I.

CONFIDENTIAL

WAR DIARY
FOR
SEPTEMBER
1916.

10/11th BN.

HIGHLAND L.I.

Army Form C. 2118.

WAR DIARY
or
INTELLIGENCE SUMMARY
(Erase heading not required.)

Instructions regarding War Diaries and Intelligence Summaries are contained in F. S. Regs., Part II. and the Staff Manual respectively. Title Pages will be prepared in manuscript.

Place	Date	Hour	Summary of Events and Information	Remarks and references to Appendices
Bde. Reserve near BAZENTIN LE PETIT	1.9.16		In Brigade Reserve in O.G.I. Received orders to relieve 12th H.L.I. on following day in left Subsection of line between BAZENTIN LE PETIT and HIGH WOOD	
"	2.9.16	3.15 am	Relief Begins.	
		6 am	Relief completed. 115th Bde. on our left. 10th Sco. Rifs on our right.	
		8 am	Bombardment by our heavies begins on enemy trenches in HIGH WOOD area working on the new SWANSEA TRENCH, deepening it throughout and completing the	
Left Sub Section	3.9.16	12 noon	winders linking up the strong point. 1st Division on right of our Bde. attack enemy's position in HIGH WOOD on which heavily shelled throughout the day by the enemy particularly INTERMEDIATE TRENCH.	
			Work on SWANSEA TRENCH continued.	
		3 pm	Received order to hand over to 12th H.L.I. on following morning and return to O.G.I	
"	4.9.16	4 am	Relief Commences.	
		6 am	Relief completed. In Brigade Reserve in O.G. I.	
			Orders received to proceed on following day to Divisional Reserve in PEAKE WOOD AREA	
			on relief by 8th Seaforth Highlanders 44th Inf. Bde.	
Bde. Reserve	5.9.16	9.30 am	Relief by 8th Seaforths begins.	
		11 am	Relief completed.	
			On leaving Reserve to proceed to Bivouacs in ALBERT in lieu of PEAKE WOOD area	
ALBERT	6.9.16		In Divisional Reserve	
"	7.9.16		In Divisional Reserve	
"	8.9.16		In Divisional Reserve	
"	9.9.16		In Divisional Reserve	

Army Form C. 2118.

WAR DIARY
or
INTELLIGENCE SUMMARY.
(Erase heading not required.)

Instructions regarding War Diaries and Intelligence Summaries are contained in F. S. Regs., Part II. and the Staff Manual respectively. Title pages will be prepared in manuscript.

Place	Date	Hour	Summary of Events and Information	Remarks and references to Appendices
ALBERT	10.9.16		In Divisional Reserve	NIL
	11.9.16		In Divisional Reserve. Received orders to relieve the 25th Northumberland Fusiliers 103rd Inf. Bde. in following day in GOURLAY TRENCH and NEW TRENCH near CONTALMAISON.	NIL
"	12.9.16	4 a.m.	Relief begun. Battalion marches out of bivouacs.	
		6 a.m.	Had quarters at PEAKE WOOD	
		8 a.m.	Relief complete. In Support. 12th H.L.I. in front system. 14½ HLI in communication trench junction of HIGHLAND TRENCH and GORDON ALLEY	
GOURLAY TR.	13.9.16		During the day 13/14th received preliminary instruction with reference to fort coming operation to be undertaken against MARTINPUICH	NIL
"	14.9.16	6 a.m.	Orders received with reference to operation on following day. Battalion to attack in front of CAMERON TRENCH linked in front of CAMERON TRENCH was MARTINPUICH and linked to MARTINPUICH to attack with 2nd Canadian Inf. Bn on the right. Final Objective — SUNKEN ROAD Drawn on the left and 7/8 & KOSB's on the right. Final Objective — trench joining BOTTOM TRENCH to M 36 c 6.2. Three objectives — linked between M 32.a 1.0. and M 31 b 74.3.	Reference Sheet 57 c S.W.
		9.30 p.m.	Battalion leaves GOURLAY TRENCH to take up position in the proximity of winches.	NIL
Lt Colin MARTINPUICH AREA.	15.9.16	6.30 a.m.	Battalion leaves trenches for the assault	
		7 a.m.	Final Objective gained. For account of operation see Appendix A	Appendix A
			Day spent in consolidating. Orders received to hand over on capture trenches to 12th H.L.I.	
		9.30 p.m.	Relief begins. Battalion returns to GOURLAY TRENCH.	NIL

Army Form C. 2118.

WAR DIARY
or
INTELLIGENCE SUMMARY.
(Erase heading not required.)

Instructions regarding War Diaries and Intelligence Summaries are contained in F. S. Regs., Part II. and the Staff Manual respectively. Title pages will be prepared in manuscript.

Place	Date	Hour	Summary of Events and Information	Remarks and references to Appendices
GOURLAY TRENCH.	16.9.16		Received orders to relieve 9th Yorks & Lancs in Right Sub-Section in MARTINPUICH area.	
		7 p.m.	Battalion leaves GOURLAY TRENCH	
		10.30 p.m.	Relief completed. As a result of information received re enemy massing battalion "Stands to" throughout the night	
MARTINPUICH	17.9.16	4 p.m.	Officers patrol goes out from PUSH ALLEY to HAMMERHEAD WOOD in M.26 central but is not held. M.G. fire heard but has to return.	9pm
			Orders received to hand over to 9th Black Watch and proceed on relief to Divisional Reserve in SCOTT'S REDOUBT	
		7 p.m.	Relief begins.	
		11 p.m.	Relief completed. Orders received to hand over on following day to 8th Yorks & Lancs and proceed to Red Billets in LAVIEVILLE.	9pm
SCOTT'S REDOUBT	18.9.16	9.30 a.m.	Battalion marches out of SCOTT'S REDOUBT	
		1.30 p.m.	Arrives LAVIEVILLE	9pm
			Orders received to proceed on following day to Red Billets in BEHENCOURT	
LAVIEVILLE	19.9.16	7.50 a.m.	Battalion marches out of LAVIEVILLE	9pm
		11.30 a.m.	Arrives BEHENCOURT	
BEHENCOURT	20.9.16		In Red Billets.	9pm
"	21.9.16		In Red Billets.	9pm
"	22.9.16		In Red Billets. Training commences	9pm

WAR DIARY
or
INTELLIGENCE SUMMARY.

Army Form C. 2118.

(Erase heading not required.)

Place	Date	Hour	Summary of Events and Information	Remarks and references to Appendices
BEHENCOURT	23.9.16		In Rest Billets. Training	8am
"	24.9.16		In Rest Billets. Training	8am
"	25.9.16		In Rest Billets. Training	9am
"	26.9.16		In Rest Billets. Training	9am
"	27.9.16		In Rest Billets. Training	9am
"	28.9.16		In Rest Billets. Training	9am
"	29.9.16		In Rest Billets. Received orders to proceed on following day to billets at ALBERT	9am
"	30.9.16	10 am	Battalion marched out of BEHENCOURT	
		1.30 pm	Arrived ALBERT.	pm

R. Spybes Lieut-Colonel
Commdg 10th A.I.F.

APPENDIX. "A".

10/11th (S) B'n. Highland Light Infantry.

REPORT ON THE RECENT OPERATIONS 13th to 17th September. 1916.

On September 12th preliminary instructions were received with regard to forthcoming operations against the enemy's trenches in and alongside the village of MARTINPUICH. All units of the Brigade were to combine in digging jumping-off trenches in front of CAMERON TRENCH. In the actual attack, to take place about September 15th this Battalion was to attack with the 2nd. Canadians on its left and the 7/8th. Bn. K.O.S.B. on the right. Our first objective would be the SUNKEN ROAD from its junction with BOTTOM TRENCH to the Divisional Boundary at M.36.c.6.2. (Reference Sheet 57c.S.W.) and our final objective, the enemy trench known as the FACTORY LINE from M.32.a.1.0. to M.31.b.7½.3.

During the night 13/14th September the Battalion worked on the jumping-off trenches on our front. The work was much interupted by enemy shell-fire but fair progress was made. At 6 am. on September 14th. final orders were received confirming the preliminary arrangements of September 12th. and giving in detail the programme of attack. Only Zero time remained to be notified later. The Battalion was then in GOURLAY TRENCH and NEW TRENCH and the front system from which the attack was to be launched was held by the 12th H.L.I. The day was spent in resting the men and equipping them with all necessary supplies of ammunition and general equipment for the following day. At about mid day we were informed that Zero hour would be 6-20 am on September 15th and orders were received to march out of GOURLAY TRENCH at 9-30 pm. and take up the allotted position on a three platoon front in the jumping-off trenches.

Capt. R.P. Easton with the Signalling officer and a staff of runners set out for an advanced Headquarters in GORDON ALLEY near its junction with the new POSTᴺ LINE to which a telephone wire had been already laid and so a double means of communication was established between the companies in action and Battalion Headquarters in O.G.1. By midnight the Battalion was reported in position in the jumping-off trenches in six waves and on a three platoon front. Throughout the night the enemy shelled our position intermittently especially with gas and tear shells which caused considerable discomfort, and at one period the linesmen at work on the wires found it necessary to use their helmets. About 3 am. the sound of bombing was heard on our left and an officer of the 21st. Canadian Regiment reported that the enemy had entered his front line and were bombing their way towards us. A bombing-block was established on our left flank and a Vickers Gun brought up in readiness, but nothing further took place and a patrol showed that the enemy had already left the trench.

At 6-20 am. the Battalion left the trenches for the attack with a three platoon front and in six waves. There was no hesitation and no confusion and the first objective was taken without much difficulty. The "Tank" which was to have gone over in advance of the Infantry came into sight at CAMERON TRENCH at 5-50 am but did not actually cross our foremost line until our troops had left it. Eventually it reached the SUNKEN ROAD at a point S.W. of the village of MARTINPUICH and destroyed a machine gun which was causing some annoyance to one of our companies in its advance. The "Tank" had a considerable effect on the enemy's morale, but apart from that altogether they showed no desire to fight and prisoners came in in large numbers. The first of these were in our lines within a few minutes of the actual assault. There was no special artillery preparation immediately before the attack but for days beforehand MARTINPUICH and the surrounding trenches had been shelled by guns of every calibre, and when the actual attack was made the Infantry advanced under a creeping barrage which lifted 50 yards every minute, and the objective until reached was subjected to an intense fire. In the SUNKEN ROAD there were many indications that the enemy had been completely taken by surprise. Rifles and equipment were stacked by the side of dug-outs and it appeared that rations had been issued just before our attack. In this first objective there were numerous dug-outs cut n

/cut.

into the side of the road and these were found to contain a fair number of Germans who immediately surrendered. Two machine guns were also taken, one of them in good condition.

At 34 minutes after Zero the 1st, 3rd. and 4th. advanced to attack FACTORY LINE the 5th wave bringing up the rear in readiness to reinforce if necessary, construct strong points in support of the position. Meanwhile the 2nd. and 6th. waves began the work of consolidation on the first objective. This attack on the second objective involved the change of front which was successfully undertaken, and great credit is due to certain Sergeants who handled their platoons with great skill after the officers who lead them had become casualties. Here again little opposition was encountered and by 7 am. the FACTORY TRENCH was in our hands. Dug-outs were cleared and many more prisoners taken. In this trench the attacking troops were considerably mixed but these were gradually sorted out and consolidation began in earnest. Strong points were constructed in support of FACTORY TRENCH and every precaution was taken to ensure its being held in event of strong hostile counter attacks. A Vickers gun was brought into position on either flank and Lewis Guns were pushed out in front to protect the line. Meanwhile the enemy shelled the whole captured area promiscuously, a particularly heavy fire being directed upon the slope in rear of the SUNKEN ROAD and between it and our jumping-off trenches. Connection was established by us with the units on our right and left in the final objective and three hours after Zero the artillery barrage lifted from the northern end of the village to enable patrols from the Battalions on our right to reconnoitre. At 3 pm. in accordance with instructions received we pushed forward patrols to GUNPIT TRENCH which was found to be practically empty and accordingly occupied. A few more prisoners were taken and another machine gun which was found in a dug-out with the sole survivor of the team. This trench was likewise cleared and the work of improving the general position went on apace until the Battalion was relieved about 9-30 pm. in the captured trenches by the 12th H.L.I. whereupon we returned to GOURLAY TRENCH.

About mid-day on the 16th we received instructions to leave GOURLAY TRENCH at 7 pm. and relieve the 9th Yorks. & Lancs. in PUSH ALLEY and its support trench N.W. of MARTINPUICH, and the 12th H.L.I. in a line of posts within the village itself.

In the afternoon a party of officers and N.C.Os. set out to reconnoitre the area to be taken over. These unfortunately found the whole region under shell fire and seven officers became casualties including the medical Officer and the four Coy. Commanders. Three officers were killed and four wounded. Hasty re-arrangements were made and at 7 pm. the Battalion left GOURLAY TRENCH. By 10-30 pm. the relief was complete, and an advanced Battalion Headquarters was established in a dug-out in the village not far from the junction of PUSH ALLEY with GUNPIT ROAD

About this time a message was received from the Brigade to the effect that troops and transport had been seen in quantity proceeding Southwards in the direction of MARTINPUICH. We were instructed to send out patrols and keep a particularly sharp look out. This was followed later by a message which said that a hostile counter attack seemed imminent and were accordingly to "stand to". Throughout the night we stood to but by morning no enemy attack had materialised and we were instructed to stand down. The earlier part of the day was quiet and the enemy's shelling although fairly constant was not heavy.

In the afternoon in consequence of a report to the effect that trenches on the slope N.W. of MARTINPUICH were unoccupied we were ordered to send out an Officer's patrol to reconnoitre. A later report stated that the trench in question was unoccupied and we would therefore proceed to occupy it, but when the patrol advanced in the direction of the trench it was met with heavy rifle and machine gun fire, and PUSH ALLEY AND MARTINPUICH itself were simultaneously shelled. The patrol had to retire and other similar patrols sent out by the units on our right and left met with the same reception and came in, but the enemy seemed apprehensive of attack because the shelling continued and a barrage was created over MARTINPUICH and the adjoining valley.

/valley.

We then recieved orders to hand over to 9th. Black Watch, and proceed to SCOTT REDOUBT. This relief which began at 7 pm. was carried out with considerable difficulties and was not completed until about 11 pm.

But for the illstarred expedition of the afternoon of the 16th. the casualties throughout the operation were not great and the percentage of killed was remarkably small.

R.S. Forbes
Lieut-Colonel
Comdg 1/4 H.L.I.

10/11th. (S). Bn. Highland Light Infantry.

REPORT ON RECENT OPERATIONS 13th.-15th. September, 1916.

On the night of the 13/14th. the Battalion was at work on the jumping-off trenches in front of CAMERON TRENCH.

About 9-30 p.m. on September 14th. the Battalion left GOURLAY TRENCH and took up its position in the jumping-off trenches on a three platoon front. During the night the enemy shelled the position with Tear Shells and a small bombing attack was made on the CANADIANS on our left.

At 6-20 a.m. on the 15th. the Battalion left the trenches for the attack with a three platoon front and in six waves. The CANADIANS were on our left and the 7/8th. K.O.S.B. on our right.

The Tank which was to have gone over in advance of the Infantry came in sight at CAMERON TRENCH at 5-50 a.m. but did not actually cross over our foremost line until the troops had left it. The first objective was the SUNKEN ROAD South West of MARTINPUICH and this was taken without much difficulty. Our Infantry had advanced close under the creeping barrage which lifted 50 yards every minute, and the objective until reached was subjected to an intense fire.

The enemy showed no desire to fight and the first prioners were in our lines within a few minutes of the actual assault.

The position of the Rifles, equipment, etc. in the SUNKEN ROAD goes to shew that the enemy was taken by surprise. At (25) ? 34 minutes after Zero the assault on the final objective commenced and by 7 a.m. (FACTORY TRENCH had been taken. There were a considerable number of the enemy in this trench but these crowded up towards the left and some took refuge in dug-outs until eventually taken prisoners. Practically no oposition was encountered.

Meanwhile the second wave was at work on consolidating the first objective. Strong Points were now constructed in support of FACTORY TRENCH and the work of clearing and consolidation began in earnest. The enemy meanwhile shelled the whole area promiscuously but did not seem to have the trenches marked down.

In particular the area in rear of SUNKEN ROAD was heavily shelled. At 3 hours after Zero the barrage lifted and patrols were sent out by the Battalions on our right to reconnoitre the village. We established connection with the units on our right and left in the final objective. About 3 p.m. we pushed forward patrols to GUN PIT TRENCH which was found to be empty and was accordingly occupied. The work of constructing strong points and consolidating the whole position went on steadily until the Battalion was relieved about 9-30 p.m. by the 12th. H.L.I.

During the attack 3 Machine Guns were taken, 2 in the SUNKEN ROAD and one in FACTORY TRENCH. Of these, two were in good condition and must recently have been in action.

Considering the magnitude of the operation the casualties were not great and the percentage of killed was remarkably small.

Lieut. Colonel,

19-9-1916.   Commanding 10/11th. (S). Bn. High: L. I.

"A" Form.
MESSAGES AND SIGNALS.

Army Form C. 2121.
No. of Message ....

Prefix .... Code .... m.	Words	Charge	This message is on a/c of:	Recd. at .... m
Office of Origin and Service Instructions.				
....	Sent		.... Service.	Date ....
....	At .... m.			From ....
....	To			
....	By		(Signature of "Franking Officer.")	By ....

TO {

| Sender's Number. | Day of Month. | In reply to Number. | A A A |

(Hand-drawn trench map showing compass rose with N, W, E, S; labelled features: GORDON ALLEY, D Coy, C Coy, B Coy Bn H.Q., GOURLAY TRENCH, CONTALMAISON VILLA, YORKSHIRE ALLEY, A Coy, NEW TRENCH, THE CUTTING)

From ....
Place ....
Time ....

The above may be forwarded as now corrected.

(Z)

.... Censor. .... Signature of Addressee or person authorised to telegraph in his name.

* This line should be erased if not required.

225,000. W 14042—M 44. H, W & V., Ld. 12.15.

"A" Form.
MESSAGES AND SIGNALS.

Army Form C. 2121.

TO 4.6" D.

Sender's Number.	Day of Month.	In reply to Number.	A A A
Rh. 334	13th		

Herewith sketch showing
disposition of this Battalion

From O.C. 10/11 HLI.
Place
Time 11.30 am

CONFIDENTIAL

WAR DIARY

for OCTOBER 1916.

10/11th H.L.I.

WAR DIARY
or
INTELLIGENCE SUMMARY

Army Form C. 2118

Place	Date	Hour	Summary of Events and Information	Remarks and references to Appendices
ALBERT	1.10.16		In Rest Billets with Batt HQ in RUE DE TRAIRIES. Church parade was held in CINEMA HALL	pm
"	2.10.16		Batt. started training in ground between BERNANCOURT and AMIENS roads. Practising attack in waves. Musketry on range S. of AMIENS ROAD School E.8.	pm
"	3.10.16		Training continued.	pm
"	4.10.16		Training	pm
"	5.10.16		Training as before. Concert in evening in CINEMA HALL by Canadians.	pm
"	6.10.16		Battalion practice attack with objective marked by flags.	pm
"	7.10.16		Training	pm
"	8.10.16		Church parade. Orders were received to proceed on following day to Divisional Reserve Area. Batt. to be in LOZENGE WOOD CAMP SOUTH, 44th and 45th Bdes in huts (LE SARS) area.	pm
"	9.10.16	7am	Battalion marched out of ALBERT and proceeded to LOZENGE WOOD CAMP taking on from 9th Yorks and Lancs who had only arrived at the camp at 6am and had come direct from LE SARS having been engaged in the fighting of the previous day.	pm
LOZENGE WOOD	10.10.16		In Divisional Reserve. Work was consisted mainly in doing a certain amount of training and in finding working parties. Carrying stores to MARTINPUICH and CONTALMAISON etc.	pm

WAR DIARY
or
INTELLIGENCE SUMMARY

Army Form C. 2118

(Erase heading not required.)

Instructions regarding War Diaries and Intelligence Summaries are contained in F.S. Regs., Part II. and the Staff Manual respectively. Title Pages will be prepared in manuscript.

Place	Date	Hour	Summary of Events and Information	Remarks and references to Appendices
LOZENGE WOOD	11.10.16		In Divisional Reserve in LOZENGE CAMP. Training of bombing Squads in conjunction with Lewis Gunners in the German trenches.	JMcA
"	12.10.16		Training and reconnoitering the forward area around MARTINPUICH in view of having to reoccupy forward Posts positions during operations of the 11th and 45th Bdes.	JMcA
"	13.10.16		Received orders to relieve 11th A. and S. Highr. on the following night in support area in 26th AVENUE between MARTINPUICH and LE SARS	JMcA
"	14.10.16 4.30 pm		At our 4.30 pm the battalion left LOZENGE WOOD and proceeded by CONTALMAISON to CONTALMAISON VILLA where we were met by guides from the ARGYLLS and marched MARTINPUICH along the tram line. Three enemy shells at open must and up by shell fire to 26th AVENUE. Relief was complete about 10.30pm and the battalion came under the orders of the G.O.C. 45th Infantry Bde. The front line battalion was the 6/7 Royal Scots Fusiliers and behind were three battalions in support, in support, we got no without casualties. The night was very quiet.	JMcA
26th AVE. Bde Support	15.10.16		Sunday. The enemy shelled LE SARS and DESTREMONT FARM where we had one platoon of B Coy. About 5.30 pm the 7/8 KOSB came up from MARTINPUICH and relieved the 6/7 R Royal Scots Fusiliers.	JMcA
"	16.10.16		A fairly quiet day. We had fairly heavy working parties at work on GILBERT ALLEY a communication trench the the front line, while in the front line working parties carried relief to our relief by hand lamp to near GUNPIT TRENCH and carried forward the open.	JMcA

1875 Wt. W593/826 1,000,000 4/15 J.B.C. & A. A.D.S.S./Forms/C.2118.

WAR DIARY or INTELLIGENCE SUMMARY

Army Form C. 2118

Place	Date	Hour	Summary of Events and Information	Remarks and references to Appendices
In Support LE SARS AREA.	17/10/16		Another fairly quiet day. There was heavy shelling of LE SARS and DESTREMONT FARM and about 7 p.m. there was a lively artillery duel on our left on the CANADIAN front. In the German which was received to relieve the 7/P. CONS in the front line. The relief started about 5.30 p.m. but was not complete until after midnight. Owing to heavy rain the state of the trenches was very bad and movement of troops was very difficult, then we lost our to line the CANADIANS were on our left and the 14th BDE on our right.	
In front and LE SARS AREA.	18/10/16		H.Q. was to 26 L AVENUE and B Coy occupied CHALK TRENCH. "A" was in O.G.1 & "D" to near to O.G.2. Lt R.A. PEERS LINE. "C" in LE SARS itself and "D" to the right of the GIR Division on the right of the 15th Div. Artillery.	
		3.40 a.m.	At 3.40 a.m. the GIR Division on the right of the 15th Div. Artillery TRENCH had been not very successful. During the attack the Lewis Gun and bombers of the enemy located in our front line operation with Lewis Gun and after the fire. The enemy retaliated by shelling LE SARS and the GIR Division had no steam gun train fairless on our R.L. & D.D Beals and R. Glennel were bombed. Throughout the day there was a considerable amount of MS artillery fire.	
"	19/10/16		There was much greater day, but had few Casualties during the period in the front line the Coy's of 5 platoons from the last 9 the trenches the front line the Coy was considerable labour during to the broken state of the ground and the involved heavy rain. In the afternoon we receive notice to be Rand over to the 11th A. and J. Hygh. to and proceed to the NINTH Camp to LOZENGE WOOD. The relief started from at 5.30 p.m. and carried on with great difficulty.	

WAR DIARY or INTELLIGENCE SUMMARY

Army Form C. 2118

Place	Date	Hour	Summary of Events and Information	Remarks and references to Appendices
LOZENGE WOOD CAMP.	20/10/16		And the last complete batch 3.20 a.m. About 4.30 p.m. the enemy attacked the 9th Division on our right but were repulsed. During the attack the right portion of our front line [heavily] shelled.	
"	21/10/16		At 7 a.m. the men were still carrying in from the front-line and the work of cleaning up both a considerable time. The men had much and got ripe and equipment in men clean & programme in charge of their [?] and Company Commander. The [?] handling of brushes & equipment will be resumed. Leave [Berm]. Training began and the basis for the parties was drawn from the Company of [?] certain number of men were employed on the road in the region of MARTIN PUICH. A certain number of men were employed on the road in the region of BAZENTIN LE PETIT.	
"	22/10/16		Training continued.	
"	23/10/16		Instructions were received to proceed to [Allenby] Camp to march to indicate to be ready to intertake the left of [Villa?] and the Batt. to march to undertaken by 44th and 45th Bdes heavy to full Corps forward area to the vicinity of LITTLE WOOD Division Agreed. The WARLENCOURT LINE to be the [reserve?] [?] position was then sure from the ADMS. 15th Div. Operation fixed for moving of 25th Oct.	9 p.m.
"	24/10/16		Operations postponed 24 hours. Batt. orders to prepare to move into fire line close above 4.30 p.m. About 2 p.m. orders were received to relieve the 6/7th R.S.F. in front LE SARS AREA, Batt. orders were [?] to relieve the 6/7th R.S.F. in front LE SARS AREA.	9 p.m.

WAR DIARY
or
INTELLIGENCE SUMMARY

(Erase heading not required.)

Army Form C. 2118

Place	Date	Hour	Summary of Events and Information	Remarks and references to Appendices
Bn. Hqrs. and Le Sars Area	25.10.16	7 am	Bombs, S.A.A. [S.A.A.] and S.A.A. were distributed about 4.30 p.m. the Batt. moved off. The night was quiet and in spite of heavy rain roadlin. the ground had begun drying out and relief was complete by 10.30 p.m. From the 6/7 R.S.F. we took over instructions with respect to an attack on REGINA TRENCH the left on conjunction in the CANADIANS. At 7 am the following morning Canadians on our right in the CANADIANS. on our left with Bn. on an attack on a relief was complete we relieved the GOC 25th 14 Bde. Canadians attacked REGINA TRENCH. From O.G.2 when in conjunction with our Bn. front the attack appeared successful. The attack was on our front was not great. The Canadian on succeeded in gaining their objective but by 12 noon no reports information was being had their wounded to hold it and were again in their own lines & the former major C.E. ANDREWS temporarily commanding the Battalion was killed it 26th AVENUE. They actually the they pulled back previously to the left. Return was brought up in part front to 26th AVENUE and Canadian clear to the line.	9 pm
"	26.10.16.		A quiet day. Very little shelling on our front. Orders were received to hand over to the 6th Cameron Highl'rs and march to Reserve to MARTINPUICH to "C" Battalion with HQ. in the N.E. corner of the village with 1 Coy in STARFISH LINE, 1 in Coy in PRUE TRENCH and 2 Coys in MARTIN ALLEY and the CUTTING. About 7.15 p.m. the relief began and was Ebnreil and without great difficulty, was complete by 10.30 pm.	9 pm

WAR DIARY
or
INTELLIGENCE SUMMARY

(Erase heading not required.)

Army Form C. 2118

Place	Date	Hour	Summary of Events and Information	Remarks and references to Appendices
MARTINPUICH	27.10.16		In Reserve in MARTINPUICH Friend looking position.	9a.m.
"	28.10.16		In Reserve.	9a.m.
"	29.10.16		Orders received to change over with the 6th Cameron High[rs] and being 'D' Battalion with H.Q. to S.W. and of MARTINPUICH. Two Companies went to MAN and EGG TRENCH, 1 Coy in continuation of GUNPIT ROAD and one in continuation of FACTORY LINE. This was carried out in the evening.	9a.m.
"	30.10.16.		Operations again postponed. Received orders about 1 p.m. to return 7/6 ROSS in front line. It rained most of the day and the still of the ground was such that relay we attempted with great difficulty and we met Cambrai. It was about 7.45 a.m. Cameron again in and left and took Bde in the night. After relief of ROSS we stood and had afternoon Munro patrol from SCOTLAND TRENCH and there both reported that the enemy was not holding entirely between GALLWITZ TRENCH and Munro. The 24 hours spent in the line were fairly quiet but the fatiquies were very hot and the line had been had to keep them from all going whipsters. About 9.30 relief began by 11th A and S.H. being mg to relations difficulty of getting down the hot completed till 3 a.m. Batt. then returned to SCOTT'S REDOUBT.	9p.m. 9p.m. A Maybee Lt. Col. Cmdg. 10th H.L.I.

CONFIDENTIAL

WAR DIARY

NOVEMBER 1916.

10/11th H.L.I.

WAR DIARY or INTELLIGENCE SUMMARY

Army Form C. 2118.

Place	Date	Hour	Summary of Events and Information	Remarks and references to Appendices
SCOTT'S REDOUBT	1-11-16		Relieved in left sector of SCOTT'S REDOUBT by Procedure to Procedure in Bivouac near LE SARS by the 11th A and S. Highlanders. The Bivouac was very wet & the men had so far not had Scott's Redoubt out about the rain, but the men were busy to the effect that Bivouac quarters were partly 1 am. Sent an order leading to the effect that Bivouac area. About 10th postponed Bivouac. Word was on same day to MILLENCOURT AREA. About 10th order for the move was received. And at 2.15 p.m. or marched by arrival at MILLENCOURT about 4.30 p.m. The battalion was comfortably accommodated in tents.	p.m.
CONTALMAISON				
MILLENCOURT	2-11-16		The day was spent in cleaning up kit making the men. Draft of 27 men arrived from Reserve Battalion.	p.m.
"	3-11-16	10 am	Inspection of Wells. by Brigadier. Companies began training and drill training when the arrived from on the 5th.	p.m.
"	4-11-16		Training parties out took on routes and generally improving the area. Received orders to move on following day to HENENCOURT WOOD.	p.m.
"	5-11-16	2 pm	Sunday. Church Parade. Serves in forenoon. 1st Division passed through on its way up to the line. Battalion marched out of MILLENCOURT and reached HENENCOURT WOOD CAMP about 3 km east. Camp situated in open space in front on top of the hill. Battalion accommodated in AMIENS HUTS. Heavy fatigues were required to carry baggage from here and up to camp. About 7 p.m. a telegram was received instructing the Batt. would move on following day to BAIZIEUX. Situated when received. at 10 pm.	p.m.

WAR DIARY
or
INTELLIGENCE SUMMARY

(Erase heading not required.)

Army Form C. 2118.

Place	Date	Hour	Summary of Events and Information	Remarks and references to Appendices
HENENCOURT	6.11.16.	11 am	Morning spent in packing up and preparing to move. About 11 am we marched out of HENENCOURT CAMP and proceeded to BAIZIEUX in WAROY. At BAIZIEUX the Battalion was accommodated in what is "C" Camp. Here be found no furnishings of any description and set to work making chair, table etc. and shelves for blankets and water-carts.	ppm ppm
BAIZIEUX	7.11.16.		Cleaning up and resting. Sites were selected for training, parading etc.	
"	8.11.16		Training began in earnest. Drill and bayonet-fighting etc. under Company arrangements. There was a good deal of wire entanglement in the vicinity and the made it difficult to find suitable ground for practising the attack and the like. The old trenches in the Corps Defence line were helpful for working Close to hand. Six officers arrived from Reinforcement Camp. Practise etc.	ppm
"	9.11.16		In the forenoon information was received that the Commander in Chief would carry out an informal inspection of the Battalion about 3.30 p.m. About two companies were at the trenches but the remainder were lined up outside the camp to Clean fatigues for the inspection.	ppm
"	10.11.16		During the sunday forenoon two companies were at bath, and the remainder carried on training. At 11 am their was a route march by BRESLE and HENENCOURT. Lt. Col R.J. Forbes Scot. to 7.A. Capt R. Macwillie takes over Company Command	ppm ppm

WAR DIARY
or
INTELLIGENCE SUMMARY

(Erase heading not required.)

Army Form C. 2118.

Place	Date	Hour	Summary of Events and Information	Remarks and references to Appendices
BAIZIEUX	11.11.16		Anything attaching in town in vicinity of old Corps hunt. Instruction in Bombing for young Officers under Bde. Bombing Officer.	p.m.
"	12.11.16		Sunday. Church Parade. Two companies inoculated.	p.m.
"	13.11.16		Attack forestalled. Continued. During the morning Sounds of fierce bombardment heard Information received that Bde. would move on following day. Appointment for inspection by Brigadier on following day.	p.m.
"	14.11.16	7 a.m.	Early morning inspection by C.O. Inspection of Battalion by Brigadier.	
		11 a.m.		
		9.30 p.m.	Orders received to move to NAOURS at 9 a.m. 15/1/16.	
"	15.11.16	9 a.m.	Battalion handed out of BAIZIEUX and proceeded by BEHENCOURT, MONTIGNY and MULLIENS AU BOIS to the neighbourhood of VILLERS-BOCAGE where a horse halt was made for luncheon. At 2 p.m. the march was continued to TALMAS & NAOURS. The billets handed out and practically to no fell out. At TALMAS be formed the 11th Division Group up. Battalion Competently recommended to commo etc.	p.m.

WAR DIARY
or
INTELLIGENCE SUMMARY
(Erase heading not required.)

Instructions regarding War Diaries and Intelligence Summaries are contained in F. S. Regs., Part II. and the Staff Manual respectively. Title Pages will be prepared in manuscript.

Place	Date	Hour	Summary of Events and Information	Remarks and references to Appendices
NAOURS	16.11.16		Day spent in resting and cleaning up. There were no latrines or wash-places and these had to be constructed.	P.M.
"	17.11.16		Training Re-commences. Excellent ground for manoeuvring was found on the high ground N. of the village.	P.M.
"	18.11.16		Training Continues. Remainder of inoculations carried out. At 6p.m. a Batt. concert was held in the Divisional Canteen.	P.M.
"	19.11.16		Church Parades.	P.M.
"	20.11.16		During the forenoon a practice attack was carried out on the high ground N. of the village. Batt. Inspection by C.O. Force below up to an Australian Artillery Brigade.	P.M.
"	21.11.16		Another practice attack.	P.M.
"	22.11.16		In the forenoon practice attack on ground N. of the village and in the afternoon on the high ground between VILLERS BOCAGE on site chosen for Brigadier's inspection of attack.	P.M.

WAR DIARY
or
INTELLIGENCE SUMMARY

(Erase heading not required.)

Army Form...

Instructions regarding War Diaries and Intelligence Summaries are contained in F.S. Regs., Part II. and the Staff Manual respectively. Title Pages will be prepared in manuscript.

Place	Date	Hour	Summary of Events and Information	Remarks and references to Appendices
NABOURS	23/4/16	10 a.m.	The Brigadier inspected the battalion carrying out a practice attack in waves on specially constructed dummy trenches on the high ground towards VILLERS BOCAGE. The battalion ammunition sent to front and acted as a barrage. In the afternoon the Brigade to be inspected by the Army Commander. The inspection was followed by a march-past.	A/m
"	24/4/16		Training Continued.	A/m
"		6 p.m.	Night Operations. Advancing in open country at night was practised.	A/m
"	25/4/16		During the forenoon inspections of kit and ammunition equipment was carried out.	A/m
"	26/4/16		Church Parades. Orders received to move to WARLOY on following day.	A/m
"	27/4/16	10 a.m.	Battn. marched out: A halt for dinner was made after passing TALMAS and we then proceeded by RUBEMPRE, HERISSART, CONTAY, to WARLOY arriving there about 5 p.m. Battalion accommodated in billets.	A/m
WARLOY	28/4/16		A scheme for protecting communication with enemy aircraft was arranged for the afternoon but has been abandoned because of weather. Preparing for inspection on following day by Divisional Commander.	A/m

1875 Wt. W 593/826 1,000,000 4/15 J.B.C. & A. A.D.S.S./Forms/C. 2118.

Army Form C. 2118

WAR DIARY
or
INTELLIGENCE SUMMARY
(Erase heading not required.)

Instructions regarding War Diaries and Intelligence Summaries are contained in F.S. Regs., Part II. and the Staff Manual respectively. Title Pages will be prepared in manuscript.

Place	Date	Hour	Summary of Events and Information	Remarks and references to Appendices
MARLOY	29/4/16	9 am	Inspection of battalion by Divisional Commander. For this inspection 2 Companies were in marching order, 1 in drill order and 1 in fighting order. During the forenoon one Company was inspected in Coy. drill, one in bayonet fighting and physical drill and another in musketry and firing a falling-point. In the afternoon the remaining Coy. was inspected on the rifle range.	9 am 3 pm 3 pm
"	30/4/16		Finding working parties. Orders received to move on following day to BECOURT CAMP.	

R. Ransom Major.
Comdg. 10/u H.L.I.

CONFIDENTIAL

Vol 18

WAR DIARY

10th/11th H.L.I.

From
1st December 1916
To
31st December 1916

WAR DIARY
INTELLIGENCE SUMMARY

Army Form C. 2118.

Place	Date	Hour	Summary of Events and Information	Remarks and references to Appendices
WARLOY	1/12/16		About 10 am the Battalion marched out of WARLOY and marched via HENENCOURT and MILLENCOURT to ALBERT and on to BECOURT NEW CAMP.	
BECOURT	2/12/16		Here the battalion was accommodated in Nissen Huts and formed part of 17th Division in Corps Support. The camps were nearly completed but required a considerable amount of work. That went in covers for cookers, flat duck boards and more hut to be cleaned out drains and latrines constructed. All these details being working parties and in addition there was much to be done in the Coal area or more Construction under R.E. Supervision. The system adopted by Brigade to this area was to employ battalions on fatigues on alternate days and leave the other days free for the continuing of training. Programme of training was submitted daily to Brigade. Apart from specialists, the Batt. had about 320 men available for fatigue, fatigue parties averages 300 so that U. was usually possible to permit — Lewis Gunners, snipers and Stretcher bearers to work their training. Church Parades. Working parties under R.E. and Town Major.	Mm
"	3/12/16			Mm Mm

WAR DIARY
or
INTELLIGENCE SUMMARY.

Army Form C. 2118.

Place	Date	Hour	Summary of Events and Information	Remarks and references to Appendices
BECOURT	4/12/16		Brigadier inspected Camp. Training in progress. Practising attacking in waves touching the Reconnoitring the approach to Rt. and Left. Divisional area so to the rear of called on.	am
"	5/12/16		Finding parties for work on FRICOURT - CONTALMAISON road, and parties for work in BECOURT CAMP. Specialists at work in vicinity of camp, training. Bayonet fighting etc. Lewis Gunners going to BOISELLE CRATER.	pm
"	6/12/16		General Training continued	am
"	7/12/16		Finding same working parties. Moved Band of Brigade flamp School. Training continued. Work on a cruciform shring point constructed as a trial near the the German line.	pm
"	8/12/16			am
"	9/12/16		Working Parties. Intriguing a shell-hole for inspection of Brigadier in morning.	pm
"	10/12/16		Church Parades.	am
"	11/12/16		Working Parties. In the afternoon the Brigadier inspected the shring point and fortified shell-hole.	am
"	12/12/16		Training and preparing Bags to launches when reaches trenches 1/6 "Gloucesters" in Support. battalion area of Rt. Bde. Left Division.	pm
				pm

WAR DIARY
or
INTELLIGENCE SUMMARY.

(Erase heading not required.)

Army Form C. 2118.

Place	Date	Hour	Summary of Events and Information	Remarks and references to Appendices
BECOURT	13/12/16		Finding working parties. Making up books, SAA &c in preparation to moving to front area.	
SHELTER WOOD NORTH	14/12/16	11.30 am	Travelled out of BECOURT CAMP. Arrived SHELTER WOOD NORTH CAMP. Battalion had dinners and teas here.	
		12.15 pm		
		4.30 pm	Battalion moved off to relieve 1/6 Gloucesters in Support of the right Subsection of Divisional Front.	
SEVEN ELMS M.29.d.3.b.		9.15 pm	Relief Complete. 2 Lt. H.A. Garson was killed in MARTINPUICH on the way up; in O.R. killed and two wounded at the same time. Shortly after arrival in PRUE TRENCH C Coy had 6 N.C.O.s wounded by a shell. Battalion was disposed as follows. D Coy in RUTHERFORD ALLEY and SEVEN ELMS, C Coy PRUE TRENCH (right), B Coy PRUE TRENCH (left) A Coy STARFISH TRENCH Bn. H.Q. at SEVEN ELMS.	P.S.
	15.12.16		Finding Working parties & reconnoitring Right Section & routes thereto	P.S.

WAR DIARY or INTELLIGENCE SUMMARY

Army Form C. 2118.

Place	Date	Hour	Summary of Events and Information	Remarks and references to Appendices
SEVEN ELMS	16.12.16.		In view of relieving 7/8 K.O.S.B. on 17.12.16. Finding working parties. Improving Trenches and Shelters occupied by the Battalion.	
	17/12/16	4.30 p.m.	Battalion moved off to relief 7/8 K.O.S.B. in right Section of Divisional right Subsection	R.A.
M.22.d.6½.9/8.12.16		2 a.m.	Relief Completed. Line taken over simply a series of posts in very bad condition. C & D Coys in front line. A Coy in Support. B Coy in Reserve. Battn. H.Q. at M.22.d.6½.0. Work of wiring & improving posts carried on with. Wiring in front between posts. New post dug at M.16.A.8.2½. Post improved. Traverses commenced	R.A.
	19/12/16		Same.	R.A.
		5.30 p.m	Relief by 7/8 K.O.S.B. commenced	
		8.15 p.m	Relief Complete. Battalion proceeded to P 10 NEEER CAMP. During this hour 5 O.R. were killed & 8 Wounded.	R.A.

WAR DIARY
or
INTELLIGENCE SUMMARY.
(Erase heading not required.)

Army Form C. 2118.

Place	Date	Hour	Summary of Events and Information	Remarks and references to Appendices
PIONEER CAMP	20.12.16		Resting & getting cleaned up.	M.
	21.12.16	3.30pm	Battalion moved off from Camp to relieve 7/8 K.O.S.B. in right Section.	M.
1.22.d.6 4.0.		8.15pm	Relief Complete. K.O.S.B. remained working until 12 midnight. Work on wiring & improving posts continued. Posts were worried with aerial darts and Lights. Trench Mortars. Retaliation by 18 Pdrs was obtained for this.	M.
	22.12.16		Work carried on with wiring and improving posts. Received orders that Battn. would be relieved by 13th Royal Scots on night 23rd/24th inst.	M.
	23.12.16		Work carried on with wiring and improving posts. Posts again worried with Light Trench Mortars.	M.
		5.39pm	Relief by 13th Royal Scots commenced.	M.
		11.39pm	Relief complete. Battalion proceeded to Scots Redoubt South.	M.

WAR DIARY
or
INTELLIGENCE SUMMARY.
(Erase heading not required.)

Army Form C. 2118.

Place	Date	Hour	Summary of Events and Information	Remarks and references to Appendices
SCOTS REDOUBT SOUTH	24/12/16		Resting and cleaning up	R.S.
SOUTH	25/12/16		Christmas Day	R.S.
	26/12/16		Finding fatigue parties. Received orders for Batt'n to relief 8/10 Gordons at VILLA CAMP on afternoon of 27th inst.	R.S.
	27/12/16	2.30 pm	Marched off from SCOTS REDOUBT SOUTH	R.S.
		3.30 pm	Relief complete.	R.S.
	28/12/16		Finding working parties. Casualties 4 killed & 2 wounded in Coy. 4 wounded on working party. Received order to relieve 7/6 Ross in left section of left sector Regt Sub-sector of Divisional Front.	R.S.
	29/12/16	7.45 pm	Battalion moved off from VILLA CAMP.	R.S.
		9.15 pm	Relief complete.	
	30/12/16		Front covered by series of piquets & posts. Work carried on wiring and improving posts. Weather very bad.	R.S.

WAR DIARY or INTELLIGENCE SUMMARY

Army Form C. 2118

Place	Date	Hour	Summary of Events and Information	Remarks and references to Appendices
26th AVENUE	31.12.16		Working on wire continued also work on pigeon & posts.	R.1.
		5.30 p.m.	Relief by 7/8 H.O.S.B. commenced	
		7.45 p.m.	Relief complete. Battalion moved back to ACID DROP SOUTH CAMP.	

R. Chromill Major
Cmdg 14" H.L.I.

10/11th Batt'n,
The Highland Light Inf'y.

January, 1917

G.L
12 sheets

WAR DIARY or INTELLIGENCE SUMMARY

Army Form C. 2118

Place	Date	Hour	Summary of Events and Information	Remarks and references to Appendices
ACIDDROPS.	1/1/17		New Years Day.	T.Y.B.
" —	2.1.17		Time given to preparation for relief. Major J.C. Grahame D.S.O. took over Command of Bn.	
		3.45 p.m.	Bn. moved off to relieve 7/8th K.O.S.B. in Bde. left front Subsection (26th Avenue)	
		8.20 p.m.	Relief Complete. K.O.S.B's remaining behind to assist in wiring etc.	T.Y.B.
26th AVENUE.	2.1.17		All time given to improvement of trenches & Shelters. Front line practically no wire in front + with few Shelters. A Series of posts with all available time during night given to the Blething of wire.	T.Y.B.
" — "	3.1.17	10 a.m.	Received orders for Bn. to be relieved by 11th A+S. Highrs tonight. Improvement of Trenches, Shelters & Posts continued. Coys in Reserve in MARTIN POICH. carried up wiring material at dusk prior to relief.	
		5. p.m.	Relief Commenced. Casualties Three men wounded. During relief Bn. moved back to SCOTS. REDOUBT. SOUTH	T.Y.B.
T.Y.B.
SCOTS.REDOUBT	4.1.17	7.45 p.m.	Relief Complete.	
SOUTH.	5.1.17		Resting and Cleaning up. in preparation for emergencies. Finding Working Parties for road repair work in vicinity of CONTALMAISON.	T.Y.B.
"	6.1.17		Finding Working parties for road repair work in vicinity of CONTALMAISON. Received police order for new billets for Bn. in Royal Section to night 8/7th 2nd F.Y.B.	T.Y.B.

299

WAR DIARY or INTELLIGENCE SUMMARY

Army Form C. 2118

(Erase heading not required.)

Place	Date	Hour	Summary of Events and Information	Remarks and references to Appendices
SCOTS REDOUBT SOUTH.	7.1.17.		Finding working parties – road repair work. Received orders for relief of 44th Inf Bde. by 46th Inf Bde. in Right Sector of Divisional Front.	J.J.B.
"	8.1.17		Times given to preparation for move into Trenches to right. Maj J. Graham D.S.O. took over command of 17th Bn. H.L.I. Maj R. Nasmith took over command of 10th H.L.I. Bn. to Relieve 9/10th Gordons in Support Area of Bde. Right Sub-Sector SEVEN ELMS.	J.J.B.
"		3-30 pm	Bn. moved off from SCOTS REDOUBT SOUTH.	
"		4-45	Relief commenced.	
SEVEN ELMS		7-42.	Relief complete. Bn. dispositions as follows. Bn. H.Q. + C Coy in SEVEN ELMS and RUTHERFORD AVENUE. A Coy. PRUE TRENCH RIGHT; B. Coy. STAR FISH TRENCH; D Coy. PROE TRENCH. LEFT. No Casualties incurred during relief.	J.J.B.
M28.d.3.6. Gourvenant Avenue	9.1.17.		Improving of trenches and shelters. New shelters constructed. Two parties consisting of 1 NCO and 20 men each supplied twice daily by Bn. in Support for pushing R.E. Stores to E. Dump. R.E. Stores for right of 10th/11th Bn. Reserve.	J.J.B.
"	10.1.17.		General improvement of trenches and shelters and salvaging of equipment etc. lying in vicinity of trenches. All Dug-outs fitted with gas proof curtains. Finding working parties to carrying of R.E. material from MARTINPUICH to Forward Dump.	J.J.B.

300

WAR DIARY
INTELLIGENCE SUMMARY.
(Erase heading not required.)

Army Form C. 2118.

Place	Date	Hour	Summary of Events and Information	Remarks and references to Appendices
Rt. Bn. Support Area (SEVEN ELMS)	10/1/17	5.15 pm	Relief by 10th Scottish Rifles commenced	J.J.B.
PIONEER CAMP	11/1/17	8.10 pm	Relief Complete. – Bn. moved back to PIONEER CAMP. Finding of working parties for road repair, also work with R.E. in MARTINPUICH. Received orders to relieve 7/8th K.O.S.B. in RIGHT. Subsection of Bde front on night 12/13th inst.	J.J.B.
"	12/1/17	4 pm	Preparation for relief tonight. Bn. moved off from camp	
"	"	4.45 pm	Relief commenced.	
Bde. Rt. Sub-Section	"	8.10 pm	Relief Complete. Disposition of Coys as follows :- D. Coy. Rt. front; C. Coy. Left front; A. Coy. Support (FLERS LINE) B. Coy. Reserve FLERS SWITCH.) Bn. Hqrs. M.2.D.6.4.0.(Ref- Geudecourt 1/10000). On Completion of relief work was immediately commenced in the park and preparation. Wiring was made impossible by Hostile M.G. fire. Wire in front of posts is weak and thin in places.	J.J.B.
"	13/1/17		Work carried on in strengthening and deepening of posts at daylight 6 am garrison of posts of the two front Coys were withdrawn to SUPPORT TRENCH	301

WAR DIARY
or
INTELLIGENCE SUMMARY

Army Form C. 2118.

Place	Date	Hour	Summary of Events and Information	Remarks and references to Appendices
Bn Rt Sd. Sector J. Divl Front	13/1/17		in rear of post knwn to a bombardment commencing at 9-30 am That morning object of bombardment to destroy enemy's front trenches from M.17.b.0.2.5 to M.16.b.9.9. (Ref:- GUEUDECOURT 1/10000). The Bn took every opportunity of causing loss to the Enemy by Rifle Mn. Gun fire. At dusk posts were reoccupied by their garrisons work having continued work continued by two front Coys in improving posts & constructing shelter. Reserve & Support Coys occupies in similar work. Inter Coy relief to take place at dusk. B Coy relieved D Coy in Rt Front, A Coy relieved C Coy in Rt Front, C Coy. Bty moves back to Reserve Line. A Coy moves back to Support. (FLERS LINE). Casualties during relief - one officer and 9 O.R. wounded - 2Lt D.C. Ferguson.	J.F.B. J.F.B. 302
	14/1/17	9-10pm	Inter Coy Reliefs complete. Coys in Support & Reserve carrying up wiring & revetting material. A party of 1 Officer and 25. OR supplied to R.E's for work in MAXWELL Support trench. Strong parties of wire between the front of post carriers by the two forward Coys. Hostile Shelling heavy at times during the day throught.	J.F.B.

Army Form C. 2118

WAR DIARY
or
INTELLIGENCE SUMMARY
(Erase heading not required.)

Instructions regarding War Diaries and Intelligence Summaries are contained in F. S. Regs., Part II. and the Staff Manual respectively. Title Pages will be prepared in manuscript.

Place	Date	Hour	Summary of Events and Information	Remarks and references to Appendices
Bde. Rt. Sub. Section of Brit Front.	15/1/17		Carried on wiring and improvement of posts. All dug out entrances fitted with gas-proof curtains. Working party of 1 Officer + 25 men supplied to R.E.'s for work in Maxwell Support Trench — (near of strong Post). Corps in Reserve + Support Carried up. wiring + R.E material to the two forward Coys.	
"	16/1/17	5.30am	Orders for relief of 46th J.Bde. by 45th Inf. Bde received 1. 10/11 1/17 – L.1.5. The relieving bn. 13th R.S. Taking over party proceeds to S.15.a.1.7 to take over camp. Improvement of posts etc carried on.) all stores etc collected and Checked for handing over to relieving Bn. – 13th R.S.	T.J.B.
"		5.30pm	Relief commenced.	
		8-42	Relief complete. Bn moved back to Camp at S.15.a.1.7. Known as CINQUE PORTS. – lying between BAZENTIN LE GRAND and BAZENTIN LE PETIT. Weather cold with snow falling.	303
CINQUE PORTS CAMP	17/1/17		Resting + cleaning up. Weather suddenly turns very cold. heavy snowfalls.	T.J.B.
"	18/1/17		Finding working Parties for repair work on roads. Weather bell. + freezing hard.	T.J.B.

Army Form C. 2118

WAR DIARY
or
INTELLIGENCE SUMMARY
(Erase heading not required.)

Instructions regarding War Diaries and Intelligence Summaries are contained in F. S. Regs, Part II. and the Staff Manual respectively. Title Pages will be prepared in manuscript.

304

Place	Date	Hour	Summary of Events and Information	Remarks and references to Appendices
INGO. PORTE CAMP.	9/1/17		Finding of working Parties for road work etc. Relief orders for relief of 4th & 6th Bdes. by 46th Bde. in Left Section of Div. Front received. Weather cold. Frosty haze.	J.F.B.
"	20/1/17		Preparation for Bn. move to VILLA Camp at 2.P.M.	J.F.B.
VILLA Camp	2.p.m.	Bn. moved to VILLA Camp. from Third Two Corps C-D proceed to relieve 2 Corps 9th Black Watch in Shelters at M 31.a.	J.F.B.
"	21/1/17		MARTINPUICH. Working party of 2 Officers and 150 O.R. for work on roads. Finding of working parties from Two Corps in VILLA Camp. for road repair work. Orders received — Bn. move to PIONEER Camp. 10th Scottish Rifles relieving. Weather Shell very cold with occasional falls of Snow.	J.F.B.
	22/1/17	3pm	Relief commences at VILLA Camp. Complete at 3-30 p.m.	J.F.B.
		7 p.m.	Relief Complete of Two Corps in MARTINPUICH at 7 p.m.	J.F.B.
GID DROP CAMP	23/1/17		Order received to relieve 1/6th K.O.S.B's. in Left Sub section of Div. Front. Finding of working parties for road work etc. Weather very cold. Frosty haze.	J.F.B.

Army Form C. 2118

WAR DIARY
or
INTELLIGENCE SUMMARY
(Erase heading not required.)

Place	Date	Hour	Summary of Events and Information	Remarks and references to Appendices
ACID DROP CAMP.	24/1/17		Preparation for relief tonight of 7/8. K.O.S.B., Tour to last four days. Return for first two days to be taken up.	
		4.30pm	Bn left camp for trenches.	
		5.50 pm	Relief commenced.	
26TH AVENUE.		9.15 pm	Relief completed. Dispositions of Coys were as follows:— D Coy right front, C Coy left front, B Coy support, A Coy in reserve in MARTIN PUICH. 10th Scottish Rifles on our Right, Essex Regt on our left. – Casualties Nil.	
		9.30pm	Working parties started work immediately after relief on improvement of food service. Weather still very cold – guns took not worn.	7.F.13
"	25/1/17		Work in front trenches continues.	
		6 pm	Party 1 of 1.N.C.O and 20 men proceeded for work in left Pln Bomb Store near junction of O.G.1 and Gilbert Alley under Supervision of 9.2nd F.Coy R.E.	
		9.30pm	Party of 6 men of others to 91st F. Coy R.E for work in Post R.16. Reserve line at M.15.c.6.8.	
		9.45	Party. H. of 10 men for carrying R.E material from R.E Store to Post 16. – Casualties Nil. Weather very cold frosty Kenn.	7.F.13

WAR DIARY or INTELLIGENCE SUMMARY

Army Form C. 2118

Place	Date	Hour	Summary of Events and Information	Remarks and references to Appendices
26th Avenue	26/1/17		Work continued. Improvement of Posts, wire etc. etc. Inter. Coy. relief to take place to night.	
		7.30 p.m.	Rations for 27th & 28th inst brought up along BAPAUME RD. to junction of ? Rd with GILBERT ALLEY.	
		8.25 p.m.	Inter. Coy. relief Complete.	
		9 p.m.	1 N.C.O. & 20 men. Supplies to R.E's for work on L.12a Bomb Store. Worked till 1 A.M.	
		9.30 p.m.	6 men to R.E's for work on Posts in Reserve Line. M.15.c.6.8. Trenches freezing etc. Casualties — nil.	T.F.B.
	27/1/17	1. A.M.	1 N.C.O. 20 men to R.E's for work on L.12a Bomb Store. Worked till 4.12 A.M. Improvement of posts shelters etc. still continues.	
" "		8.30 p.m.	An Enemy patrol consisting of a Corporal and two men were captured near the Chalk. CHALK PIT. They were of the 64th R.I.R.; much information of value were given by them including a map of the opposite trenches shewing their disposition of machine guns etc. Orders received for relief tomorrow night 28th inst by 11th A+S. Highrs. Weather extremely cold. — men sticking it well. Casualties — nil. After dusk, wiring of posts continued.	T.F.B.

306

WAR DIARY or INTELLIGENCE SUMMARY

Army Form C. 2118

Place	Date	Hour	Summary of Events and Information	Remarks and references to Appendices
1st AVENUE	28/1/17	1.a.m.	Party of 1 NCO + 20 men supplied to R.Es. for work on L.Rn. Bomb Store - worked till 4am. Work in trenches put in improvement construction of shelter continues	
		5-30 pm	Relief by 11th A.I.S. Highrs. commences. (44th Bde). Relief Complete	
		9-5 pm	At this hour. The Bn. moved back to CINQUE PORTS CAMP — BAZENTIN.	
CINQUE PORTS CAMP		11-15pm	Bn. complete in Camp. Enemy suspects that a relief was in progress as all tracks ways were subjected to a heavy bombardment. MARTIN PUICH being heavily shelled. Casualties — one man died, cause of death unknown.	T.P.B.
"	29/1/17		Day given up to cleaning of equipment etc. Weather still very cold.	T.P.B.
"	30/1/17		Cleaning up + refitting as far as possible in preparation for move back to ALBERT. Division going back for rest. 2nd Australian Div. relieving. Orders regarding move to ALBERT. Received. Weather still freezing. Condition of men good.	T.P.B.

Army Form C. 2118

WAR DIARY or INTELLIGENCE SUMMARY

Place	Date	Hour	Summary of Events and Information	Remarks and references to Appendices
ALBERT.	31/1/17		Bn. marched off from CINQUE PORTS CAMP - BAZENTIN at 10-20 a.m., route to ALBERT - via CONTALMAISON and LA BOISELLE. Bn. arrived in ALBERT billeted by 12-45.p.m. Bn. H.Q. in 22 Rue de AVELUY. Afternoon given to resting. Weather very cold.	T.J.B.
	1/2/17			

J.R. Easton. Capt.
Comndg. 10th H.L.I.

10/11th Batt'n,
The Highland Light Inf'y,
February, 1917

10.L

Army Form C. 2118.

WAR DIARY
or
INTELLIGENCE SUMMARY

(Erase heading not required.)

Place	Date	Hour	Summary of Events and Information	Remarks and references to Appendices
ALBERT	1/2/17		The work of refitting the battalion, after a period of two months in the front line, began. Strict inspections were held and clothing and boots were exchanged and repaired. Trench and washhouse equipment was examined and made up. There was a general cleaning up of clothing and equipment. At this time Capt. R.P. Eaton was in temporary command of the battalion during the absence on leave of Lt. Col. R. Mcneill M.C.	310/13
"	2/2/17		Along with the work of refitting a great deal of drill was carried out in the yard of the GENDARMERIE particularly for NCO's. An account of the recent raids on the town by hostile aircraft, two Lewis gun teams were on duty all night with views to the aim when the planes showed and made its hostility apparent by firing a bomb in the town. A battalion parade was strong as possible was held at 10 am on the GENDARMERIE yard and afforded a practical demonstration of the necessity for drill. The result of the refitting showed themselves in the uniform appearance presented by the men on parade. Orders were received to proceed on the following day to WARLOY Sunday.	
"	3/2/17			
"	4/2/17	8 am	The Battalion marched out and passed the "WARLOY" - BAC. starting point on the MILLENCOURT ROAD at 8.20 am.	

WAR DIARY or INTELLIGENCE SUMMARY

Army Form C. 2118.

Place	Date	Hour	Summary of Events and Information	Remarks and references to Appendices
WARLOY	5/2/17		The route was by MILLENCOURT and HENENCOURT to WARLOY which we reached as the church bells were ringing at about 10.20 A.m. The battalion was partly billeted on the main WARLOY-CONTAY ROAD, partly in the RUE NEUVE and partly in the RUE DU BAS BAILLON. While battalion H.Q. was in M. I. GRANDE RUE DU BAILLON. The men's billets were mainly barns and great care had to be taken to prevent fires. In WARLOY the ground used for training was that situated immediately N. of the town and to the W. of the WARLOY - VARENNES ROAD. Yor battalion parades and football matches we used a ground immediately S. of the RUE DU BAS BAILLON and adjoining his Transport Lines. The majority of the billets were only about two minutes walk from its majority of the billets. Every morning at 7am there was a battalion parade in the ground taken in alternate days by the Adjutant and the R.S.M. Forenoons were occupied with training for offensive action on the lines laid down and platoons were organised as fighting units with specialist sections and earmarked for specific functions in attack.	

WAR DIARY or INTELLIGENCE SUMMARY

Army Form C. 2118.

Place	Date	Hour	Summary of Events and Information	Remarks and references to Appendices
WARLOY	6/2/17		Similarly afternoons were consistently devoted to recreational training. Football matches were arranged and played between half companies and considerable interest was shown. Tug of war competitions were also held. Draft from Reinforcement Camp at HENENCOURT WOOD rejoined. Bn.	
"	7/2/17		Training as above.	
"	8/2/17		A short route march was held in the forenoon round by SENLIS and back by the HEDAUVILLE - WARLOY ROAD. Training continued. Major J.C. Graham D.S.O. rejoined and assumed temporary command. Information was received that the battalion would have some days of continuous marching and a preparatory route march should therefore be held.	
"	9/2/17		Training continued. Draft of about 95 recruits (Royal Scots and Royal Scots Fusiliers) physically in the main good, but training very incomplete.	

WAR DIARY or INTELLIGENCE SUMMARY

(Erase heading not required.)

Army Form C. 2118.

Place	Date	Hour	Summary of Events and Information	Remarks and references to Appendices
WARLOY	10/2/17	10.30am	Route march took place as practice for the coming move. The Route was by VADENCOURT and VARENNES and so back to WARLOY. The distance was about 11 miles in all and the men were dry and good. About 6 men fell out before the end.	
"	11/2/17		Sunday. Church Parade.	
"	12/2/17	10am	Contact Aircraft Scheme. This exercise was carried out under Bde. arrangements and took place on the ground by the WARLOY-HENENCOURT ROAD. Bde. HQ and Bn. HQ and 1 Company from each battalion took part. Bn. HQ were established at the corner of HENENCOURT WOOD by the road. At 10 am the contact plane flew over the companies representing their battalion in the first objective and called for flares. Yellow Flares were lit and the was repeated when the advance was made to second and final objectives. Message was sent and received also by Bn. HQ.	

Army Form C. 2118.

WAR DIARY
or
INTELLIGENCE SUMMARY
(Erase heading not required.)

Instructions regarding War Diaries and Intelligence Summaries are contained in F. S. Regs., Part II. and the Staff Manual respectively. Title Pages will be prepared in manuscript.

Place	Date	Hour	Summary of Events and Information	Remarks and references to Appendices
WARLOY	13/2/17	8.10 a.m.	The Battalion passed the Bde. Starting point at WARLOY Brewery and marched to billets in BEAUVAL. The route was by CONTAY, HERISSART, LE VAL DE MAISON and VERT GALAND Fme. During the march no. 1 and 1a had been returned him hospital on the previous evening. Billets in BEAUVAL were good and were practically all in the RUE DU BOURG	8 p.m.
BEAUVAL	14/2/17		The Battalion passed the starting point on the BEAUVAL – GEZAINCOURT ROAD at 10 a.m. and marched to billets in OUTREBOIS with the exception of C Coy who was up to about 250 strong which proceeded to MILLY as part of a Bde. working party under Major R. Naesmith M.C. The march to OUTREBOIS was by GEZAINCOURT, BRETEL, HEM and OCCOCHES. The march was completed shortly after mid-day and no one fell out.	8 p.m.

WAR DIARY or INTELLIGENCE SUMMARY

Army Form C. 2118

Place	Date	Hour	Summary of Events and Information	Remarks and references to Appendices
OUTREBOIS	15/2/17	About 9 am	The battalion marched out of OUTREBOIS for FORTEL and arrived there about mid-day. The route lay by MEZEROLLES, FROHEN LE GRAND and VILLERS L'HOPITAL. In FORTEL all the billets were full of sheds and extra precautions against fire had to be taken. H.Q. was situated in a house by the Railway Crossing.	
FORTEL	16/2/17	About 7:30 am	The battalion marched out of FORTEL and proceeded by PETIT FORTEL to the main FREVENT ROAD and so by FREVENT and MAGNICOURT SUR CANCHE to AMBRINES where we were to stay for the next few days train to proceeding to relieve part of the 12th Division in ARRAS. Billets in AMBRINES were good, from the point of view of the men, as most of the farms were fitted with bunks, but officers' accommodation was poor.	
AMBRINES	17/2/17		In AMBRINES training was continued on the same lines as at WARLOY with early parades on a ground just outside the village and on the right of the AMBRINES – MAGNICOURT ROAD	

WAR DIARY or INTELLIGENCE SUMMARY

Army Form C. 2118

Place	Date	Hour	Summary of Events and Information	Remarks and references to Appendices
AMBRINES	18/2/17		Other training was carried out S. of the village and E. of the AMBRINES – LIGNEREUIL ROAD. Attachment from MILLY known Major R. Naesmith M.C. rejoined. Sunday. Church Parades in barn behind the Chateau.	
"	19/2/17		Training continued.	
"	20/2/17		Training. Practising the attack. A good deal of instruction in wiring was also carried out	
"	21/2/17		Training as above	
"	22/2/17		Orders received to proceed on following day to DUISANS	
"	23/2/17		At 8.42 A.m. The battalion passed the starting point at the eastern end of the village and marched by GIVENCHY LE NOBLE	

WAR DIARY or INTELLIGENCE SUMMARY

Army Form C. 2118.

Place	Date	Hour	Summary of Events and Information	Remarks and references to Appendices
DUISANS	24/3/17		MANIN, NOYELLE-VION and HABARCQ to DUISANS where we were accommodated in No 4 Camp which had recently been constructed and was absolutely devoid of furniture. An advance party of 1 Officer and 20 O.R. who sent on to ARRAS to arrange accommodation for working parties amounting to 150 O.R. due to proceed there on the following day.	
"			Accommodation has found to the will age for 2 corps. 1 coy made up to the necessary strength proceeded to ARRAS to supply the parties mentioned above and the Hq and Bn HQ. were left in No 4 Camp.	
"	25/3/17		Lt. Col. R.F. Forbes D.S.O. rejoined from England and took over Command of the battalion. Orders were received to proceed to billets in ARRAS the following night.	

WAR DIARY or **INTELLIGENCE SUMMARY**

Army Form C. 2118.

Place	Date	Hour	Summary of Events and Information	Remarks and references to Appendices
DUISANS	26/2/17		Advance parties and cleaning parties were sent on in the forenoon and at 5.20pm the battalion left DUISANS and marched to billets in ARRAS. Bn. HQ. was at No 15 RUE GAMBETTA and the mens billets were in cellars in the GRANDE PLACE. Men rested and Officers reconnoitred the line prior to taking over.	9pm. T.J.B.
ARRAS.	27/2/17		Received orders to take over line next day.	T.J.B.
"	28/2/17		Left Billets at 8 am. to take over the line from The Royal Sub-Section of the Bde. Front. Relief complete at 9-35 am. Dispositions of Bn. as follows :- B Coy: Front Line, C Coy in Support Arm: half Coy in billets in Rue St. Michel. "A" & "D" Coys in Reserve — In cellars in GRANDE PLACE. Working parties were supplied from the two Coys in Reserve to the forward Coys. Casualties 1 killed, 2 wounded. M.G.R. shelled more than usual between 9pm +10-30 pm	T.J.B. T.J. Goughtrie Lt. Col. Commdg 10/11 H.L.I.

Confidential

Vol 21

War Diary
of
10th Sqn Highland Light Inf

From 1st March 1917
To 31st March 1917

Vol.

11.L.
13 sheets

WAR DIARY or INTELLIGENCE SUMMARY

Army Form C. 2118.

Place	Date	Hour	Summary of Events and Information	Remarks and references to Appendices
ARRAS	1.3.19		Battalion still in the line. There were no active operations of any sort. Large working parties were taken from the own Coys. for clearing country, the front line trench which had been allowed to fall into a very bad state of dilapidation by the last occupants. An experimental gas entertainment had been arranged for the night Feb 28/Mar. 1st, but was cancelled. Things were is have been discharged from our lines in to no mans land. Still in the line. Situation very quiet. Work continued on the front and support lines.	
"	2.3.19			
"	3.3	5.30 am.	The Battalion was relieved by the 6/7th R. Scots. Frs., the Coys. in the front and support lines were relieved at about 5.30 am. marched back to billets in the GRAND PLACE, Headquarters moved from the RUE ST. MICHEL to the 15 No 15, RUE GAMBETTA. The Coys. in reserve moved to a different set of billets. (Most of their time had been spent in moving from one set of billets in Arras.) In the evening the Battalion moved out	

WAR DIARY

INTELLIGENCE SUMMARY

Place	Date	Hour	Summary of Events and Information	Remarks and references to Appendices
ARRAS	3.3 (cont)		ARRAS. The starting point — PORTE BAUDIMONT — was passed at 6.50 p.m. The Bath. marched about 10.30 p.m. Billets were, on the whole, good. Unfortunately the transport was delayed and all the blankets were left at ARRAS.	
HABARCQ	4.3		The day was spent in rest, and after's Units were moved for 13th Coy to proceed on a permanent working fatigue with the 25th Canadian Fron. Coy.	
"	5.3	9.00 a.m.	Paraded in the morning under NCRs. to steady & chief. Handling of arms, training was carried out under Coy. arrangements: Bombers, Snipers, Lewis Gunners & under their own officers. Attack in Artillery formation was practiced. "B" Coy moved in the afternoon to BLAVINCOURT to take up work under the Canadian Tunnel Corps.	
"	6.3		Training continued as above.	

WAR DIARY
INTELLIGENCE SUMMARY

Army Form C. 2118.

Place	Date	Hour	Summary of Events and Information	Remarks and references to Appendices
HABARCQ	7.3		Training continued. Officers were now chiefly matched. Advantage was taken today of the baths in the village. An afternoon class for N.C.O. Readers was started a few days ago by Major R. Naismith, M.C.	
"	8.3		Training continued, as far as possible, much interfered by large working parties, detachments re: BOX RESPIRATORS &c. At last issue Spittis Bothie came for "C" Coy to proceed in a permanent working party similar to that on which "D" Coy is employed. A canvas screen held in the Church Army tent, at which the Divisional Band was present.	
"	9.3		Training chiefly bombing continued. The 44th Bn carried out a machine attack on trenches laid out at LIGNEREUIL. The C.O. and Adjutant attended for instructional purposes. Capt. R.P. EASTON was attached to the 12th R.I. to act as Second in Command.	

Army Form C. 2118.

WAR DIARY
or
INTELLIGENCE SUMMARY
(Erase heading not required.)

Place	Date	Hour	Summary of Events and Information	Remarks and references to Appendices
HABARCQ	10/3		Training was carried out as follows:- 7.0am. Rev[eille]." Parade under R.S.M., 9.30am. Lewis Gunners to parade under their own officers. All officers not otherwise employed, under the Bombing officer, for instruction in the use of the S.I.Bead Bomb, & clearing dug-outs. In the afternoon the Bn marched to billets in IZEL-LEZ-HAMEAU. The starting point was passed at 2.0pm.,& the destination reached shortly after 4.0pm. Rations for both officers and men [being] food. Again there were some troubles with the transport, which did not arrive till 10pm. G.	
IZEL-LEZ-HAMEAU	11/3		Church Parade in the morning. In the afternoon Major R. NASMITH, M.C. gave a lecture to all officers in which preliminary instructions were given with regard to the coming offensive. G.	

WAR DIARY
or
INTELLIGENCE SUMMARY
(Erase heading not required.)

Army Form C. 2118

Place	Date	Hour	Summary of Events and Information	Remarks and references to Appendices
IZEL-LEZ-HAMEAU	12.3		Training. The attack - including capture, exploitation of supply dumps during attack a.s.o - was practised on ground near LIGNEREUIL and DENIER, where trenches have been laid out there in the fac-simile of those which Division will advance during the coming offensive. Kitchen is bad; no recreational training possible.	
"	13.3		& raining. Was again carried out as above.	
"	14.3		As above, the whole attack was carried out;	
"	15.3		Training. The attack which had thoroughly been practised by every Battalion was now carried out by the Brigade, the preliminary practice was clearly shown, as the whole of the Bouclecliers was a distinct success. The Brigadier himself tried a slight formed with the whole of the troops which he himself is carrying orders to given to ARRAS on the 19th instant.	

WAR DIARY or INTELLIGENCE SUMMARY

Army Form C. 2118

Place	Date	Hour	Summary of Events and Information	Remarks and references to Appendices
ZEL-LEZ-HAMEAU 16.3				
"	17th		There was no field training. Or noon the Brigadier addressed the officers on the coming operations, after this there was a demonstration of methods of using live cutters Anselow. In the afternoon Box Respirators were issued to those who required it.	
"	18.		A "Divisional" field day was held; the 8th Brigade was imagining an "Unforeseen Situation" was provided, they dealt with it as well [illegible] to heaven, but were not individually consulted, on share to the satisfaction country of they still in a wood. [illegible] the German retirement on the Somme continues. News came last of the fall of BAPAUME. Arrival Mathieson has been given command from the 25th Division. Reaction March at 11 tampm. Lt. Col. the Brigadier however addressed, H ordered great regrets at leaving the Brigade, but offered to the great take done by the Brigade. In conclusion he gave some advice on the coming offensive. Loud fretted in the afternoon. Abdication of the CZAR has caused much comment speculation.	

1875 Wt. W 593/826 1,000,000 4/15 J.B.C. & A. A.D.S.S./Forms/C. 2118.

WAR DIARY
or
INTELLIGENCE SUMMARY

Army Form C. 2118

Place	Date	Hour	Summary of Events and Information	Remarks and references to Appendices
IZEL-LEZ-HAMEAU	19th		The Battalion left IZEL-LEZ-HAMEAU and marched to billets in ARRAS. It moved off at 1.30 p.m. and arrived at 6 p.m. when the Bn. bivouacked in a field just off the road. Rain which had been threatening for some considerable time came on, and made the march very disagreeable. It reached ARRAS at about 6.25 p.m. The men again are billeted in cellars, not far from the PETITE PLACE. Bn. Hd. at 46 RUE DES TROIS VISAGES.	
ARRAS	20th		As the Battalion is in Brigade Reserve just now, we have nothing to do but working parties. There are daily going on. Men working parties. Orders were received to be in readiness to counter attack at short notice if necessary. Rifles were in GRANDE PLACE; bomb & store dumps started there.	
"	21st		Casualties, 1 wounded.	
"	22nd		Heavy working parties continued. Firing of Stumps carried on. A draft of 100 from the 3rd Entrenching Bn. arrived: few quality. Casualties, 1 wounded.	

WAR DIARY or INTELLIGENCE SUMMARY

Army Form C. 2118.

Place	Date	Hour	Summary of Events and Information	Remarks and references to Appendices
ARRAS	23rd		The 27th Brigade carried out a raid in the early morning. Taken into it was a failure. The Germans were waiting for them, and casualties were severe that day. Parcel Sjt: Smith's workers parties were continued. Casualties 2 wounded. The 10th Scot. Rif. secured extra rest just N. of the RAILWAY. It	
	24th		was fairly successful, but no identification was secured. The fort lines were almost deserted. It was found that the men were worked. Casualties were fairly heavy, mostly caused by staying out too long and being caught by the morning light. Returned to the post lines. Rest of the day passed quietly. Bags water parties out. Much digging going on at night. Casualties 1 wounded.	
	25th		Fairly quiet day. Stokes artillery shelled the supports and also the CEMETERY DEFENCES. A lot of work was done namely cleaning, deepening communication trenches which between shelling and rain had got into a bad state. Casualties 2 wounded.	
	26th		The men wounded yesterday died in hospital. Battalion still in the line. Hostile artillery fairly active. In the afternoon there was a sharp bombardment about A.29h., which did a lot of damage to the posts and support line and caused some casualties. Heavy working parties continued clearing and repairing trenches. Casualties 9 wounded.	

WAR DIARY

INTELLIGENCE SUMMARY

Place	Date	Hour	Summary of Events and Information	Remarks and references to Appendices
ARRAS	27		Hostile Artillery and action. Work continued. The C.T's especially received a good deal of yesterday's bombardment. The CEMETERY and T.M. attacks during incoming the day. Our continue wire cutting. From patrol reports, the results are good. Casualties. 9 wounded.	
" "	28		Thursday. Passed fairly quietly, but about 5.30 P.M. the enemy shelled somewhat of the town very heavily, watch the STATION. Last night (and — a working hat was engaged in removing "LOUSE WALLERS" (and all empty — home a dug out in the support area. This rift it were finished, else were in the accidents: a great relief. Casualties. 1 wounded.	
" "	29		A Silent Raid was carried out at 2.0 a.m. by 6th R. Warwicks on our right. At about 3:15 a.m. the Germans placed a heavy barrage on our front and support lines. A little later they sent up a rocket which burst into two green lights, and its remarks combination the German thought was mistaken for an S.O.S. in taking a definite fire, which lasted for about any	

WAR DIARY
or
INTELLIGENCE SUMMARY

(Erase heading not required.)

Army Form C. 2118.

Place	Date	Hour	Summary of Events and Information	Remarks and references to Appendices
ARRAS	29	cont.	An immense amount of enemy ammunition was found in his half. A good deal of damage was done to our trenches by the enemy fire, but casualties were few. With almost his last shell, he blew up a dump of bren trench mortar ammunition. The result was a tremendous explosion; the supervising hymn complete destroyed, and a large crater formed. The 1st Scots. Rif. lost his three platoons, who were on guard. He was relieved by the 12th K.O.S.L.I. and marched back to his former billets, with spread guards at 46 RUE DES TROIS VISAGES in the station, present guard quickly looking having again carried on. Rest of the Battalion Ocrup in the GRAND PLACE was completed by	Casualties 1 wounded 1 killed
ARRAS	30		the addition of 4000 rounds S.A.A. In the evening we were relieved by the 6th CAMERONS, and moved out to the reedgrove on the FAUBOURG DES BAUDIMONT, by a complicated back-road which had a at transport through the newspark. The Battalion then marched to billets at NOYELLETTE. Here in a NISSEN Hut, comfy and quite comfortable. In the third time, the blanket wagon failed us, and it was not till 6.0am that the blankets of a Coy of arrived.	Casualties 2 wounded 2 missing (also a Bomb Dump) 1 chief wounded

WAR DIARY

Army Form C. 2118.

Place	Date	Hour	Summary of Events and Information	Remarks and references to Appendices
HÉNU	31		The day was spent in resting and cleaning up.	

R.P. Parker
Lieut-Colonel
Comdg. 1/4 R.B.

46/15

10/11th (S) Bn. High. L.I.

Vol 22

WAR DIARY
APRIL 1917

CONFIDENTIAL

12. L.
25 sheets

Army Form C. 2118.

WAR DIARY
or
INTELLIGENCE SUMMARY
(Erase heading not required.)

Instructions regarding War Diaries and Intelligence Summaries are contained in F. S. Regs., Part II. and the Staff Manual respectively. Title Pages will be prepared in manuscript.

Place	Date	Hour	Summary of Events and Information	Remarks and references to Appendices
NOYELLETTE	April 1st		Sunday. Church parade in the morning. The Battalion paraded on the road outside the camp, and marched down where to HABARCQ, where the service was held.	
"	2nd		Training was carried out on the ground at K13 b 3.5. Training was under Coy. arrangements, and included attacking in the open, and breaking from into Artillery formation into HABARCQ was obtained, and practically the use of the Baths at HABARCQ was obtained, and practically the whole Batn was able to get a clean up. During the morning Coy. Commanders reconnoitred a back road into ARRAS, via. the SCARPE VALLEY and ST. CATHERINE.	
"	3rd		Training was continued during the forenoon but had to be broken off by a hostile 9 in. gun which shell the town very severely to ARRAS on the 1th inclusive of the 5th. All the final arrangements were made prior to settling down in cellars for the period of the bombardment. pm.	

WAR DIARY or INTELLIGENCE SUMMARY

Army Form C. 2118.

Place	Date	Hour	Summary of Events and Information	Remarks and references to Appendices
NOYELLETTE	6/4/17		Preparation for operation. Surplus personnel left and 9 officers under Section XXX S.S. 135 were sent to DUISANS some to be accommodated there at the first line transport. Remainder disposed to the Corps Depot Battalion at FREVENT for the period of the action. At about 6.30 p.m. the Battalion marched out of NOYELLETTE about 680 strong and proceeded to ARRAS via the ST. POL – ARRAS road, the SCARPE VALLEY, ST CATHERINE and the BASSIN. The bombardment had started on the morning of the 4th but the enemy was not retaliating to any great extent and we reached ARRAS without casualty. The Battalion was accommodated in cellars 76 – 683 in the GRANDE PLACE (Western Side). Till Zero day (9th inst.) we remained in the cellars and collected all the materials to be carried into action and there were distributed amongst the men. There always to the cellars was a complete road; Every morning there was a hour for physical drill and afterwards packs of playing cards were issued both hour concert was arranged and everything was done to keep the men amused. Meanwhile the bombardment	

Army Form C. 2118.

WAR DIARY
or
INTELLIGENCE SUMMARY
(Erase heading not required.)

Instructions regarding War Diaries and Intelligence Summaries are contained in F. S. Regs., Part II. and the Staff Manual respectively. Title Pages will be prepared in manuscript.

Place	Date	Hour	Summary of Events and Information	Remarks and references to Appendices
ARRAS	5/4/17		Continued ous the entry knowledge to that has been hithedr to know the cellars.	A.m. P.m
"	6/4/17		In the cellars.	A.m. P.m.
"	7/4/17		In the cellars.	P.m.
"	8/4/17		Sunday. In the cellars. There were Easter from Services and a celebration of the Communion.	A.m. P.m.
"	9/4/17	5.30 a.m.	Operations commenced. See Battalion Operation No 78 and Report on Operations attached	See Appendices "A" and "B" A.m. P.m.
FEUCHY	10/4/17		Operations continued	
MONCHY	11/4/17		Operations continued.	
"	12/4/17		Relieved at 6 am by 10th Yorks. 17th Division. The batt. then proceeded first to the RAILWAY TRIANGLE and remained there for about two hours after which it proceeded to ARRAS to billets in the RUE GAMBETTA	

WAR DIARY or INTELLIGENCE SUMMARY

Army Form C. 2118.

Place	Date	Hour	Summary of Events and Information	Remarks and references to Appendices
ARRAS	13/4/17		When we took stock of our losses. Our total casualties were 8 Officers and 216 O.R. killed & our officers wounded and respectively few had been killed. The officers were Capt W.B. Henderson killed, Lieut W. Rae killed, 2/Lt. J. Mathers killed, 2/Lt. G. Ross wounded, 2/Lt. P.C. Hutcheon wounded, 2/Lt. T. Allan wounded, 2/Lt. A.B. Roger wounded, 2/Lt. A. Gildner wounded. The work of refitting began sharply away, and a battalion dump was formed in cellar 8 RUE GAMBETTA in rear of public quarters. A draft of 100 O.R. arrived from FREVENT, together some of the Battalion details. The Defunt Batt. Commander did not sit our fit to let our how our Regimental workshops in Rand.	Mm
—	14/4/17		In the morning we had the usury of the bath at the BOOTS COMMUNAL and an issue of clean clothing was made by the Brigade. In look of cleaning up the Batts. was carried on vigorously and with very good effect. In the afternoon we marched to FILLIEVES, DUISANS, we moved off at 2.30 pm in order of march C.D.A.B. The Divisional Commander took the salute of the Brigade on DUISANS. In spite of the hard time then had first come through, the men presented a	

WAR DIARY or INTELLIGENCE SUMMARY

Army Form C. 2118.

Place	Date	Hour	Summary of Events and Information	Remarks and references to Appendices
DUISANS	15/4/17		very small afternoon but were accommodated officially - in four long huts 3 for the Bn and one for the officers. All ranks were severe, but by judicious use of these not allotted to us we reached a degree of comparative comfort. Sunday Church parade. The Divisional Priest Canon Scott gave a performance in the concert hut which was well attended. Church church service only by their absence. Physicians, hut was very conspicuous only by their absence. Physicians, hut thus were some who seemed to be "Roused" and rest in the Pew with all possible speed.	28
	16/4/17		All effort to carry out the much needed training were successfully foiled by the weather, which was still extraordinary, the ground was covered with some inches of wet snow, which rapid thaws chief and muddy slush. The use of the Baths at AGNEZ-LES-DUISANS was secured but morning staff training carried a further outbreak of cleaning.	29 30

2449 Wt. W14957/M90 750,000 1/16 J.B.C. & A. Forms/C.2118/12.

WAR DIARY
or
INTELLIGENCE SUMMARY

Army Form C. 2118.

Place	Date	Hour	Summary of Events and Information	Remarks and references to Appendices
DUISANS	14.4.17		The threatened inspection was put owing to the weather. It was decided it would be best not obey. Turning out of clean kit was impossible, and it had to be confined to helmets &c.	
"	16.2.17		The General's Inspection was again postponed, this time indefinitely. During the morning training was again impossible. Early in the afternoon we suddenly got orders to evacuate the camp by 6 p.m. and go to No 4 camp, at the far end of the village, to lift immediately after tea and were settled down before dark. This time we were on Nissen Huts.	
"	19.4.17		Training was carried out under Cy. arrangements. Special attention being given to practising semi-open warfare and breaking from artillery formation into waves. The draft had special parades with the R.S.M. at 4.0 c.m. and 2 o'p.m.	
"	20.4.17		Training was carried out as on the 19th. Arrangements made for move to ARRAS tomorrow.	

WAR DIARY
or
INTELLIGENCE SUMMARY.

(Erase heading not required.)

Army Form C. 2118.

Place	Date	Hour	Summary of Events and Information	Remarks and references to Appendices
DUISANS	21-4-17		The Battalion moved to billets in ARRAS. Bn. moved off at 10.20am in order of march D,A,B,C Coys. Bn. was billeted in cellars in and round the RUE GAMBETTA. In the afternoon Coys. were completed with bombs &c from the Batt's Dump.	
ARRAS	22-4-17		Sunday. Church Parade at 10.20am. At 8.20pm the Battalion paraded in the RUE GAMBETTA and marched to its position S. of TILLOY known as the HARP where was to be accommodated until Zero hour on the following day. M.M.	
TILLOY	23/4/17		In action. For account of the operation on 23/4/17 and 24/4/17 see Operation Order No. 81 attached and Report on Operations. M.M.	Appendices B and D
	24/4/17		In action.	
BROWN LINE	25/4/17		The day was spent in Divisional Reserve in the BROWN LINE holding the men after the strenuous fighting of the preceding days. Companies were hurriedly reorganised and filled out with S.A.A. and other S.S. At first it was very difficult to form an accurate estimate of our Casualties. A small party continued to come in from other regiments to right and left of	

WAR DIARY
or
INTELLIGENCE SUMMARY.
(Erase heading not required.)

Army Form C. 2118.

Place	Date	Hour	Summary of Events and Information	Remarks and references to Appendices
			he with elsewhere they had become mixed up. Casualties among Officers were found to total 12 and were as follows:-	
			Lieut. J.L. Forbes Killed 23/4/17	
			" J.H. Campbell " 24/4/17	
			2/Lieut. J.M. Bell " 24/4/17	
			" A. Scott, Missing believed killed 24/4/17	
			2/Lieut. R.J. Law Wounded 23/4/17	
			" W.W.C. Miller " 23/4/17	
			" A.B. Stewart " 23/4/17	
			" W.S. Reid " 23/4/17	
			" D.R. Intosh " 23/4/17	
			" A.L. Hay " 23/4/17	
			" J. Miller wounded at Dury 23/4/17	
			" J.A. Smith " 24/4/17	
			During the period in which we remained in the BROWN LINE rather ever reliable came up to a point close by on the TILLOY - WANCOURT road and were easily collected there.	9pm
BROWN LINE	26/4/17		Shell & Drummond Reams. Work of reorganisation continued.	am

A5834 Wt.W4973/M687 750,000 8/16 D.D.&L.Ltd. Forms/C.2118/13

WAR DIARY
or
INTELLIGENCE SUMMARY.
(Erase heading not required.)

Army Form C. 2118.

Place	Date	Hour	Summary of Events and Information	Remarks and references to Appendices
BROWN LINE	27/4/17		In Divisional Reserve. Shortly after 9 p.m. we were relieved by the 3rd London Regt. and proceeded to billets in ARRAS via TILLOY. The relief was accomplished without casualty. In ARRAS we were billeted in the RUE DE TRIPOT, RUE DU PIGNON BLANC and RUE DES TROIS VISAGES all near the Cathedral. A warning order was received that the battalion would move to DUISANS about noon on the following day.	PM.
ARRAS	28/4/17		The morning was spent in preparing for the move. Shortly a/c 10 a.m. a hostile aeroplane was brought down on the first part of a large aeroplane was dropped a large bomb on the RUE DES TROIS VISAGES occupied by the nearby room, the in the RUE DES TROIS VISAGES occupied by a number of the Battalion Headquarters. he direct hit which rendered them killed and a number of the guard who Both melted rubble were killed. Six were killed and 10 wounded, some known in the cellar of the house. At 11.50 a.m. the Battalion marched via the RUE DE TRIPOT for DUISANS and about a mile out of ARRAS we passed the Divisional Commander. A halt will was held in the afternoon and no casualties were found to be known to 24th.	PM.

WAR DIARY
or
INTELLIGENCE SUMMARY

(Erase heading not required.)

Army Form C. 2118.

Place	Date	Hour	Summary of Events and Information	Remarks and references to Appendices
OUTRANS	29/4/17		Sunday. Church parade were held in the morning and afternoon the day was spent in writing and Cleaning up equipment.	9pm
"	30/4/17		Training Commenced. Specialists were made up and there was sheeting drill and handling of arms for the recruits. Aug/4. A draft arrived 145. O.R.	9pm

J. Carter Capt.
Comdg. 10/11 High. L.I.

SECRET.   10/11th (S) B'n. Highland Light Infantry. Copy No. 10

Ref. 51B N.W.3.)
51B N.W.4.) 1/10,000. Operation Order No. 78.   3.4.1917.
Secret ARRAS Maps.

1. **GENERAL**   Operations on a large scale will shortly be carried out against the enemy trenches, E. of ARRAS.
   The object of the 15th Division attack will bbe to capture the enemy third line from the road in H.28.c.8.2. northwards to the R. SCARPE in H.32, also to capture the high ground in H.29.c. and a. i.e. the Northern slope of ORANGE HILL. The Divisional boundaries and the objectives of the Division are shown on secret map already issued to Coys.

1st Objective	BLACK LINE.
2nd. Objective.	BLUE LINE.
3rd. Objective.	BROWN LINE.

2. (1)   The 15th Division is attacking on the left of the VI Corps with the 12th Division on its Right and the 9th Division (XVII) Corps) on its Left.   The 37th Division is in Corps Reserve and after the BROWN LINE and ORANGE HILL have been taken, will advance through the 15th Division and attack MONCHY.
   (2)   The 15th Division will attack with the 44th Inf. Bde. on the Right, the 45th Inf. Bde. on the Left and the 46th Inf. Bde. in Reserve.   The dividing line between the two leading Brigades will run from S. of SAP 66b (G.24.c.5.6.) parallel with Railway to H.19.b.5.2.
   The advance from the BLACK LINE will probably commence about ZERO plus two hours 20 minutes and from the BLUE LINE about ZERO plus 6 hours 40 minutes.
   (3)   The attack will be preceeded by a bombardment lasting four days.   During the bombardment the 44th and 45th Inf. Bdes. will each have two Battalions in the front system and behind it, and two Battalions in cellars in sewers in ARRAS.
        The 46th Inf. Bde. will be in cellars and sewers in ARRAS with Brigade Hd. Qrs. at G.23.c.4.6.
   (4)   At ZERO hour the Division will be disposed:-
   (a)   Headquarters   DUISANS.
   (b)   44th Inf. Bde. (H.Q. G.29.a.7.8.)
         Right Battalion on front SAP 62 to South of SAP 65a.
         Left Battalion SAP 65a to 66b (exclusive.)
         Support Battalion in the area north of the Railway, N.W. of the CEMETRY.
         Reserve Battalion in the area north of the CEMETERY ROAD and West of the CEMETERY.
   (c)   45th Inf. Bde. (H.Q. G.23.c.4.0.)
         Right Battalion on front SAP 66B (inclusive) to road in G.24. a.6.1.
         Centre Battalion on front G.24.a.6.1. to IRON STREET (inclusive).
         Half Battalion on the Left from IRON STREET to the River.
         Support Battalion West of WOOD in G.23.Central.
         Reserve Half Battalion in Sewers.
   (d)   46th Inf. Bde. (H.Q. G.23.c.4.6.) In Sewers and Cellars in ARRAS.
   (e)   Royal Engineers and Pioneers in Sewers and cellars in ARRAS.

3. Tasks are allotted as under :-
        The 44th and 45th Inf. Bdes. will capture both the BLACK and the BLUE LINES.
        Tanks will co-operate in the attack on the RAILWAY TRIANGLE.
        The 46th Inf. Bde. will advance from ARRAS by the Sewer (or by the streets if enemy bombardment permits) and move to a position of assembly near the captured BLUE LINE.   From here an attack will be launched on FEUCHY REDOUBT and the BROWN LINE in conjunction with tanks.

4. In these operations the 46th Inf. Bde. is therefore first in Reserve, to the 44th and 45th Inf. Bdes. and afterwards proceeds to attack the Third Objective. For this attack the Brigade will be disposed as under :-
   Left Battalion 7/8th K.O.S.B.
   Centre Battalion. 10th Sco. Rifs.
   Right Battalion. 12th High. L.I.
   Reserve Battalion 10/11th High. L.I.
   Boundaries between front Battalions are shewn on Secret map referred to above.

5. The Brigade will be quartered from 5th inst. in cellars in GRANDE PLACE and will remain there till "Z" day. Units are arranged so that they march from the cellars into the Sewer in the following order :-
   Left Battalion   N. Exit.
   Right Battalion. S. Exit.
   Centre Battalion. S. Exit.
   Reserve Battalion. S. Exit. (A. or B.)

6. As each Company debouches from the sewer it forms up in the vicinity of the exit and manoevres from there to a place of assembly between O.G.1. and the BLACK LINE. The Bde. remains there for about one hour 40 minutes and then advance to the BLUE LINE which will be crossed about six hours 40 minutes after ZERO. The attack on the BROWN LINE then commences. The first phase of the attack will be the capture of FEUCHY REDOUBT and the trenches S. of the Railway in H.21.c. This will be followed by a halt of about an hour after which the attack will be launched on the BROWN LINE.

7. Throughout the operations the 10/11th High. L.I. will be in Bde. Reserve and will be employed as follows :-
   "A" and "B" Coys. will provide carrying parties and supply dumps in accordance with detailed instructions already issued to these Coys. "A" Coy. less 1 Platoon detailed for "A" Dump will join the 7/8th K.O.S.B. before ZERO. "B" Coy. will follow the 10th Sco. Rifs. from the sewer and the platoon of "A" Coy. detailed for "A" Dump will follow immediately after "B" Coy. There two Coys. carry out their appointed tasks without further reference to Battn. Headquarters and the Coy. Commanders concerned must be prepared to act on their own initative should any emergency arise. Action taken should at once be reported to Battn Hd Qrs .
   "C" and "D" Coys. will act as Brigade Reserve and follow in rear of the 10th. Sco. Rifs. On receipt of orders from Battalion Headquarters they will be prepared to reinforce at any point on the Brigade front or fill any gap that may arise.

8. The following will be the programme for the Battalion on "Z" day. Before ZERO the Battalion will be quartered in cellars in the GRANDE PLACE (76 - 68b inclusive W. side.) By ZERO hour the three platoons of "A" Coy. will have reported to O.C. 7/8th K.O.S.B. as detailed above.

TIME.	ACTION.
(a) ZERO plus 30 minutes.	The Battalion begins to follow the 10th Sco. Rifs. down the Sewer.
(b) ZERO plus 1 hour 30 minutes.	As soon as possible after this hour the Battalion debouches from the Sewer, Southern Exit (A and B) and Coys. move to position of assembly in O.G.1. and 2. The carrying Coys. take up positions in rear of the attacking units that they follow. O.C. Coys. may manoeuvre their Coys. to the position of assembly by whatever routes they select.

TIME	ACTION
(b) Contd.	Trenches have been prepared as already described and these may be used if it is thought necessary. Otherwise Coys. may move in Artillery formation over the open.
(c) ZERO plus 5 hours 40 minutes.	The Battn. will advance to the HERMES TRENCH area.
(d) ZERO plus 6 hours 40 minutes.	The Bde. attack on the intermediate objective (FEUCHY REDOUBT etc) begins. "C" and "D" Coys. will not cross the BLUE LINE until the attacking units have left the intermediate objective, when the Coys. will advance to the vicinity of HOKHOY LANE provided they have not previously been called upon to reinforce.

9. During the action Battn. H.Qrs. will be situated as follows:-
   (a) Till ZERO in cellars 73 GRANDE PLACE.
   (b) During the wait of 1 hour 40 minutes in the O.G. area, at Brigade report Centre in dug-out North of the Railway and West of the Support Line, (G.24.c.3.4½) Meanwhile an advanced Hd. Qrs. will be established in the O.G. area by Capt. R.P. Easton who will establish connection between the Coys. and Battalion Hd. Qrs.
   (c) In HERMES TRENCH Battalion Hd. Qrs. will be marked if possible by a GREEN FLAG with a YELLOW BUGLE and orderlies should be instructed to look out for this flag.
   (d) A final Hd. Qrs. will be established in FEUCHY SWITCH near the BLUE LINE.

10. Details of dress and equipment with particulars of what is to be carried have already been communicated to Coys. During the action leather jerkins will be worn. Greatcoats and one blanket per man will be taken the cellars and left there at the Battalion Dump when the Battalion goes into action.

11. Rations will be brought up in the usual manner till Y/Z night. One day's rations and water will be established at "A" Dump Men will go into action with:-
    (a) Unconsumed portion of day's rations.
    (b) One day's rations.
    (c) One Iron Rations.
    The Quartermaster and the C.Q.M.Ss and 1 cook per Coy. will join "A" Dump after ZERO on "Z" Day following in rear of T.M. Batty. Reserve from the GRANDE PLACE and will supervise and assist in the distribution and loading of supplies for the Battalion in the evening.
    Pack ponies each with a Transport man under the Transport Officer will, before "Z" Day be stabled in a place to be notified later and will probably proceed to "A" Dump at ZERO plus 8 hours.

12. LIVEN's PROJECTORS. 415 of these have been allotted to the Division and Gas Bombs will be fired from them 15 minutes before the Artillery bombardment commences on "V" Day. If the wind is unfavourable on that day the first suitable opportunity for discharge before ZERO minus 6 hours will be taken.

13. SIGNALLING ARRANGEMENTS. No wire will be laid out until the final Hd. Qrs. is established. During the action, communication between Coys. and Battalion H.Qrs. will be by visual signalling and by runner. Wherever possible an advanced Battn. H.Q. will be established to receive reports etc. from Coys. and this centre will be connected with Battn. H.Qrs. by a chain of runners.

-4-

14. **PRISONERS.** Prisoners will be sent under escort to Battn. Hd. Qrs. Officers and N.C.Os. will be searched and the documents found handed over to the N.C.O. in charge of the escort.

15. **MEDICAL ARRANGEMENTS.** Walking wounded after being dressed make their way down the old communication trenches to South Side of BASSIN then Westward by SOURCE VIVIER - RUE JULES FERRY - RUE MCADAM crossing RUE BAUDIMONT to the BASTION (Corps Dressing Station for walking wounded) G.20.b.6.4. Signs indicating route are being put up.
Lying cases will be taken by stretcher bearers to relay posts and finally by wheeled stretcher to 15 Divn. A.D.S. NOUVEAU QUAI.

                                                  B. Marshall. 2nd. Lieut.
                             Adj. 10/11th (S) B'n. Highland Light Infty.

Distribution:-
Copy No. 1. File.
         2. "A" Coy.
         3. "B" Coy.
         4. "C" Coy.
         5. "D" Coy.
         6. Lewis Gun Officer.
         7. Signalling Officer.
         8. Quartermaster.
         9. Transport Officer.
       10. 46th Inf. Bde.

SECRET   10/11th. (S). Battalion Highland Light Infantry.   Copy No. 10

Corrections and Addenda to
Operations Order No 48.   7-4-1917.

1. **Correction.** Ref. para 11, delete from "After Z" down to "GRANDE PLACE" and substitute "on the morning of Zero plus 1 day".

2. **Addenda.**
   1. The attacking Battalions of the Bde. will leave the INTERMEDIATE objective for the attack on the BROWN LINE at Zero + 7 hrs 55 minutes.
   2. Companies will report arrival and approximate casualties on reaching
      (a) O.G. Area.
      (b) HERMES TRENCH.
      (c) BLUE LINE.
      (d) HOKHOY LANE.
   3. **Signals to Artillery.**
      From now onwards the firing of green lights in quick succession will be the signal to the artillery to open fire. This will therefore constitute the S.O.S. Signal, and with so many persons in possession of the means of giving the signal, great care will have to be taken in its use.
      A succession of White Lights will be the signal to the artillery to lengthen range.
   4. The signal in use in the 12th Division when bombing parties are working toward each other in a German trench, is the waving of a sandbag on the end of a bayonet.
   5. While the Battalion is proceeding along the sewer, rifles will be carried slung and butt up.
   6. 2/Lieut. J. Miller will be in charge of an officer's patrol to which will be attached 2 Signallers. This patrol will keep in touch with the attacking Battalions & report progress to Battn. Hd. Qrs.
   7. O.C. Coys will send reports at every available opportunity, even if only to say that there is nothing to report. It is only in this way that complete communication can be established and every emergency met.
   8. The carrying parties must work forward to the best of their ability and salve as they go. The importance of getting up ammunition cannot be exaggerated.
   9. On reaching HOKHOY LANE, the best defensive position in that area is to be taken up. O.C. Coys will bear in mind that they must be prepared to go forward at a moment's notice.
   10. The Reserve Coys at Battalion Headquarters must be prepared to act on the defensive wherever they go, unless ordered forward to reinforce.

B. Marshall. 2nd Lieut.
Adj. 10/11th (S) Bn. H.L.I.

SECRET. A

10/11th. (S). Bn. Highland Light Infantry.

Appendix A

OPERATION ORDER NO. 78.

COPY No. 1.

Reference 51 B.N.W.3.)
51 B.N.W.4.) 1/10.000.
Secret ARRAS Maps.

3/4/1917.

1. **GENERAL.** Operations on a large scale will shortly be carried out against the enemy trenches E. of ARRAS.

   The object of the 15th. Division attack will be to capture the enemy third line from the road in H.28.c.8.2. Northwards to the RIVER SCARPE in H.22., also to capture the high ground in H.29.c., and A., i.e., The Northern slope of ORANGE HILL. The Divisional Boundaries and the objectives of the Division are shewn on Secret Map already issued to Companies.

   1st. OBJECTIVE. BLACK LINE.
   2nd. OBJECTIVE. BLUE LINE.
   3rd. OBJECTIVE. BROWN LINE.

2. (1). The 15th. Division is attacking on the left of the VI. Corps with the 12th. Division on it's right and the 9th. Division (XVII Corps) on it's left. The 37th. Division is in Corps Reserve and after the BROWN LINE and ORANGE HILL have been taken will advance through the 15th. Division and attack MONCHY.

   (2). The 15th. Division will attack with the 44th. Infantry Brigade on the right, the 45th. Infantry Brigade on the left and the 46th. Infantry Brigade in Reserve. The Dividing Line between the two leading Brigades will run from S. of SAP 66B. (G.24.c.5½.6.) parallel with Railway to H.19.b.5.2.

   The advance from the BLACK LINE will probably commence about ZERO plus 2 hours 20 minutes and from the BLUE LINE about ZERO plus 6 hours 40 minutes.

   (3). The attack will be preceded by a bombardment lasting 4 days. During this bombardment the 44th. and 45th. Infantry Brigades will each have two Battalions in the front system and behind it, and two Battalions in Cellars and Sewers in ARRAS.

   The 46th. Infantry Brigade will be in Cellars and Sewers in ARRAS with Brigade Headquarters at G.23.c.½.6.).

   (4). At ZERO Hour the Division will be disposed:-
   (a). Headquarters. DUISANS.
   (b). 44th. Infantry Brigade (H.Q., G.29.a.7.8.).
   Right Battalion on front SAP 62, to South of SAP 65A.
   Left Battalion. SAP 65A. to 66B. (exclusive).
   Support Battalion in the area North of the Railway N.W. of the CEMETRY.
   Reserve Battalion in the area north of the CEMETRY ROAD and West of the CEMETRY.
   (c). 45th. Infantry Brigade. (H.Q., G.23.c.44.0.).
   Right Battalion on front SAP 66B. (inclusive) to road in G.24.a.6.1.
   Centre Battalion on front G.24.a.6.1. to IRON STREET (inclusive).
   Half Battalion on the left from IRON STREET to the RIVER.
   Support Battalion, West of WOOD in G.23.Central.
   Reserve ½ Battalion in SEWERS.
   (d). 46th. Infantry Brigade (Headquarters G.23.c.½.6.)
   In SEWERS and CELLARS in ARRAS.
   (e). Royal Engineers and Pioneers in SEWERS and CELLARS in ARRAS.

2.

3. Tasks are allotted as under:-
The 44th. and 45th. Infantry Brigades will capture both the BLACK and the BLUE LINES.
Tanks will co-operate in the attack on the RAILWAY TRIANGLE.
The 46th. Infantry Brigade will advance from ARRAS by the SEWER (or by the Streets if enemy bombardment permits) and move to a position of assembly near the captured BLUE LINE.
From here and attack will be launched on FEUCHY REDOUBT and the BROWN LINE in conjunction with Tanks.

4. In these operations the 46th. Infantry Brigade is therefore first in Reserve to the 44th. and 45th. Infantry Brigades, and afterwards proceeds to attack the third objective.
For this attack the Brigade will be disposed as under:-
LEFT BATTALION.   7/8th. K.O.Sco.Bords.
CENTRE BATTALION.   10th. Sco. Rifles.
RIGHT BATTALION.   12th. Highland L.I.
RESERVE BATTALION.   10/11th. Highland L.I.
Boundaries between Front Battalions are shewn on SECRET MAP referred to above.

5. The Brigade will be quartered from 5th. instant in Cellars in GRANDE PLACE and will remain there till Z Day.
Units are arranged so that they march from the Cellars into the Sewers in the following order:-
LEFT BATTALION.   N. EXIT.
RIGHT BATTALION.   S. EXIT.
CENTRE BATTALION.   S. EXIT.
RESERVE BATTALION.   S. EXIT. (A. or B.).

6. As each Company debouches from the Sewer it forms up in the vicinity of the Exit and manoeuvres from there to a place of assembly between O.G.1. and the BLACK LINE. The Brigade remains there for about 1 hour 40 minutes and then advances to the BLUE LINE which will be crossed about 6 hours 40 minutes after ZERO. The attack on the BROWN LINE then commences.
The first phase of this attack will be the capture of FEUCHY REDOUBT and the Trenches S. of the Railway in H.21.c.
This will be followed by a halt of about an hour after which the attack will be launched on the BROWN LINE.

7. Throughout the operations the 10/11th. Highland L.I. will be in Brigade Reserve and will be employed as follows :-
xAxxandxxBxxCoyxx "A" and "B" Coys. will provide carrying parties and supply dumps in accordance with detailed instructions already issued to these Companies.
"A" Coy. less 1 Platoon detailed for "A" Dump will join the 7/8th.K.O.Sco.Borders before ZERO.
"B" Coy. will follow the 10th. Scottish Rifles from the Sewer and the Platoon of "A" Coy. detailed for "A" Dump will follow immediately after "B" Coy.
These 2 Companies carry out their appointed tasks without further reference to Battalion Headquarters and the Company Commanders concerned must be prepared to act on their own initiative should any emergency arise. Action taken should at once be reported to Battalion Headquarters.
"C" and "D" Coys. will act as Brigade Reserve and follow in rear of the 10th. Scottish Rifles. On receipt of orders from Battalion Headquarters they will be prepared to re-inforce at any point on the Brigade Front or fill any gap that may arise.

3.

8. The following will be the programme for the Ba[ttle]
Z. day. Before ZERO the Battalion will be quartered [in]
cellars in the GRANDE PLACE (76-68b. inclusive W. Side).
By ZERO hour the 3 Platoons of "A" Coy. will have repo[rted]
to O.C. 7/8th. K.O.Sco.Bords. as described above.

TIME.	ACTION.
(a). Zero plus 30 minutes.	The Battalion begins to follow the 10th.Sco.Rifs. down the Sewer.
(b). Zero plus 1 hour 30 minutes.	As soon as possible after this hour the Battalion debouches from the Sewer, Southern Exit (A. and B.) & Coys. move to position of assembly in O.G.1. and 2. The carrying Companies take up positions in rear of the attacking units that they follow. O.C.Coys. may manoeuvre their Companies to the position of assembly by whatever routes they select. Trenches have been prepared as already described and these may be used if it is thought necessary. Otherwise Coys. may move in Artillery Formation over the open.
(c). Zero plus 5 hours 40 minutes.	The Battalion will advance to the HERMES TRENCH area.
(d). Zero plus 6 hours 40 minutes.	The Brigade attack on the intermediate objective (FEUCHY REDOUBT etc.) begins. "C" and "D" Coys. will not cross the BLUE LINE until the attacking units have left the intermediate objective when these Coys. will advance to the vicinity of HOKHOY LANE provided they have not previously been called upon to re-inforce.

9. During the Action Battalion Hd.Qrs. will be situated as follows :-
(a). Till ZERO in Cellar 73. GRANDE PLACE.
(b). During the wait of one hour 40 minutes in the O.G.AREA at Brigade Report Centre in dug-out N. of the Railway and W. of the Support Line (G.24.c.3.4½.). Meanwhile an advance H.Q. will be established in the O.G. Area by Capt.R.P.Easton who will establish connection between the Companies and Battalion Hd.Qrs.
(c). In HERMES TRENCH. Battn.Hd.Qrs. will be marked if possible by a GREEN FLAG with a YELLOW BUGLE and Orderlies should be instructed to look out for this Flag.
(d). A Final Headquarters will be established in FEUCHY SWITCH near the BLUE LINE.

10. Details of Dress and Equipment with particulars of what is to be carried have already been communicated to Companies. During the action Leather Jerkins will be worn. Greatcoats and One Blanket per man will be taken to the Cellars and left there at the Battalion Dump when the Battalion goes into action.

11. Rations will be brought up in the usual manner till Y/Z night. 1 Days's rations and water will be established at "A" Dump.
Men will go into action with :-
(a) Unconsumed portion of day's rations.
(b) One day's rations.
(c) One Iron Ration.
The Quartermaster the C.Q.M.Ss. and 1 Cook per Company will join "A" Dump after ZERO on Z.Day following in rear of T.M.Battery Reserve from the GRANDE PLACE and will supervise and assist in the distribution and loading of supplies for the Battalion in the evening. *on the morning of Z+1 Day*

Pack Ponies each with a Transport man under the Transport Officer will before Z. Day be stabled in a place to be notified later and will probably proceed to "A" Dump at ZERO plus 8 hours.

12. LIVEN'S PROJECTORS. 415. of these have been allotted to the Division and Gas Bombs will be fired from them 15 minutes before the Artillery bombardment commence on Y. Day. If the wind is unfavourable on that day, the first suitable opportunity for discharge before ZERO minus 6 hours will be taken.

13. SIGNALLING ARRANGEMENTS. No wire will be laid out until the final Headquarters is established. During the action, communication between Companies and Battalion Headquarters will be by visual signalling and by runner. Wherever possible an advanced Battalion Headquarters will be established to receive reports, etc. from Companies and this centre will be connected with Battalion Headquarters by a chain of runners.

14. PRISONERS. Prisoners will be sent under Escort to Battalion Headquarters. Officers and N.C.Os. will be searched and the documents found handed over to the N.C.O. in charge of the escort.

1. MEDICAL ARRANGEMENTS. Walking wounded after being dressed make their way down the old Communication Trenches to South Side of BASSIN then Westward by SOURCE VIVIER-RUE JULES FERRY-RUE MCADAM crossing RUE BAUDIMONT to the BASTION, (Corps Dressing Station for Walking wounded) G. 20.b.6.4. Signs indicating route are being put up.

Lying cases will be taken by stretcher bearers to Relay Post and finally by wheeled stretchers to 15th. Division A.D.S., NOUVEAU QUAI.

Marshall. 2/Lieut.,
Adjt. 10/11th.(S).Bn.H.L.I.

DISTRIBUTION :-
Copy No. 1. File.
2. "A" Coy.
3. "B" "
4. "C" "
5. "D" "
6. Lewis Gun Officer.
7. Signalling Officer.
8. Quartermaster.
9. Transport Officer.
10. 46th. Infantry Brigade.

B   Appendix B

Headquarters,
    46th. Infantry Brigade.

    Reference your B.M./100/10 (S). of this day's date, herewith report on the recent operations.
    On Monday April 9th. 1917. the Battalion was in position by 10 a.m. in the O.G.Area and the Carrying Companies "A" and "B" were in touch with the Battalions they had to follow, and armed with Stokes bombs for "C" and "D" Dumps. During the progress from the Sewer Exit to this area only two slight casualties were sustained, but while the fighting for the BLUE LINE was going on, the enemy shelled the O.G.Area fairly heavily and "B" and "C" Coys. had each about 20 casualties. The delay in this area was unfortunate. One Officer was killed and three others wounded before the real work of the Battalion had commenced. Shortly after 1 p.m. orders were received that the Brigade had to be in position in the BLUE LINE area by 2 p.m. and launch an attack in accordance with the original plans on the INTERMEDIATE Objective and subsequently the BROWN LINE.
    At 2 p.m. the Battalion was in position in the HINDEN TRENCH area with the carrying Companies forward and establishing "C" and "D" Dumps. The remaining Companies followed in rear of the attacking battalions and conformed to their movements and dispositions. The work of carrying was performed without any hitch and "B" Dump was established in BATTERY VALLEY about 200. yards S. of the Railway. Supplies to the 46th. Advanced Dump were rather slow in arriving and delayed the filling up of "D" Dump.
    Meanwhile "C" and "D" Coys. had established themselves in HONGRY LANE area and taken up a defensive position there with Lewis Guns pushed forward. Battalion Headquarters was established on Observation Ridge at H.20.c.85.96. At 6-50 p.m. an order was received to send "C" and "D" Coys. to fill a gap in the BROWN LINE between the Right of the 10th. Scottish Rifles and the Left of the 12th. H.L.I. By this time the enemy was apparently taking his guns back as hostile fire altogether ceased on our front. The night was extraordinarily quiet. "C" and "D" Coys. were occupied with the work of consolidation. "D" Coy. after completing the course of carrying as laid down, took up a defensive position on the ridge N. of BATTERY VALLEY and S. of the RAILWAY and the 4 Lewis Guns at H.Q.were sent to join them there. "A" Coy. took up a similar position N. of the Railway Arch. At 6 a.m. an order was received that the three front Battalions of the Brigade were to hold a position on the general line H.23.c., H.22. A. & C. and the Battalion was then to be in Brigade Reserve in the BROWN LINE.
    "A" and "B" Coys. were moved up and Battn.Hd.Qrs. was established in a dug-out in FEUCHY VILLAGE about H.21.c.d.6.
    The remainder of the day was quiet and uneventful.
    A small Reserve Dump of S.A.A. was formed in the BROWN LINE.
    At 3-30 a.m. 11/4/17. orders were received that the Battn. would attack at 5 a.m., the objective being the enemy line of trenches N. of MONCHY and stretching from I.31.b.7.8. to I.31.d.3.2.
    At 5 a.m. the Battalion was to pass through the leading troops of the 63rd. Brigade holding a line in the region of the terraces in H.36.a. The 45th. Brigade were to attack on our left from LONE COPSE to the River and the 111th. Brigade on our right were to deal with MONCHY. The 7/8th.K.O.S.B. were in Support to us and the 10th. Scottish Rifles and 12th.H.L.I. in Reserve. Company Commanders met in a dug-out by the Railway N. of the BROWN LINE and the situation was explained and instructions given. At 4 a.m. the Battalion formed up in Column of Route on the E. side of the BROWN LINE and marched with a hundred yards distance between Companies Southwards along the BROWN LINE for about 1000. yards, then left wheeled by Coys. and marched on a compass bearing due East, arriving just short

of the terraces at 5 a.m.   By this time there was signs of approaching daylight and we deployed into position for advancing to the attack.   There were 3 Companies in front in order from left to right "B" "D" "C" Coys. each in two waves about 50 yards apart.   "A" Coy. followed in Support at a distance of about 150 yards from the front Coys.   During the march from the BROWN LINE everything was quiet except for occasional bursts of Machine Gun Fire from the direction of MONCHY.   While we were deploying one of our own heavies fired a succession of duds which fell within a 100 yards of the deploying troops.   The 45th. Brigade came up too far to their right and considerably S. of LONE COPSE.   When the advance started it was still fairly dark but a rattle of Machine Guns was heard along the whole line, those being most active which appeared to be situated in the SUNKEN ROAD in X.25.d.   The 45th. Brigade still bore to the right and forced our men out of their original direction.   The change of direction was accentuated by the line advanced because of heavy Machine Gun Fire from MONCHY and the enclosure.   The enemy had 4 Guns in a trench about 400 yards N.W. of the VILLAGE in H.36.d. and N.6.b. and these caused many casualties.   Our first line swept round to meet this fire and found themselves making straight for the trench.   "C" and "D" Coys. were held up by Machine Gun Fire from this trench when they were near the hedge in H.36.c.   The Company Commanders of "D" and "P" Coys. were both killed near this spot and the advance was momentarily checked until "B" Coy. under 2/Lieut. J.R.Campbell succeeded in carrying out a flank attack on the left of the trench when the enemy abandoned it and made for the Village, closely followed by our troops.   Seeing that the 111th. Brigade on the right had not yet come up "A" Coy. which had been in Reserve led round to the right and entered the village from the S.W. just in rear of the front Companies clearing cellars and houses as they went

By this time the 45th. Brigade were also in the Village and the 111th. Brigade entered immediately after.   The enemy were cleared from the village and work of consolidation was largely undertaken by the 111th. Brigade.   The surviving Officers of the Battalion collected as many men as they could and endeavoured to advance upon the original objective.   For this purpose they left the Village by the N. but when they attempted to advance Eastwards it was found impossible to do so because of the heavy Machine Gun Fire and the barrage which the enemy now placed on the Village and the general line North of it.   They therefore took up a position in a line of shell-holes immediately to the left of the 10th.Yorks and Lancs.Regiment and maintained this position throughout the day.   Towards evening about 7 p.m. it was found possible to collect the men from the shell-holes and occupy a position N. of the Village, which had apparently been the main enemy line when we launched our attack in the morning.

With regard to the day's operations I would draw attention to the following points:-   It was understood that the attack would be carried out under cover of Artillery Fire and when no barrage was placed on the enemy position it made it doubly hard to deal with his Machine Guns, also an excellent opportunity of inflicting heavy loss upon him was wasted because during the very early stages of the operation the enemy could be plainly seen moving back in large numbers over the ridge in rear of his front position.   Later, when he rallied and returned no fire was brought to bear upon him by the Artillery.   He could even be seen standing firing on the MONCHY-PELVES ROAD.   If the two Vickers Guns allotted to the Battalion had reported I feel that full advantage might have been taken of these targets and that the advance of the Battalion might have been covered.

The fact that the 45th. Brigade swung over to their Right might have proved serious as for a considerable time the left flank of the Division was completely in the air.   Further, an advance on the left would have resulted in the withdrawal of the Guns in the SUNKEN ROAD in H.25.d. which were responsible for a good many of our casualties.   An enemy counter-attack from this flank would probably have proved serious.

The spirit of the men throughout the operation was excellent. They advanced under heavy fire the whole way and passed through the hedge with great dash to the assault on the enemy trench. That many should find themselves committed to exploit with other Units was inevitable. In the Village and engaged in clearing cellars, etc. there was a mixed crowd of soldiers of all units and by and by these sorted themselves out in different directions in groups of varying size to hold and consolidate shell holes and strong points round the Village. That these stragglers did excellent work I am convinced and one Lance Corporal was discovered by an Officer of "D" Coy. holding a shell hole with a Lewis Gun and the remnant of a Team about 100 yards in advance of any Infantry position E. of the village and here he remained with his men oblivious of any relief taking place behind and came down in the early morning of the 13th. with a party of the 10th. Hussars.

Excellent work was done by the 18.Pounder Battery that came into action early in the afternoon on the Southern slopes of ORANGE HILL.

J.Marshall Lt.Adjt.
for Lieut. Colonel,
14/4/1917. Commanding 10/11th.(S).Bn. Highland Light Infy.

C / 10/11th. (S). Bn. Highland Light Infantry.
                                                                    Appendix C

SECRET.
                    OPERATION ORDER No. 81.   22-4-1917
Reference 51.b. N.W.
          51.b. S.W.
  1/20,000.

1. The enemy is holding the following general line on the Third Army front :-
FONTAINE-LEZ-CROISELLES-GUEMAPPE-ROEUX-GAVRELLE.
    On the front of the 15th. Division (according to information from prisoners) the 176th. Regiment, 35th. Division, holds GUEMAPPE and north of GUEMAPPE is the 18th. Bavarian Infantry Regiment, 3rd. Bavarian Division. The relief of the latter is suspected.

2. The Third and First Armies are continuing their advance at zero hour on April, 23rd.
    On the right of the 15th. Division is the 50th. Division (Vll Corps) on front N.30.b.2.8. to COJEUL River at N.24.a.4.8.
    On the left of the 15th. Division the 29th. Division (Vl Corps) on front LA BERGERE (exclusive) round the eastern outskirts of MONCHY-LE-PREUX.
    The 3rd. Division (H.Q. WARLUS) is in Vl Corps Reserve.
    A map shewing the objectives (Blue Line and Red Line) of the 50th, 15th and 29th. Divisions has already been issued.

3. Dividing Line between :-
(a) 15th and 50th.Divisions - The COJEUL River.
(b) 15th and 29th.Divisions - N.12 central to small copse in O.8.central to south edge of BOIS DU VERT to road in O.9.b.central (Road to 15th. Division).

4. (1). The 15th.Division will attack at zero hour on April,23rd.
    The advance will be simultaneous along the whole front of the Division.
        44th. Inf. Bde. (H.Q. N.16.b.1.8.) on the right.
        45th. Inf. Bde. (H.Q. N.10.d.3.7.) on the left.
        46th. Inf. Bde. (H.Q. H.31.central) in Reserve.
    Dividing Line between 44th. and 45th. Inf. Bdes :- from bend in road N.18.a.6.7½. to north of buildings in O.14.a.central, to point of spur on second objective about O.15.b.3.4½.
(2). (a). The 44th. and 45th.Inf.Bdes. are to capture both the first and second objectives.
     (b). The advance from the first to the second objectives will commence at zero plus seven hours.
     (c). After the capture of the RED Line, patrols will be sent forward to cover the consolidation of the captured position and to obtain observation with a view to a further advance at a later date.
(3). The 44th. Infantry Brigade are detailing one battalion to deal with GUEMAPPE, the remainder of the Brigade pushing forward to the capture of the BLUE Line.
(4). The 45th.Infantry Brigade are to advance against the first objective-Right battalion in line with the 44th.Infantry Brigade and left battalion in echelon forward to connect with the flank of the 29th.Division.
(4). The advance of both Brigades will at first be at the rate of 100 yards in three minutes, and subsequently at 100 yards in four minutes.
    The 18 pr.barrage maps will be issued later.
    The leading Infantry will advance as close to the barrage as possible.

5. (1). (a). The Battalion will move to the 46th. Brigade position of assembly S. of the CAMBRAI ROAD and West of BOIS DES BOEUFS to-night and Coys. will occupy the areas already allotted to them.

(b). The Battalion will parade in the RUE GAMBETTA ready to move off at 8-20 p.m. in order of march- "A" "B" "C" "D" Coys.

1st. Platoon of "A" Coy. will pass Battalion H.Q. at 8-20 p.m. and the remainder of the Battalion by Platoons at distances of 75 yards between platoons. The route to be used is ARRAS STATION G.28.b.3.2.) through STATION Road leading S.E. from G.28.b.3½.0. to G.29.c.3½.½. thence along track.

(c). Platoon Commanders will reconnoitre route this afternoon.

(d). Surplus personnel will be accommodated as already detailed.

(e). Blankets, greatcoats and Officers' Valises will be stored under arrangements to be notified later.

(f). Surplus Company Money and Conduct Sheets will be handed in to the Orderly Room this afternoon.

(g). Men detailed for carrying under instructions given to the Lewis Gun Officer will report to 2/Lieut. Stafford at Battalion Dump (Cellar 8.RUE GAMBETTA) at 7-30 p.m. to-night, i.e., 15 men per Company.

(h). Snipers going into action must have their sniping rifles exchanged for ordinary ones, at Q.M.Stores.

(i). Men are to be warned that the Emergency Ration (Iron) is only to be eaten on the order of an Officer and disciplinary action will be taken in the case of men coming out without one.

(j). Arrangements are being made by Brigade to take the names of men walking wounded without arms or equipment who are reported fit to have carried above, the same also as men who arrive with trivial wounds or without reasonable cause. All such men will be Courts-Martialled.

(k). Arrival in area to-night to be reported at once to Battalion Headquarters (N.1.a.6.2.).

(2). The Brigade is to be prepared to move to the BROWN LINE when vacated by rear battalion of leading Brigades on receipt of orders.

In the first instance the 10/11th. Highland Light Infantry will occupy the portion of the BROWN LINE in rear of the 45th. Brigade (FEUCHY CHAPEL S. to N.10.c.8.8.), and the 10th. Scottish Rifles in rear of the 44th. Brigade.

Order of Coys. will be from Left to Right- "A" "B" "C" "D" Coys.

6. When the Battalion moves out to-night, rations for "Z" Day (23rd.) and Z plus 1 day will be carried. Cooked rations to be eaten on "Z" Day.

7. Orders for synchronisation of watches will be issued later.

Marshall 2/Lieut.,
Adjt. 10/11th. (S). Bn. Highland Light Infy.

D/   OPERATIONS 1917.   Appendix D.

2nd. PHASE.

REPORT ON OPERATIONS (23-4-1917 - 26-4-1917.).

Reference 51B. S.W. 1/20.000.
VIS-EN-ARTOIS Sheet.
         1/10.000.
Special GUEMAPPE SHEET.

       At Zero hour (4-45 a.m.) on 23-4-17. the battalion was accommodated in the HARP South of TILLOY in Divisional Reserve.
       At 8 a.m. orders were received to advance to the vicinity of the BROWN LINE and occupy the area held by the Reserve Battalion of the 45th. Infantry Brigade as soon as it should be vacated by them. Apart from occasional shells the enemy did not concern itself with the area in rear of the BROWN LINE and no casualties were sustained in getting there. In due course we occupied the line vacated by the 6th. Cameron Highlanders, meanwhile the attack of the leading Brigades had met with varying success and although the BLUE LINE remained untaken a line of sorts was held for some time East of GUEMAPPE. A further attack was arranged for 12 noon to be carried out by the 44th. and 45th. Infantry Brigades. Our orders were to occupy the old British Front Line as soon as vacated by the 45th. Brigade and be prepared to support their attack on the BLUE LINE.
       But the 12 noon attack had to be postponed because the enemy counter-attacked and heavily shelled the new positions.
       Some time later the 50th. Division on our right and the right of the 44th. Brigade were reported back in the old front line. At 2-15 p.m. a warning order was received that the Brigade would probably take over the line that night from the two leading Brigades. But some progress was made during the afternoon and by 4 p.m. the line was roughly along SHOVEL TRENCH in O.7.d. At 4-15p.m. verbal orders were received that we were to pass through the front line of the 45th. Brigade and attack the BLUE LINE at 6 p.m. Company Commanders were assembled at Battalion Headquarters in the BROWN LINE, the position explained and orders given. "A" Coy. was to attack on the left and "B" Coy. on the right with "C" Coy. in support and "D" in Reserve. At 5-10 p.m. the Battalion left the BROWN LINE in artillery formation to make its way to SHOVEL TRENCH prior to attacking the BLUE LINE on the front O.8.central to junction of road with BLUE LINE at O.14.a. 70.95. All went well till we crossed the ridge South East of LA-BERGERE and South of the ARRAS CAMBRAI ROAD. At this point we were evidently seen by the enemy who immediately placed a heavy barrage along the ridge and brought machine gun fire to bear upon our troops from the direction of CAVALRY FARM and the ground to the South of it. "A" Coy. succeeded in getting through the barrage without heavy loss and without becoming seriously disorganised, but "B" Coy. suffered considerably and was temporarily thrown into confusion. "C" Coy. coming up took "B" Coys. place as right front Company and "B" became the Support Company while "D" remained in Reserve. At 6-7 p.m. "A" and "C" Coys. left SHOVEL TRENCH for the assault. Meanwhile orders had been received that Battalion Headquarters that the advance was not to go further than the line of TANK TRENCH and SHRAPNEL TRENCH without further orders, but we were to consolidate there under cover of our barrage. An Officer and runners were immediately despatched with instructions to Companies, but,

inevitably arrived too late to stay the advance.

"A" and "C" Coys. much depleted reached their objective about 6-30 p.m. and commenced to consolidate. On arriving at the BLUE LINE they succeeded in inflicting considerable loss on the retreating enemy by means of Lewis Gun and rifle fire, although a few snipers remained in shell holes and seriously hindered the work of consolidation until they were eventually silenced by our snipers. From about 6-30 p.m. until 8 p.m. we held a line from approximately the Copse in O.8.central to a point about O.14.a.O.7. on our right. About 8 p.m. taking advantage of the pockets in the ground the enemy began to mass in considerable numbers to right and left of us and continued to carry out a flanking movement in spite of the Lewis Gun fire that we brought to bear on them.

The 20th. Division on our left were found not to be on the BLUE LINE and the Scottish Rifles on our right who had received the orders mentioned above were holding the line to be consolidated on our right and in rear. Our numbers were insufficient to prevent the enemy from getting round on the flanks and on our left he succeeded in getting behind us so that we were compelled to withdraw to SHOVEL TRENCH, but succeeded in taking our wounded with us. SHOVEL TRENCH was held and consolidated under very heavy and continuous shell fire until our relief on the following night when we withdrew to the BROWN LINE. Our casualties amounted to about 250, and included three Company Commanders, two of whom were killed on the day after the attack while we were holding SHOVEL TRENCH.

Vol 23

13.L.
11 sheets

CONFIDENTIAL

10/11th (S) Bn. High. L. I.

WAR DIARY

MAY 1917.

WAR DIARY / INTELLIGENCE SUMMARY

Army Form C. 2118.

Place	Date	Hour	Summary of Events and Information	Remarks and references to Appendices
OUSIGNIES	1.5.17		Training continued. QMS Parade at 6.15 am. Training under Coy arrangements during the morning. One of the Baths at AGNEZ-LES-DUISANS was obtained, and the whole Battalion was able to have a clean of the afternoon this was a permutation of violet ribbons by the Corps Commander at Divisional HQ at WARLUS. This was attended by a party of 50 men under Capt. J. JOHNSTON. Unfortunately out of 8 recipients of the Military Medal in the Bn. none were able to be present, as 3 were killed, 4 wounded and one on leave.	M.P.
"	2.5.17		Training continued as above. The C.O. held a marching order inspection of 'A' Coy at 10.30am.	35
"	3.5.17		Training as above. 'A' Coy fired a grouping practice on a range at 2.15. The C.O. inspected 'B' Coy in the afternoon at an issue of the second round of the Bn. football competition and played in the second round of the 4/5 K.O.S.B. by 2-1.	D/0. 51. C (1/40000)
"	4.5.17		'B' Coy was on the range (grouping) 'C' Coy was inspected by the C.O., who also inspected all lunch and visibility etc. Infantry Reftg completed by drawing a Branch of L.A.A. Grenades from Bde. Baths in the afternoon.	20

Place	Date	Hour	Summary of Events and Information	Remarks and references to Appendices
OUISANS	5.5.17		Firing was begun at 6.0 a.m. and finished by 11.30. Owing to the heat of the day, firing was such Coy. arrangements chill attack, inability to "C" Coy. was on the range, and "D" was infield by the C.O.	
	6.5.17		Sunday. There was a march Bn. Church Parade. The ground N.W. of Bn. H.Q. was used for it. After the Bn. marched past the Divisional General, having only received by B.H.Q.	
	7.5.17		At 9.55 a.m. an order of march C.D.A.B. Road was b. t. 19. a. 70 Refs s/c. —1. 24. a. 96. —15. 2. Cunchy— MONTENESCOURT—HAUTEVILLE—FOSSEUX 21 owd—BARLY. This road as far as HOULE HAUTEVILLE was a track across the fields, and by falling uh the roads the tack was very rough in fair traffic and dust & probably than for by & that left than a by or dry. D— in huts. 6 men fell out, probably from Coy. —D— in huts. Billets. Good.	

Army Form C. 2118.

WAR DIARY
or
INTELLIGENCE SUMMARY.
(Erase heading not required.)

Place	Date	Hour	Summary of Events and Information	Remarks and references to Appendices
BARLY	6.5.17		As no space of any sort could be found near at hand, all having had to be cleared out subsequently by Corps. Steady and extended order drill, attack in practice.	
"	9.5.17		Training continued much as previous. B Coy fired grouping on the range. A good deal of time devoted to drill and handling of arms.	
"	10.5.17		In the afternoon, all the men of Bn. were given an Aux. at GRAND RULLECOURT. a normal attack (Trench to trench) was practised. The Divisional Sgts. N.C.O.'s gave exhibition of arms drill. Bn. was on up.	
"	11.5.17		Training as on the 9th. "A" Coy on the range.	
"	12.5.17		A Tactical scheme was carried out on ground near GRAND RULLECOURT. The Bn. made H. at 4.30 a.m. All stages of the attack were practised, advancing to artillery formation. Breakfasts about 8.15. The attack was then refined again, paying attention to subdivision of the first practice.	

Place	Date	Hour	Summary of Events and Information	Remarks and references to Appendices
BATLY.	13.5.17		Sunday. Church Parade. Preparation handed in for Battalion sports - to be held on Tuesday.	
"	14.5.17		A Brigade Tactical Scheme was carried out as a Coy) N.W. of GRAND RULLE COURT. The Batt inarched off at 6.30 a.m. Zero hour was at 6.30 p.m. The attack was made up all a skeleton trench system. Bob. was obtained a follow:- Front line 4/6 R.O. 100 Bomb, 1/5 Suff L.I.s outpost 1st Sco. Rif. Reserve 2nd Suff L.I. Lewis Guns, Stokes Mortars and rifle grenades were all demonstrated in this attack.	
"	15.5.17		Regimental sports are held today. It was very fortunate in the weather, some rain had fallen the previous night and the ground was in good condition. Staff was run off in the morning. The Cup & was was won by "C" Coy, who have putted well C.Q.M.S. McLean	

WAR DIARY
or
INTELLIGENCE SUMMARY.
(Erase heading not required.)

Army Form C. 2118.

Place	Date	Hour	Summary of Events and Information	Remarks and references to Appendices
			won the 5/m 100 yards. In the Band comp. Pte. Rawson the 1st prize for the best turn out, & Pte Bob. Pte. Major Richardson 2nd & 3rd. won the Piping Competition. Amongst the Judges were Brig Gen. F.G. Logan D.S.O. Lt. Col. McLeod, and Major Drummond. Dan Monroe. Major Sinclair Thom, & F.W. McCracken C.B. D.S.O. kindly presented the prizes.	
BARLY.	16/8/17		A Bugler. The Regt. was n/a in N 165 but this stopped short was n/a N 165 but this Babb C.Y.F.K.O. 2nd Bn. to 2 Coys Rifles. 1st Hufp. L.I.) were in fact him inf. Inf. L.I. were engaged — Lule Army The attack was successfully carried out.	
	17/8/17		Let the Field trains arranged for the morning were postponed the afternoon and left inspection & substitute as Sheep in all of this good hot dinners for troops to breakfast and the remainder of gun and trumpery was cleaned down.	

WAR DIARY
or
INTELLIGENCE SUMMARY.

Army Form C. 2118.

Place	Date	Hour	Summary of Events and Information	Remarks and references to Appendices
BARLY.	18.5.17		Battn: under Batt:n arrangement at ROELLECOURT. Coys moved off at 9.0am till noon. Coy worked independently. Coy wore parthin was a Bt. /naker attack. Bt'l alarm till 3.45 — the Bn was spent in Marching into Contraction with the attack and a wash past in Correction with the attack.	
	19.5.17		Firing much Coy. arrangements. "B" Coy fires an application practice on the range.	
	20.5.17		Sundays. Church Parade. Baths at Pernkimon	
	21.5.17		Battalion marched bREILLY & OUS-ST-LEGER. Moved off at 9.0.5 am. Bus was reached about 11.35am. The distance being about 5 miles. Billets were good. Company took flat of room. Is was fit out in Billet in each. In part hen for a long while. The B's sea health in Ordn g road.	

A 5834 Wt. W4973/M687 750,000 8/16 D.D. & L. Ltd. Forms/C.2118/13.

WAR DIARY
or
INTELLIGENCE SUMMARY.

Army Form C. 2118.

Place	Date	Hour	Summary of Events and Information	Remarks and references to Appendices
SUS-ST-LEGER	22.5.17		The march was continued. The time to FORTEL, when about a night on the way, was from the SOMME BATTNS. It was a hot day, and only 6 men fell out — not many considering the heat and length of the march (12 mls.) Billets quite good. The Health condition also not appear too bad on the night, and were not well tried down in tts. on arrival of destination	
FORTEL	23.5.17.		The last stage from march was accomplished, and settled down in LE PONCHEL with A Coy at VAULX about 1½ miles away. Billets good though scattered. Rout by VACQUERIE - LE - BOUCQ — RUINS-au-BOIS — VAULX. Shortly aft. arrived a fatigue place was found at the R. AUTHIE, and the Batt. had a wash down.	

WAR DIARY
or
INTELLIGENCE SUMMARY

Army Form C. 2118.

Place	Date	Hour	Summary of Events and Information	Remarks and references to Appendices
Le Poucret	24.5.17		Training was carried on this am. A Coy. were Musketry and bombing on range and ground W. of VAUX. B Coy. on similar having 300 yards SW of VILLEROY SUR AUTHIE. C & D Coys. on general training on grounds S. of VAUX.	
"	25.5.17		Physical training in early morning. Training as above. B & C Coys. on musketry. (Appendices) A riding school for Officers started.	
"	26.5.17		Training as above.	
"	27.5.17		Sunday. Church Parade. In the absence of the Padre a learn. Lt. Prosky conc. divine service late H.Q. Adjutant.	
"	28.5.17		A Batln. practice attack was carried out on the training ground at VAUX. Attacking in reserve & supports, the objective being an imaginary trench line practised. Lts. Osborn &

WAR DIARY
INTELLIGENCE SUMMARY

Army Form C. 2118.

Place	Date	Hour	Summary of Events and Information	Remarks and references to Appendices
LE PONCHEL	29.5.17		Brick kiln covered by line of trees front. Training under Coy. arrangements steady drill advancing - firing to 75 Coy. practice musketry (various stages) & 70 Coys on the range, 4 Coys in a new 600 yards range of Vickeroy application and short shooting practice.	
"	30.5.17		An inspection was held in preparation for an inspection by General PETAIN. Owing to practices the General's inspection was put back and cancelled.	
"	31.5.17		Training under Coy. arrangements, chief advancing by Coys, musketry, lectures NCOs, training divisional Gas NCO.	

R. Naismith Major
for Lt Colle
Comdg 10th HLI

CONFIDENTIAL

14.L
10 sheets

(6202) W 11186/M1151 350,000 12/16 McA. & W., Ltd. (Est. 731) Forms/W 3091/3.   Army Form W. 3091.

Cover for Documents.

Nature of Enclosures.

10/11th (S) Bn. High L.I.

WAR DIARY

for

JUNE 1917

Notes, or Letters written.

WAR DIARY or INTELLIGENCE SUMMARY

Army Form C. 2118.

Place	Date	Hour	Summary of Events and Information	Remarks and references to Appendices
LE PONCHEL	JUNE 1st 1917	9 a.m.	A Field-Firing Practice was carried out on "A" and "B" Training areas just E. of VAULX. At 9 a.m. we formed up for attack N. of the VAULX - BUIRE AU BOIS road and advanced in a westerly direction toward the hill slopes. "A" Coy on the right in the front line and "B" Coy on the left. "C" Coy supporting "A" and "D" supporting "B". Overhead fire was provided from a Vickers gun section of the 216 M.G. Corp. Lewis Gun Scouts reconnoitring entrenched enemy and M.G. positions were deployed along the front. The practice in fairly accurate and the shooting was quite good.	Nil.
"	JUNE 2nd 1917		An ordinary day's training was carried out. Two companies practised open warfare and attack of on the Training area, "C" Coy firms supporting practice on the VAULX range and the Scouts rifle grenade firing. "D" Coy fired on the Range at VITZ-VILLEROY. In the afternoon a number of Officers attended an interesting demonstration of an Infantry Field Practice held near AUXI LE CHATEAU.	Nil.
"	JUNE 3rd 1917		Sunday. Protestant Church parade was held on the trade of the AUTHIE. The Church of England had a service in the School opposite the battery area and the Roman Catholics marched to the Parish Church at GENNE NERGNY.	Nil.
"	JUNE 4th 1917		A Bn. practice attack was carried out on the VAULX training area. Zero hour was 9 a.m. Bn. Organisation were as follows: 10/11 Hyd. L.I., Aff. Fund. 10th Sco. Rif., Centre, 7/8th K.O. Sco. Bord. Rgt. front. The 12th Hyl L.I. in positron in the area of the BACHIMONT WOODS.	

WAR DIARY or INTELLIGENCE SUMMARY

Army Form C. 2118.

Place	Date	Hour	Summary of Events and Information	Remarks and references to Appendices
	JUNE 5th 1917		Reported to the Brigade. The Battalion was rested by Lewis & Lodges W. of the AUXI - QUEUX road. A Contact Aeroplane Exercise and flare were held as the Division.	Appx.
"	JUNE 6th 1917		Training was carried out in the same Area as above on the lines marked out on the Training Area. In the afternoon a Rifle meeting organised by the 10th Sea. Rgt. was held at ROUSSEAUX. No one but a few officers and a few NCOs were permitted to be present for the evening the hangars.	Appx.
"	JUNE 7th 1917		Training continued on the morning. Firing and musketry classes were started at the "A" Company area. Musketry in instructing the given by Mr. W.S Maxwell. "C" and "D" Coys on the Training Area, "B" Coy firing and musketry. A and B Coys firing on the Ranges. Ammo Drivers on Range at VITZ VILLEROY.	Appx.
"	JUNE 8th 1917		Brigade Practice attack was held near QUATREVAUX and GALAMETZ. The Battalion paraded at 6.30 am and marched via ROUTE MAINIL Bill area 10/11.4.M.S. attack on the right and on the 10th Sea. Rgt on the left with the 1st Rgt. L.I. in Support. The 7/8 R.O. Sco. Borde represented the enemy. Their was three Aeroplane assembled and 12 Tanks supported in the attack. Armored Aeroplanes for flown during the attack. All has represented an land and flat cumulated in field by the enemy. During time which to the backward of the Division to which was HAUT MAINIL and in expense to reinforce line within the Check.	Appx.

WAR DIARY
INTELLIGENCE SUMMARY

Army Form C. 2118.

(Erase heading not required.)

Place	Date	Hour	Summary of Events and Information	Remarks and references to Appendices
"	JUNE 9th 1917		The Battalion marched to EUMONVILLE and carried out an outpost scheme covering the line along the road from the line north to north N. of the N of NEUVLLY to the village of ACQUET.	Ref. LENS Sheet 11. App.
"	JUNE 10th 1917		Sunday. Church parade for Protestants in the new hut, for Roman Catholics in LE PONCHEL Chalet. In the afternoon "B" Coy marched to BACHIMONT and relieved a coy. of 7/8 K.O.S.B. Both incoming and outgoing parties used Canadian Huts, "A" Coy came to LE PONCHEL from VAULX and outposts were vacated by "B" Coy.	App.
"	JUNE 11th 1917		Training. Arrangements had to be suspended for a account of the heavy rain and the fracas the spain in being platoon clothing, musketry initiation etc. in billets.	App.
"	JUNE 12th 1917		The Battalion paraded at 9 a.m. and marched to BACHIMONT. Rain however for the coy. from the 10th Sea. Reg. he carried out an attack through the wood and became ground scouts.	App.

WAR DIARY
or
INTELLIGENCE SUMMARY

Army Form C. 2118.

(Erase heading not required.)

Place	Date	Hour	Summary of Events and Information	Remarks and references to Appendices
"	JUNE 13th/1917		"A" Coy carried out a practice attack on the hairpin area. "C" Coy practised wiring and mortar and D Coy commenced an elementary musketry course on the ranges at VAULX.	Nil
"	JUNE 14/4/1917	At 10 am	A Battalion inspection was held by the Commanding Officer on the ground by the huts. This was to be a rehearsal for the G.O.C. 18th Division to be on the following day.	Nil
"	JUNE 15th/1917		Inspection was promised for about 7pm that the inspection had been postponed but arrived too late please on 16th instant. The day was spent in cleaning clothes and equipment and was of the inspection in the following day. A small carrier party was dispatched to POPERINGHE to take over supplies for all to be sent to FREVENT for loading and storing up and sent to the Army school at AUXI LE CHATEAU. Information about the G.O.C.1 inspection has been cancelled.	Nil
"	JUNE 16/6/1917		The day was spent in preparation for impending Battalion movement.	Nil
	JUNE 17th/1917	1 am	The Battalion marched out of LE PONCHEL for FREVENT and proceeded by VAULX, BUIRE AU BOIS, VACQUERIE LE BOUCQ and PETIT ROUBERS, where it arrived shortly after 3 am and then bivouacked. B Coy which did not join the Bn. Left FREVENT until 12.20 am. 1st Bn. arrived on to the distribution camps W. of FREVENT and are accommodated there for the day. The movement reached PREVENT station at	

WAR DIARY or INTELLIGENCE SUMMARY

Army Form C. 2118.

Place	Date	Hour	Summary of Events and Information	Remarks and references to Appendices
	June 18th 1917	6.20 am	Coys Commenced entraining. Entraining was completed in 50 minutes and at 9.20 am the train left for HAZEBROUCK. he Arrived at HOPOUTRE about 2.30 pm. The day was exceptionally hot and after leaving HOPOUTRE he had a long hot march to TORONTO CAMP on the BUSSEBOOM – VLAMERTINGHE Road at about 3.30pm. Battalion was accommodated partly in huts and partly in tents.	Nil.
			Day spent in cleaning up and making the men fit after the journey of the previous day.	Nil.
	June 19th 1917		Drill parades and inspection were held until noon. Coy arrangements:– he had both listed men by no left battalion and of right section of X/XIX Corps. At 8.30 pm an advance party of about 50 all ranks left for the trenches and proceeded till 7/8th K.O. Sec. Bom. (Mining Support trenches of Bn. and were later on) as far as REIGERSBURG where this and guides of the 5th King's Own and were conducted to own area. A party of about 100 O.R. were despatched for work under 254th Tunnelling Coy R.E. Everything being met in the Mivian area.	Nil.
	June 20th 1917		Preparatory to proceeding to the trenches all the harness inspection lines held and huts were made up with S.A.A. and Bombs. At 8.45 pm he marched off and entrained at BRANDHOEK at about 10 pm. Guides had to as the position of Inniskilling Troops with the BRIELEN – YPRES road, and we proceeded to relieve the 5th King's Own R. Lanc. Regt. Relief was not complete till about 2.30pm. Dispositions	
			Bn. Hq. DRAGOON Fm. B. Coy Right Front C. Coy Left Front D. Coy Support in ST JAMES TRENCH A. Coy Reserve to PUTTS, POTIZZE REDOUBT and MILL COTS.	
			Our front extended from WARWICK Fm. (exclusive) on the left to PICCADILLY (inclusive) on the right.	

Army Form C. 2118.

WAR DIARY
or
INTELLIGENCE SUMMARY.
(Erase heading not required.)

Instructions regarding War Diaries and Intelligence Summaries are contained in F. S. Regs., Part II. and the Staff Manual respectively. Title pages will be prepared in manuscript.

Place	Date	Hour	Summary of Events and Information	Remarks and references to Appendices
	JUNE 21st 1917		The Battalion on our right was 7/8th K.O. Sco Bord, that relieve on our left 6th King's Own Liverpool Regt. 165th Inf. Bde. 55th Division. Relations and work were handed by Battalion to HUSSAR FM. Pt. S of POTIJZE Bm made. D Coy carried relation to the two front coys. Clothing in use in the western portion of ST JAMES TRENCH and part in carried forward to kent pure and brices. No hits on casualties during the relief and the situation is general is quite satisfactory.

Disposition as above. Enemy's artillery very active. Area in rear of ST. JAMES TRENCH was shelled fairly persistently with 4.2's, 5.9's and 8" Howte. Our artillery was very quiet and did not retaliate strongly upon enemy activity in consequence. Enemy having during our stay in the sector on enemy plane came over about 9 am and usually flew fairly low on our hivites. At 6.15 pm 6 to 8 enemy planes were premature from shelling with our hivites to it is not attempted to do the our horse light programme was as follows:- The two front Coys held out and a patrol. Each front Coy worked on its own area. by opening and statening the parapet building a firestep. Opening up the communication hitch. The Support Coy carried relation due just to the front lines and then worked on an area in the rear Coy. Carrier R.E. material etc. and then worked on a relief of the front Coys. About 3 pm two reliefs to the 7/8 K.O Sco Bord in the right portion of our front and then Swan during two new frames through a point I S to 3.0.

At about. Enemy's Artillery fired very active. We published on this unit and the right coy presumed its one of the STABLES and the MOUND. Right was fired upon from the MOUND and remained steadily that - we fired No hits of the enemy in No Man's Land. | Mm. |
| | JUNE 22nd 1917 | | | AMR |
| | JUNE 23rd 1917 | | The Enemy's Artillery was active all day and about 9.30 pm. the ECOLE and surrounding area was bombarded with Lachrymatory shells. At the time we were watching a great part of this 9 to the storm broke upon us. Bombardment continues till about 2.30 am 24th inst. | Mm. |

WAR DIARY
or
INTELLIGENCE SUMMARY.

Army Form C. 2118.

(Erase heading not required.)

Place	Date	Hour	Summary of Events and Information	Remarks and references to Appendices
	JUNE 24th 1917		Harassed by persistently heavy shelling in the morning. HALF MOON TRENCH, HUSSAR FM, LANCER FM and DRAGOON FM were all apparently shelled from 9 a.m. — 12.30 p.m. and mostly with HEAVY Shell. Two attached Stokes trench mortars fired in the MENIN ROAD area which had been shelled, a gun that moved away the previous stage. Two took its continuing on the hun direction about MILL ST in observed might through to the union leading to MILL COTS, CURZON ST. was partially cleared. Particular attention was paid to enlarging huts which were apparently on the left of the district. An advance party of officers of the 12th Highl. L.I. arrived to reconnoitre the lines prior to taking over.	Mm.
	JUNE 25th 1917		Much quieter. After however the shelling of the eylinium the enemy's artillery was not very active. At 11.15 p.m. a patrol was sent out from reconnoitre the MOUND and the STABLES. Front of Colberg was not heard from the STABLES. The Battalion was relieved by the 12th Highl. L.I. and was sent into Bde Support.	Mm.
	JUNE 26th 1917		In Bde. Support: Battalion was disposed as under. B Coy. HALF MOON TRENCH A and C Coys. ECOLE D Coy. CONVENT YPRES. Bn. HQ. in a hut on the MENIN Rd. near the ECOLE The Coys. in the ECOLE were accommodated in cellars and dugout floor cubicles, the coy in YPRES CONVENT in cellars. As the area had been working parties for the R.E. amounting to nearly three companies. These parties worked at night and were allotted various tasks in the forward areas. During the day to the vicinity of the ECOLE has to be kept at a minimum because of the shelling.	Mm.

Army Form C. 2118.

WAR DIARY
or
INTELLIGENCE SUMMARY.
(Erase heading not required.)

Instructions regarding War Diaries and Intelligence Summaries are contained in F. S. Regs., Part II. and the Staff Manual respectively. Title pages will be prepared in manuscript.

Place	Date	Hour	Summary of Events and Information	Remarks and references to Appendices
	27th June 1917		As above. Enemy artillery comparatively quiet, some intermittent action. Draft of E.O.R. received from Base and a number of Canada improvised.	Nm.
	June 28th 1917		Trading working parties as above. Situation quiet.	Nm.
	June 29th 1917		Situation normal. Heavy artillery fire from 9 to 11 p.m. Received bursts of fire on the MENIN ROAD. Working parties as before.	Nm.
	June 30th 1917		Enemy's artillery rather more active again. Heavy firing on our batteries S. of ECORE. Battalion relieved by 9th Black Watch. Reliefs previous to advanced reserve in TORONTO CAMP. Relief complete at 1.30 a.m. At 1.10 a.m. 185th Bg. Bde. Carried out a minor enterprise on enemy trenches in trenches of WHITE COTTAGE. During the time the battalion was to support as had only about a dozen casualties.	Nm.

A. Norton
Lieut. Colonel
Comdg. 10/11 Highrs. L. I.

35807. W16879/M1879 500,000 3/17 R.T. (1074) Forms/W3091/3   Army Form W.3091.

15.L.
Vol 25
46/15

Cover for Documents.

Nature of Enclosures.

10/11th (S) Bn. HIGH L.I.

WAR DIARY
JULY 1917.

CONFIDENTIAL

Notes, or Letters written.

WAR DIARY
or
INTELLIGENCE SUMMARY

Army Form C. 2118.

Place	Date	Hour	Summary of Events and Information	Remarks and references to Appendices
ECOLE YPRES.	1/7/17		About 1.30 am the Battalion was relieved in Brigade Support by the 9th Black Watch and withdrew to TORONTO CAMP near BRANDHOEK in Divl. Reserve. Information was later received that on the following day we would march to WATOU area and commence training there. The day was accordingly spent in making preparations for the move and in getting men and equipment cleaned.	Mn.
TORONTO CAMP.	2/7/17	At 6.55 am	the battalion marched out of TORONTO CAMP and proceeded to POPERINGHE by the main VLAMERTINGHE – POPERINGHE POPERINGHE rd. From POPERINGHE we went to our new Condition and ran S.S.W. by the INN and the FORGE. Billets situated about 2 miles south of WATOU were reached at Main. Companies and Bn. HQ were billeted in scattered farms. Accommodation for men in Barns etc was good. Officers' accommodation was very scanty and billets were some length back. Billets had been known to the Bde Comd. at AREELE and Bent and Companies as the best supply we were poor. Training to them was to consist of Company and Platoon training principally, the morning the Bn elementary part of a training scheme to be carried out in one of the proposed objectives E. of YPRES. The area to be used was STEENVOORDE NNE Training area and the area was reconnoitred during the afternoon. Most of the area was under Crops so her general plans to fixed a Stayg plan to each Company to be taught the elementary principles of attack practise the elementary principles of attack.	Mn.

WAR DIARY
or
INTELLIGENCE SUMMARY.
(Erase heading not required.)

Army Form C. 2118.

Place	Date	Hour	Summary of Events and Information	Remarks and references to Appendices
WATOU	3/7/17		Training Commenced. A physical drill and running parade in the vicinity of billets was held at 6 am. At 8 am Companies moved to their allotted areas and carried on platoon training in the attack. A great deal of attention was paid to the training of specialists particularly Lewis Gunners and Scouts.	JMc
"	4/7/17		Training was conducted on the same lines as the previous day. Some practice in day-patrolling was included.	JMc
"	5/7/17		This has been a day devoted to Shooting drill and Company training moving to the vicinity of billets on the a. or else right during the forenoon. Platoons being so divided and an small attention was devoted to patrolling. Platoons busy in practice and in practical movement into the pockets.	JMc
"	6/7/17		Same devotion to specialist and their training. A definite class of Men was now on introduced to Physical Training and bayonet-fighting. At 11am the Reg.t Sergt. Major held a kit parade	JMc

Place	Date	Hour	Summary of Events and Information	Remarks and references to Appendices
WATOU	7/7/17		During the morning the Brigadier saw each company in turn & gave his Brigadiers at 2.30 told paradin for attack in recent areas & performing instructions wanted with regard to forth coming operations. This practice took place on the ground round "C" Coy Billets. The Remainder of the day was spent in preparation for turn known here Rifles places on following day.	MM
"	8/7/17		The battalion marched out of billets at about 1.40 am. Men's packs were sent on motor lorries. Route was by WATOU, DROGLANDTS, WINNEZEELE, WEMEARS CAPPEL and LE MENEGAT to POINT DU JOUR & the CASPEL – LEDERZEELE Road. Heavy rain fell from the trip to left DROGLANDTS & made the march rather heavier than I would otherwise have been. At 6 am a half of an hour was a half was made for 10 am and so too Breakfast was ANGE Cros ment. Billets were reached before 10 am. And so too breakfast was again accommodated in reddies farms, three accommodation fell out. Men were again accommodated before the Bn. arrived in this area been most readily them before. During the period the Bn. Remained in this area been hunt scarcely than before. Operations which were carried out. The training area has arranged for but carrying operations which were up to the area, Ft RUBROUCK area with practice breaches from the BLUE line to the BLUE line, and the BROXEELE area with breaches from the BLUE line and the BLACK line. The area has been reconnoitred with a view to halts and preparations been have 6 carriers operations on the following days.	MM

WAR DIARY or INTELLIGENCE SUMMARY

Army Form C. 2118.

Place	Date	Summary of Events and Information	Remarks and references to Appendices
POINT DU JOUR	9/7/17	Training in RUBROUCK area. Time was devoted to Company and Platoon training. Forming up for practice and having the sections, fire and support Coys working together. The training area in length was Coy Rn manoeuvre which divides together. It was difficult to carry out as it was very much more similar than the area we have just left at STEENVOORDE front.	AM.
"	10/7/17	During the morning parades and inspection were carried out with Coy. arrangements. Trench and musketry equipment were inspected. Instruction was given to laying and answer bow shing points. In the afternoon training in continues to resume lines as a previous class, in the BRIXEELE area.	AM.
"	11/7/17	9.30 am. A Bn. practice attack was carried out in the RUBROUCK area. The Coy of 10th Bn. Rly. carried forth battalion to hopping-up. Artillery also the Vickers guns and a Stokes mortar. The attack was carried out as far as the BLUE line.	AM.
"	12/7/17	In the afternoon the second phase of the attack was practised in the BRIXEELE area.	AM.

WAR DIARY
or
INTELLIGENCE SUMMARY.
(Erase heading not required.)

Army Form C. 2118.

Place	Date	Hour	Summary of Events and Information	Remarks and references to Appendices
POINT OU TOUR.	13/7/17		Bde. practice attack on RUBROUCK area. Final scheme of Practicing on practices up to capture of BLUE line. 7/8 K.O. Sco. Borr. attacked on right. 10/11 Inf. Bn. in reserve. Practice shewed a left. 12th Inf. Bn. in Support. 12th W'inf. B.I. in reserve. Practice shewed a lack of 7th Sco. Ry. were to assault. area to man this time on heavy Ltyping on the part of the assaulting waves to run this time on heavy Ltyping on the part of the assaulting waves to run this time Cm. arr trench happened to require more defence. Wireline, telephone, pigeon, visual were experimented. M—	M—
"	14/7/17		Bde. practice continued on BROXEELE area. Recce plan for practice up to capture and consolidation of BLACK line. Two leads cooperation in the practice. M—	M—
"	15/7/17		Sunday. Forenoon Church Parade. Presbyterians at C. Coy's Field. C.Q.E. in field at Bde. HQ. Roman Catholics at BROXEELE parish church. In the afternoon 6 officers attended a pill practice at TIQUES. At 10 p.m. A and D Coys along with the Coy of 7th Sco. Rif. practiced forming up to battle position as given here to the Bde. A Coy were front parties and the other behaviours occupied parties men actually less more than the man carrying parties. M—	M—
"	16/7/17		Forenoon. Parade and inspection under Coy. Arrangements. Afternoon. RUBROUCK area. Training of Gas sent Instruction in Tactics Lecture of Lewis Guns. M—	M—

Army Form C. 2118.

WAR DIARY
or
INTELLIGENCE SUMMARY.
(Erase heading not required.)

Place	Date	Hour	Summary of Events and Information	Remarks and references to Appendices
POINT DU JOUR	17/7/17		Bn. parade in vicinity of billets. Bn. parade under R.S.M.	Bn.
"	18/7/17		Training in LEDERZEELE area. Practising stacking with farm and stabling of a similar nature.	Bn.
"	19/7/17		Similar training in RUBROUCK area. Platoon of B and C Coys sent later in the Ground and practice in drill of happens of.	Bn.
"	20/7/17		Preparation for transport to move. R.S.M. held a parade at 10.15 am on ground N. of C. Coy billet. 11.30 am Adv. gd. NCOs & Pickets reported.	Bn.
"	21/7/17		Bn. marched off at 5.15 am and marched by ARNECKE and HARDIFORT to WINNEZEELE. Bn. accommodated in huts. 7.10 Critics per N. of WINNEZEELE.	Bn.
WINNEZEELE	22/7/17		Bn. paraded M & W's Church 6 am and marched to Camp. S. of WATOU arriving there shortly after 9 am. Church Parade was held in Camp at 5.30 pm.	Bn.
WATOU	23/7/17		Bn. marched to ERIE CAMP leaving WATOU area at about 7 am. Men were warned this be not to touch We left E Camp in H16.C and relieve 10th Sea. Reg. in Bde. Reserve. Bn. reached M from ERIE CAMP at 8.45 pm	Bn.

Army Form C. 2118.

WAR DIARY
or
INTELLIGENCE SUMMARY.
(Erase heading not required.)

Instructions regarding War Diaries and Intelligence Summaries are contained in F. S. Regs., Part II. and the Staff Manual respectively. Title pages will be prepared in manuscript.

Place	Date	Hour	Summary of Events and Information	Remarks and references to Appendices
H16.c.2.2	24/7/17		Area relief was completed shortly after 10 p.m. Bn. HQ and A and B Coys. situated at H16.c.2.2., C and D Coys. in huts and shelters about H16.c.3.3 p.m.	3 p.m.
			Bn. found working parties to BIVOUACK Camps S.E. of VLAMERTINGHE. Bn. now in Bde. Support. Men invited with Lee-Enfield Rifle & short S.A.A. boots etc.	9 p.m.
"	25/7/17		Bn. was later relieved 17th Kings L.I. in front line but then went into Cancelled and was transferred to Bn. Support at H16.C. Arrange for physical drill, hands etc. in early morning, bayonet practice at night - to becoming well preparation on	9 p.m.
"	26/7/17		In Bde. Support. Scheme Continued.	9 p.m.
"	27/7/17		In Bde. Support. A Considerable number of gas shells from 10 p.m - Daybreak Bn. and D Coys put covers for training to know a permanent 11.30 p.m.	9 p.m.
"	28/7/17		In Bde. Support. Preparation made for going up into line on following day. Line in trucks front line. Num 10th Res Regt.	9 p.m.
"	29/7/17		Sunday. Run formed and made movement difficult. Bn. left VLAMERTINGHE Camp at about 8.15 p.m. and marched by KRUISSTRAAT and "C" Track to the trenches	

A.S834. Wt.W4973/M687. 750,000. 8/16. D. D. & L. Ltd. Forms/C.2113/13.

WAR DIARY
or
INTELLIGENCE SUMMARY.
(Erase heading not required.)

Army Form C. 2118.

Place	Date	Hour	Summary of Events and Information	Remarks and references to Appendices
	30/9/17		Bttn was relieved by 10th Sea. Regt. in the left half of the front line posn. A Coy and ½ D Coy occupied the front and support trenches, C Coy and ½ D Coy occupying ST. JAMES WOOD and B Coy was in reserve in the region of HUSSAR FM. An advance guard company in preparation for the operations.	
	1/9/17		In addition. See Appendix A (O.O. 9hr) and Appendix B Report on Operations Brm attached.	

M. Stoles
Lieut. Colonel
Comdg. 10th Regt. L. I.

Appendix A.

SECRET.   10/11th.(S).Bn.Highland Light Infantry.   10/11th H.L.I.
                                                        No 3 Copy

References:-
Secret Map A. already
issued to Coys., Map B.
attached, Sheet 28 N.W. and
N.E. 1/20,000. St.JULIEN
Sheet 1/10,000. and
ZONNEBEKE Sheet 1/10,000.

OPERATION ORDER NO.94.   15/7/1917.

1. Offensive operations on a large scale are being commenced on "Z" Day.

2. The 15th.Division will attack on "Z" Day. The objectives and boundaries of the Division were shewn on Map "A".
   1st. Objective.   BLUE Line.
   2nd. Objective.   BLACK Line.
   3rd. Objective.   GREEN Line.

3. The 15th.Division is to attack on the right of the XIX Corps, the 8th.Division II Corps, on its right, and the 55th. Division, XIX Corps, on its left.
   The 18th. and 36th. Divisions will be in Corps Reserve.
   The 55th.Division is attacking with 2 Brigades in line, the 165th.Infantry Brigade on the right, the 166th.Infantry Brigade on the left. These Brigades will capture both the BLUE and BLACK Lines and the 164th. Infantry Brigade will advance through them and capture the GREEN Line.

4. The 15th.Division will attack with the 44th.Infantry Brigade on the right, the 46th.Infantry Brigade on the left, and the 45th.Infantry Brigade in Reserve. The 44th. and 46th. Infantry Brigades will capture the BLUE and BLACK Lines, the 45th.Infantry Brigade will capture and consolidate the GREEN Line.
   The dividing line between the two leading Brigades is shewn on Map A.
   The 44th. and 46th. Infantry Brigades will advance to the assault at ZERO Hour.
   The advance from the BLUE Line will be at ZERO plus 1 hour 15 minutes; the advance from the BLACK Line will be at ZERO plus 6 hours 20 minutes.
   The Reserve Brigade will advance at ZERO Hour to a position of assembly W. of CAMBRIDGE ROAD. From here the advance will be in Artillery Formation.

5. The 46th. Infantry Brigade will attack as follows :-
   (a). 7/8th.K.O.Sco.Bord. on the right.
        10/11th.High.L.I.   on the left.
   These Battalions will capture the BLUE and BLACK Lines.
   The BLACK Line will be consolidated after its capture, each Battalion will dig two trenches 100 yards in length, shaped as shewn below and sited at suitable points on its front. These trenches will subsequently be joined up so as to form a continuous line.

   ~~~~~~~~~~~~~~~

   (b). 10th.Scottish Rifles will place one Company at the disposal of each of the Attacking Battalions to act as moppers up for the German front system including RUPRECHT FARM. These Companies after completion of mopping up will hold IBERIA and CAMEROON RESERVE Trenches.
   (c). 10th.Scottish Rifles (less 2 Coys.) will be in SUPPORT.
   (d). 12th. High. L. I. in RESERVE.
   (e). 12th.High. L. I. will detail one Company for carrying duties.

6. The 10/11th. High. L.I. will attack as follows :-
(a). "A" Coy. on the right.
"D" Coy. on the left.
These Companies will attack and capture the BLUE and BLACK Lines. These Companies will consolidate the BLACK Line when taken, as described in para 6 above.
(b). "B" Coy. in support to "A" Coy.
"C" Coy. in support to "D" Coy.
These Companies will render assistance as required.
As the moppers up 10th. Scottish Rifles only deal with the German front system, O.C. "B" and "C" Coys. will each detail 1 Platoon to report at BLUE Line to O.C. "A" and "D" Coys. respectively for mopping up during the attack on the BLACK Line.
"C" Coy. moppers up will deal with SQUARE FARM, CAMEROON DRIVE and CAMEROON AVENUE as far as D.36.a.2.6. "B" Coy. Moppers up will continue close in rear of the first wave of the assaulting Coys. and deal with the area between SQUARE FARM and the BLACK Line objective. They will also deal with BECK HOUSE.
(c). The moppers up of the 10th. Scottish Rifles will deal with the German front system as follows :-
1 Platoon front line and area up to support line.
1 Platoon support line and area up to reserve line.
1 Platoon reserve line.
1 Platoon RUPRECHT FARM and CAMEROON AVENUE as far as BLUE Line objective.

7. (a). The Battalion will be formed up at ZERO Hour as shewn on Map B. Boundaries, frontages and objectives are shewn on Map A.
The 3rd. and 4th. waves will close up to within 50 yards of the 2nd. wave by ZERO minus 30.
(b). "A" and "D" Coys. will attack each with two Platoons in the front line.
(c). At ZERO Hour each wave will be in one line, second lines of waves gaining their positions as they cross "No Man's Land", which will be crossed at a quick step until within 100 yards of our Barrage.
(d). After capture of the BLACK Line the usual patrols will be sent out to the front as far as our barrage permits.
(e). After the capture of each objective O.C. "A" and "D" Coys. will reorganise their Companies, thin out the front line which is apt to become overcrowded, and send back to their Companies any men of "B" and "C" Coys. not required, that a Battalion Reserve may again be built up.

8. (a). On July 19/20th. the 10th. Scottish Rifles will take over the Left Section of the Divisional Front from 45th. Infantry Brigade and will be disposed as follows :-
10th. Scottish Rifles on Right.
10th. High. L.I. on Left.
(b). On V/W. night 10/11th. High. L.I. will relieve 12th. High.L.I. dispositions :-
1½ Companies in front line.
1½ Companies in reserve line.
1 Company in ECOLE or POTIJZE Defences.
(c). On Y/Z. night "A" and "D" Coys. will be in the front line. "B" and "C" Coys. in close support and CAMBRIDGE TRENCH. Battalion Headquarters will be in CAMBRIDGE TRENCH N. of HAYMARKET (I.5.a.15.35.).

9. DEFENSIVE FLANKS. In the event of the troops on the Left of the Brigade not being able to advance to the BLACK Line in line with the Brigade, "C" Coy. will be prepared to form a defensive flank as it advances. This will be formed along CAMEROON AVENUE up to BLUE Line. O.C. "C" Coy. will select suitable positions at other points should occasion arise.

3.

10. LATERAL COMMUNICATION. With a view to the maintenance of touch with the 55th. Division on our left, meeting places have been arranged where the left platoon and section commanders of "D" and "C" Coys. will communicate with corresponding personnel of the 165th. Infantry Brigade as follows :-
   (a). Where Northern Boundary cuts German Reserve Line. C.29.d.C.9.
   (b). Point on HANEBEEK where BLUE Line cuts Northern Boundary C.30.a.2.3.
   (c). Point where FREZENBERG ~~tr~~ URG line cuts ZONNEBEKE stream D.19.c.75.74.
   (d). IBERIAN FARM.
   (e). Where Boundary crosses German Front Line C.29.d.35.79.

11. TANKS. Two Companies of Tanks will co-operate in the attack on the Divisional Front.
   One Company will operate against the BLACK Line of which one section will work on the Brigade Front.
   One Company will operate against the GREEN Line.

12. ARTILLERY. (1). Six Brigades of Field Artillery will support the attack of the Division.
   (2). Heavy Artillery will support the Division under Corps Orders.
   (3). (a). The opening bombardment will last twelve days.
   (b). The creeping barrage will start on the enemy's front line and will lift off the enemy's front line at ZERO plus six minutes and will move forward at the rate of 100 yards in 4 minutes. It will remain stationary 300 yards beyond the BLUE and BLACK Lines until the hour fixed for the advance from that line, therefore the leading waves of attacking Battalions must time their advance from the BLUE Line so as to be within 100 yards of the barrage when it moves on.

13. MACHINE GUNS. The attack of the Division will be covered by Machine Gun Barrages from 38 Guns.

14. MOVEMENTS OF BATTALION HEADQUARTERS. Until the BLUE Line is taken Battalion Headquarters will remain in CAMBRIDGE TRENCH at I.6.a.45.35., but an advanced Headquarters will be established as early as possible at about C.29.d.8.7.
   When the BLUE Line is taken Battalion Headquarters will be at this spot. During the attack on the BLACK Line there will be an advanced Headquarters at GREY RUIN C.30.a.9.8.
   When the BLACK Line is captured Battalion Headquarters will be established at this point.

Marshall Lieut.,
Adjt. 10/11th.(S). Bn. High: L. I.

Appendix B

10/11th.(S).Bn.Highland Light Infantry.   5/8/1917.

SECRET.

Ref: Sheets 28 N.W., N.E.
1/30.000. ZONNEBEKE and
ST. JULIEN Sheets 1/10.000.
and Situation Maps attached.

REPORT ON OPERATIONS 31st.JULY-1st. AUGUST, 1917.

The Battalion front extended from WARWICK FARM on the left to CRUMP FARM on the right and we were assembled at Zero hour as under.
The two front Coys. "A" (right) and "D" (left) had their front waves about 30 yards in front of our wire and their second waves in our old front line. Between these two waves lay "D" Coy.10th.Scottish Rifles allotted to the Battalion for the mopping up of the German front system. The Support Coys. "B" (right) and "C" (left) were in position with their front waves between CRUMP TRENCH and our front line and their second waves on or about CRUMP TRENCH. Battalion H.Q. was established in a dug-out in CAMBRIDGE TRENCH N. of its junction with HAYMARKET.
The work of getting into position was carried out in absolute quiet and almost without casualty. Zero hour was at 3-50 a.m. and at that hour our Artillery opened an annihilating barrage on the German system under cover of which our troops advanced. The Eighteen Pounder barrage remained on the German front line for 6 minutes and then crept forward with our Infantry close in rear. The ground was extraordinarily difficult and had been distorted beyond all recognition by our shell fire, but excellent progress was made and the first objective (the BLUE Line) was taken without difficulty. Casualties during this phase of the attack were unusually slight and the objective was taken absolutely to time. We did not call a halt actually on the BLUE Line but advanced close to our barrage and established ourselves on the higher ground. The action of the enemy during this phase was as follows.- About 2 minutes after our barrage commenced he placed a barrage contrary to expectations on the line of CRUMP TRENCH, but

this was almost immediately lifted and he shelled the Communication Trenches somewhat indiscriminately particularly HAYMARKET near its junction with the front line, while occasional heavies dropped on the line of CAMBRIDGE ROAD. His Infantry shewed little or no fight and prisoners gave themselves up without any fuss. At first a few machine gunners remained by their guns but soon fled in full retreat or gave themselves up. Advanced Battalion H.Q. went forward in rear of the last wave and was established at RUPRECHT FARM. As soon as the news of the capture of the BLUE Line was received Battalion H.Q. moved forward to a concrete dug-out in CAMEROON AVENUE about 200 yards from RUPRECHT FARM and Advanced H.Q. moved to GREY RUIN.

Immediately after the arrival of Battn. H.Q. at RUPRECHT FARM the old German Reserve Area including the farm itself was heavily shelled and several casualties occurred. The Battalion Lewis Gun Officer and the Medical Officer were both killed.

The attack on the BLACK Line was launched at 5-5 a.m.

The 55th Division on our left was at first held up, but soon succeeded in advancing and all went well on crossing the ridge beyond GREY RUIN. We came under very heavy Machine Gun fire both from FROST HOUSE and HILL 35, and a considerable number of casualties were caused. The two front Coys. went straight forward and by 5-50 a.m. we were 100 yards E. of SQUARE FARM. The farm itself did not offer resistance and was mopped up by a Platoon of "C" Coy. and 130 prisoners were taken. The Officer in command of the Company which took the farm was badly wounded about 150 yards in advance of it. Meanwhile on the right "A" Coy. went straight ahead in spite of the heavy Machine Gun fire from the right and maintained touch with "D" Coy. on its left. "B" Coy. coming up in Support of "A" Coy. had three Officers killed but continued to advance under command of the one remaining Officer. Under the influence of the Machine Gun fire from the right this Company tended to front the fire and moved a little to the right. A flanking movement by this Company silenced an enemy Machine Gun near LOW FARM which was causing many casualties. The Battalion Intelligence Officer arriving at SQUARE FARM within 20 minutes of its capture reported that the 7/8th.K.O.S.Bords. apppared to be on their objective and he thought that we would presently succeed in capturing ours. We were delayed for some little time longer by the fact that the 55th.Divn.

had not yet taken POMMERN CASTLE and Machine Gun fire was still heavy from HILL 35, although the enemy could clearly be seen retreating across the POMMERN CASTLE, DOCHY FARM Road. At 10-35 a.m. the one remaining Officer of "A" Coy. reported the BLACK Line taken and the work of consolidation commenced. Meanwhile the enemy had developed a heavy artillery fire and was barraging the BLUE Line area, SQUARE FARM and the vicinity between there and the BLACK Line, but the 45th. Brigade had already passed through us to attack the GREEN Line.

Up to this point we had about 180 Casualties in Other Ranks and 10 Officer Casualties. Consolidation of the BLACK Line continued but it was found that this was not being done on the most advantageous ground so our energies were directed to constructing a line which started from near IBERIAN FARM on the left and continued to the right about 150 yards in advance of BECK HOUSE. Meanwhile all was not going well in front. The 55th.Division after reaching the GREEN Line objective began to fall back leaving the flank of the 6th.Camerons in the air. The 13th.Royal Scots moved forward to reinforce and we arranged to send forward our Companies to occupy the ground vacated by them, but it seems unlikely that the move was complete when about 4-5 p.m. the S.O.S. went up on the 55th.Division Front. The troops on our left began to give ground, but we succeeded in standing firm on a general line D.19.c.80.75. D.19.d.8.5. D.19.d.5.5., which we held along with the Royal Scots. During the counter-attack there was a certain confusion of Units but when the above line was established we succeeded in reorganising and held that portion of the line which was between the Royal Scots and the remnants of the 6th.Cameron Highdrs. This line we proceeded to consolidate. Meanwhile we had contrived to establish a thin line in front of SQUARE FARM, which we manned with details from Headquarters and held during the whole period of the counter-attack. This was considered necessary because we felt that there was a complete absence of supports should the enemy's attack prove successful and our front line be pushed. In addition to these H.Q.Details we had 11 Vickers Guns in defensive positions in front of the farm. These Guns played an important part in checking the enemy's attempts at counter-attacking by firing on the DELVA FARM Ridge and along it to our left. Every possible target which appeared was successfully engaged. Ammunition and Water were sent up to the front and all preparations made to hold the line. Our patrols reported that the enemy were digging in on the ridge and that he appeared restless and uneasy. The 10th. Scottish Rifles and 12th. High. L.I. were ordered to relieve the Royal Scots and 6th. Camerons and on completion of that relief the Battalion was to withdraw to the vicinity of SQUARE FARM. This relief proved impossible as the time and daylight found us with the 12th. High. L.I. and three Companies of the 10th. Scottish Rifles well up behind the front line and to our right, but were unable to carry out a relief because of the light.

The forenoon of the first was very quiet and we succeeded in improving our position and comfort. The enemy were reported massing in D.27.c. and would there presumably counter-attack on our right. About 2 p.m. we received a message from Advanced H.Q. of 13th. Royal Scots in BECK HOUSE that the enemy could be seen advancing on our right between BECK HOUSE and BORRY FARM. As the 6th. Camerons had for some time been unable to get in touch with the 6/7th. Royal Scots Fusrs. on our right and the dispositions on our right were accordingly unknown we feared that our front might be outflanked and therefore sent up the S.O.S. and brought down the Artillery Barrage on the enemy ridge. A defensive flank was thrown back from about D.19.d.3.0. towards FROST HOUSE and we discovered that the Royal Scots Fusrs. had been relieved and that the 44th. Infantry Brigade were not holding the dispositions that had been held by them. At 3-45 p.m. a report was received from BECK FARM that the enemy was advancing past BORRY FARM. About 4 p.m. the enemy came through on our right in three waves and we were at the same time attacked in front and driven back after very heavy losses. From SQUARE FARM we could see bodies of our men apparently occupying part of the FREZENBERG Line. At 5 p.m. a patrol sent out from SQUARE FARM reported the enemy in occupation of BECK HOUSE. Patrol got to within 100 yards of the house and the enemy signalled to them to come in. When they turned to come back they were fired on. They did not meet any of our men between SQUARE FARM and BECK HOUSE. At 5-40 p.m. a message from 10th. Scottish

6.

Rifles confirmed the report that the enemy occupied BECK HOUSE. At 6-15 p.m. the enemy occupied certain shell holes in the FREZENBERG Line, but no further advance took place. At 6-40 p.m. we intercepted a message intended for "C" Coy. of the 6th.Battn.The King's, which stated that a line was being established by us from SQUARE FARM Southwards. This referred to a line we had been holding with Headquarter Details from the time we sent up the S.O.S. at 2 p.m. and which proved to be the only organised line between us and the enemy. We had 11 Vicker's Guns in defensive positions E. of the FARM covering both flanks as well as our front and they fired bursts on the ridge and directed fire on the ground in front of the BLACK Line as soon as we received definite information that parties of the enemy were established there. Several parties of the enemy shewed themselves on the ridge and were fired upon and dispersed. At 7-5 p.m. we reported that we had no Infantry in front of us and accordingly even if the situation should clear we would have no one to send forward as a fighting patrol. At 7-50 p.m. we discovered that the 44th. Brigade were standing firm in their part of the BLACK Line and that LOW FARM was occupied by neither side. To the North we could discover no Infantry in the BLACK Line and no movement of troops was anywhere visible.

At this point one Company Royal Scots Fusrs. began to come up and about 8-30 p.m. we sent them forward to construct and hold a line (FREZENBERG Sheet) from L. of LOW FARM (D.25.a.5.7.) to D.19.c.4.2. About 9-30 p.m. orders were received that 6/7th.Royal Scots Fusrs. and 11th. A. and S.Hdrs. would advance through us and occupy the BLACK Line. At 10-30 p.m. they arrived and succeeded in occupying the line and establishing connection with the 56th. Division on the left and the 12th.High.L.I. on the right. On the completion of this occupation we collected the remnants of the Battalion under the one remaining Coy.Officer and withdrew to the region of ST. JAMES'S TRENCH.

R. Stokes,
Lieut. Colonel,
Commanding 10/11th.(S).Bn. Highland L.I.

APPENDIX 11.

DUMPS, CARRYING PARTIES and EQUIPMENT.

1. **SITUATION OF DUMPS.** Explosives, Lights, R.E. Stores, etc.

   46th. INF. BDE.   M V. A.   I.1.a.7.9. ⎫ Battalion
                     M V. B.   I.5.a.4.1. ⎬ Dumps.
                     M V. C.   I.5.a.3.4. ⎭
                     M V. D.   C.30.c.5.7.

2. Before ZERO the Battalion will form its dump M V. C. from M V. A. This dump will be used throughout the early stages of the operations.

3. 1 Company, 12th. High. L.I. will provide carrying parties for the Brigade. As soon as possible this Company will establish M V. D. by carrying from M V. A. A relay dump will also be established in the vicinity of the MOUND and the Battalion Dumps mentioned above will be cleared to form it. O.C. "B" Coy. will detail 1 N.C.O. to remain in charge of the Battalion Dump until it is exhausted.

4. As soon as the BLACK Line is taken a supply of water will be carried up to M V. D. for the use of 7/8th.K.O.Sco. Bord. and 10/11th. High.L.I. The importance of sending back petrol tins whenever an opportunity presents itself cannot be over-emphasised.

5. On X/Y. night "A" and "D" Coys. will each construct a trench dump near where HAYMARKET joins the front line.
   This will be done by collecting S.A.A., bombs, Very Lights, etc., which are in the trenches. Position to be marked by shovels placed in a conspicious position on Y/Z. night.

2. **FIGHTING KIT.**
   1. Steel Helmet.
   Equipment, pack and entrenching implement and carrier.
   Respirator and P.H. Helmet.
   Mess Tins and 1 Water Bottle.
   Waterproof Sheet.
   Rations for Z. and Z. plus 1 days, plus the emergency rations.

APPENDIX 11. 2.

2. FIGHTING KIT.
    2. The following will also be carried:-

      S.A.A.Rifle. 220 rounds per Rifleman.
                   100   "   " Bomber.
                   100   "   " Rifle Grenadier.
                   100   "   " Lewis Gunner.
      S.A.A. (Lewis). 20 Drums. 1000 Loose.
        per Gun. (Remainder of drums to be kept
                     in Battalion Reserve).
    Tools. 1 Full size per man.
    Very Light Pistols to Establishment.
    Mill's Hand Grenades. 8 per bomber.
    No.23.   8 per Rifle Grenadier.
    Sandbags. 2 per man.
    Flares. 2 per man.
    "P"Bombs. 4 per platoon of moppers up.
    Wirecutters. To Establishment. 4 pairs of
            large wirecutters will be issued to
            each platoon of leading waves.
    Very Lights. 12 per Pistol.
    Rifle Bomb Signals. 4 per R.G.Section.

    Above Stores will be issued at TORONTO CAMP.

APPENDIX III.

PERSONNEL LEFT OUT OF ACTION.

Personnel will be left out in accordance with SS.135, Section 3e.
    (a). 7 Officers and 108 Other Ranks will be accommodated at TORONTO CAMP.
    (b). Surplus to above, at 13th.Divisional Depot Battn.
Personnel working under 73rd. Field Coy. R.E. will be included in above.
Each Company will leave out 1 Gas.N.C.O.

APPENDIX VII.

Special attention is directed to the following points in connection with the operations.

(a). Before ZERO the greatest care must be exercised in getting into position with as little noise as possible.

(b). Men will be warned against blind ditches filled with wire. Ground Scouts will be employed as far as possible.

(c). It seems probable from the dispositions of the enemy that the greatest resistance will be met with at or about the BRAEMEN LINE, but in the event of the enemy driving in the Division on our left, the 46th. Infantry Brigade will counter-attack from the BLACK Line towards HILL 37. in D.20.a.

SECRET.

10/11th (S) BN, Highland Light Infantry.

ADDENDA to Operation Order No. 24. of 13.7.1917.   24.7.1917.

1. Ref para 2a. "A" Coy. will construct trench at A.19.d.30.35 to fire towards BREMEN REDOUBT and DELVA FM.
"D" Coy will 3.6 trench at M.18.c.25.10. (vicinity of IBERIAN FM.) to fire towards ZEVENKOTE and HILL 35 in D.22.c.

2. (1) Ref: Appendix VI. para 2. Add:
Flares will be lit by the leading Infantry
(a) When called for by the contact patrol aeroplane by means of KLAXON-HORN and Very Lights. This call will normally only be made at times when the Infantry are believed to be on the BLUE, BLACK and GREEN LINES.
(b) When the Infantry consider it advisable to make known the position of their front line.
Flares should be lit at the rate of one to ten men and at the bottom of a trench or shell hole where possible. Clusters of three flares at 25 yds. interval are especially effective.

(2) Ref: para 3.
(a) The three following general signals will be used and all ranks should know them by heart.
2RED and GREEN Discs = Have reached my objective.
RED, RED and RED Discs = Broken down.
RED, WHITE and WHITE Discs = No enemy in sight.
(b) Helmet hoisted on bayonet means "Require assistance from Tanks".
(c) When a Tank is out of action, a white square 18"x18" will be placed on top of the Tank.

(3) DOGS. Two message dogs have been allotted to the 55th Division. All ranks should be warned that dogs carrying message pouches on their collars are not to be detained, except for the purpose of having the message read by an officer.

-2-

(4) **Runners:** All runners should be instructed to carry messages in their top right hand pockets.
(5) **Rockets:** An issue of message carrying rockets is being made.

3. Ref: Appendix 11 para 2 (2)
The two gunners per team still equipped with the old pattern buckets will be with B'n. H.Q. during the operations as a Reserve and will be used to replace casualties in teams. They will report at B'n H.Q. when the Battalion takes over the front line and their place in the team will be taken by riflemen.

4. Ref: Appendix V11.
Add: (d) It is of the utmost importance that enemy dugouts should be carefully searched as soon as possible after capture. Information of great value in the form of orders, war diaries, etc. can be found in them, and it is essential that such things should be collected before they are destroyed, or appropriated by souvenier hunters who do not realise their value. Each Coy. will arrange for a systematic search to be carried out under the supervision of an officer. Search to commence immediately the captured trench is mopped up. Books, Maps, Documents etc. will be placed in sacks, labelled where found and forwarded to Battalion Headquarters.

C O R R E C T I O N.

1. Ref: Para 7a, line 3.
Delete "and 4th"
Add to end of sub para
"and the 4th wave to within 50 yds. of the 3rd."

Mansell Lieut.
Adjt 10/11th (S) Batt'n. Highl. L. I.

APPENDIX VI.

COMMUNICATIONS.

1. **WITH BATTN.H.Q.** Battalion Headquarters will be connected by telephone with Advanced Battn.H.Q. and runners will be sent there by the Companies.

    In addition visual stations will be established wherever possible and Companies should make use of every opportunity of communicating in this way.

    It is hoped to establish a Visual Station at SQUARE FARM during the attack on the BLACK Line.

2. **WITH CONTACT AEROPLANE.** Flares will be lit by most forward troops when called for.

3. **WITH TANKS.** Tank Coloured Disc and Light Code will be used.

APPENDIX IV.

BATTLE/ STRAGGLER POSTS.

1. A Brigade Line of Straggler Posts will be established under Brigade arrangements.

2. A record of all stragglers will be kept and each case investigated.

3. Men are to be warned that all cases of avoiding duty will be tried by F.G.C.M.

4. N.C.Os. and men are to be informed that disciplinary action will be taken against all persons found looting on the battle field. Any soldier found searching for souvenirs during an action will be severely dealt with.

APPENDIX V.

PRISONERS OF WAR.

1.   All prisoners will be disarmed at once.
     Officers and N.C.Os. will be searched by their captors immediately they are captured.
     Men will be searched on arrival at Divisional Cage. Special attention should be paid to pockets in the back of the tunics and back of trousers.
     Personal belongings and decorations should not be removed.
     The SOLDBUCH should not be removed from prisoners of war.

2.   All prisoners will be sent at once to Battalion Headquarters and then passed on to 10th.High.L.I.
     Stretcher cases will be evacuated in the usual way.

APPENDIX I.

MEDICAL ARRANGEMENTS.

1. REGIMENTAL AID POSTS.
    1. Before Zero the Regimental Aid Post will be at I.5.c.2.9.
    2. After Zero the Regimental Aid Post will be at C.29.d.5.4.

2. COLLECTING POSTS. Will be on the POTIJZE and MENIN ROADS at I.4.a.7.2. and at I.9.d.3.6.

3. EVACUATION. Will if possible be by Motor Ambulance to the main dressing station at BRANDHOEK.

4. WALKING WOUNDED. There will be a clearly marked track S. of YPRES by KRUISSTRAAT to VLAMERTINGHE MILL walking wounded Dressing Station.
    There will be a soup kitchen on the road at H.18.c.9.9. and as far as possible walking wounded will be met by Char-a-bancs.

5. CARRYING will be done by Regimental Stretcher Bearers as far as Regimental Aid Post, and then by R.A.M.C. Bearers.

6. On receipt of orders personnel as under to act as auxilary bearers will be provided from personnel left out of action.
    - "A". 1 Cpl. 6 men.
    - "B" 6 men.
    - "C" 1 L/Cpl. 6 men.
    - "D" 7 men.

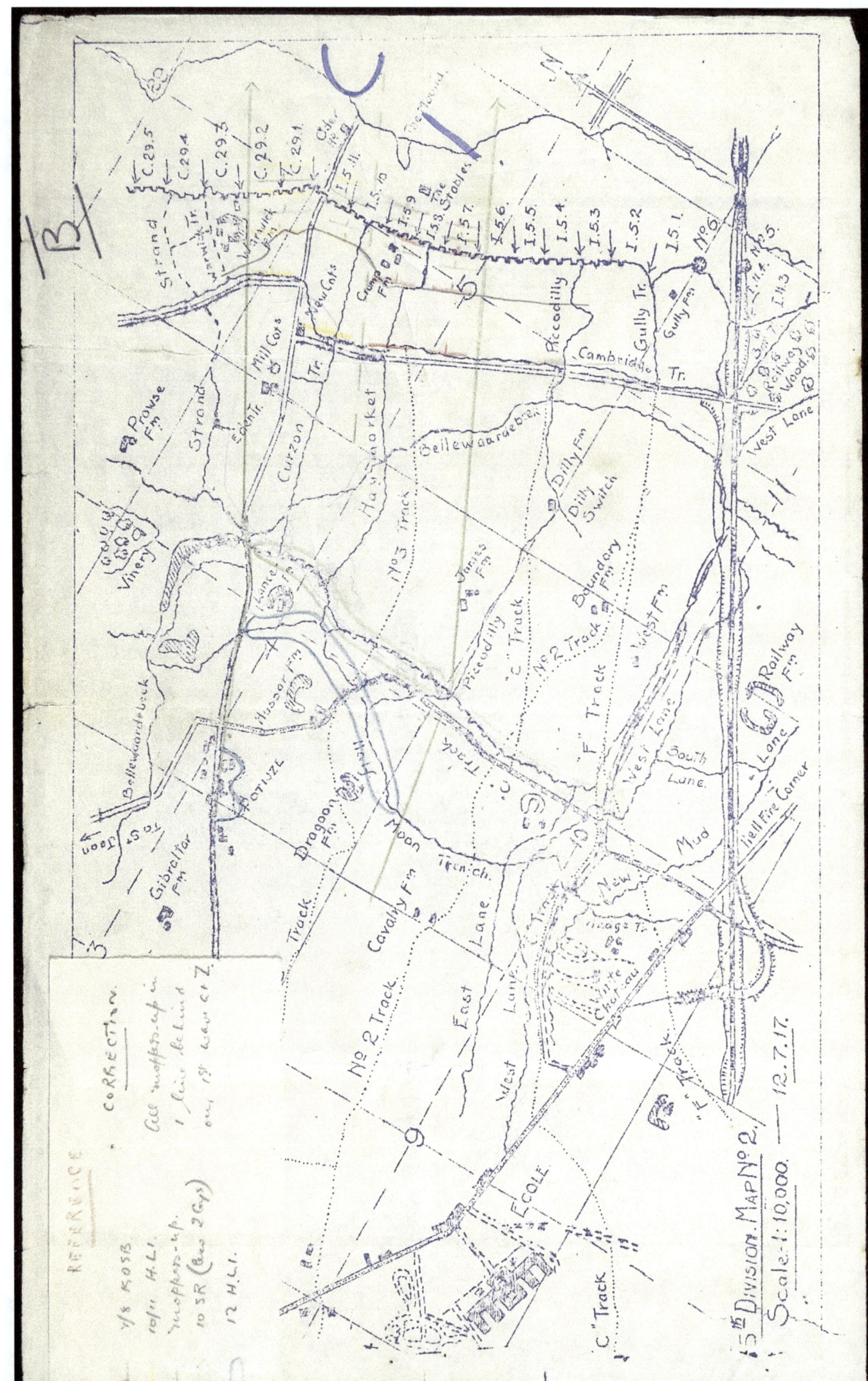

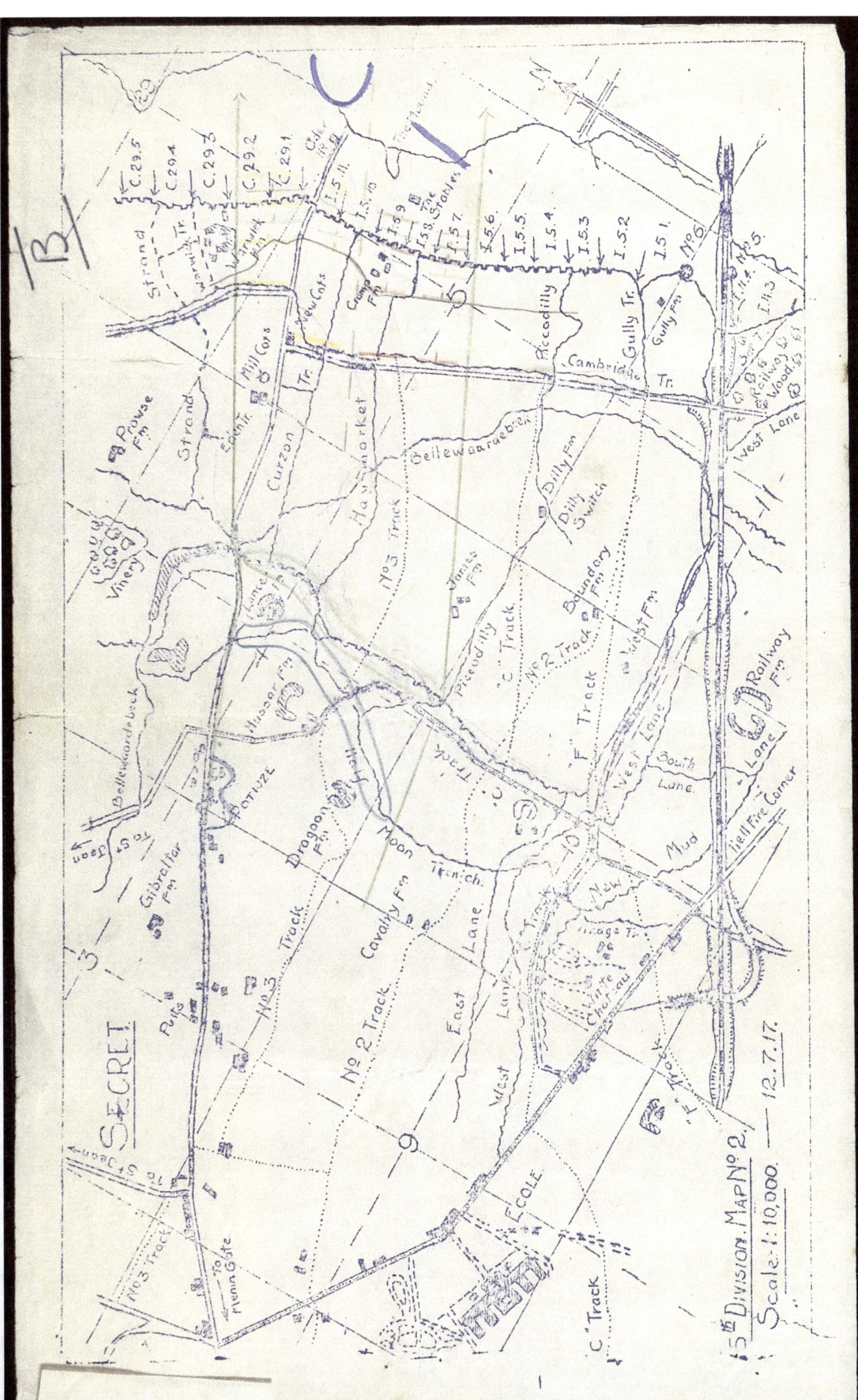

Vol 26 46/75

16.L.
15 sheets.

10/11 (S) Bn. HIGH L.I.

WAR DIARY FOR AUGUST 1917.

CONFIDENTIAL

Army Form C. 2118.

WAR DIARY
or
INTELLIGENCE SUMMARY.
(Erase heading not required.)

Place	Date	Hour	Summary of Events and Information	Remarks and references to Appendices
In action	1/8/17		In action. See Appendices to WAR DIARY for July 1917.	Am
"	2/8/17		About 3 p.m. Bn's withdrew to the lines of ST JAMES TRENCH and consolidated. Bn. HQ. at DRAGOON FM. At 5:15 p.m. an order was received that the Bn. was moving to WINNEZEELE and that the Bn. was to parade in clothing in which it fought (ECOLE) at 6:15 p.m. Bn. was hurriedly collected and on parade moved off to YPRES and entrained to a point just S.9. VLAMERTINGHE when that Bn. have to entrain to 6 WINNEZEELE. Here the Bn. had dtf[?] and then entrained and arrived at an destination abt. 1:30 a.m. 3/8/17 for H.Q. as a farm D.25.d.7.3 (sheet 27). As the men proceeded to their quarters were accommodated to farms for the night without their own Cook ranks fitted. Total casualties amounted to Officers Held on hands nil Carr. 278 O.R. about 9 men gas inhaled	Am Am
WINNEZEELE	3/8/17		(including N.C.O.) Commenced.	Am
"	4/8/17		A day spent in by inspection and cleaning parades. All Equipment and Fighting Kit was carefully checked and orders sent to	Am

A5834 Wt. W4973/M687. 750,000. 8/16. D. D. & L. Ltd. Forms/C.2113/13.

WAR DIARY or INTELLIGENCE SUMMARY

Army Form C. 2118.

Place	Date	Hour	Summary of Events and Information	Remarks and references to Appendices
WIMMEREUX	5/8/17		Sunday. Church Parade, weather fair, hot, Rustling continued.	
—	6/8/17		Sgt J. 55. O.R. arrived. Att was J about 3 months. Divine Service also held. Marched him to house. Phone from R.S.M. to W.A.	
—	7/8/17		Sgt J. 51. O.R. arrived from lifts J ran a.m. to draft store.	
—	8/8/17		The Commanding Officer inspected all Coys in full marching order. Training was continued under Coy arrangements: the chiefs of staff had two days running special instruction in chief unde the R.S.M. A performance was started by the Divisional French Corps, it had both a hundred on account of rain. A Regimental Canteen was opened. It made an excellent start.	
—	9/8/17		The morning was spent in preparing for an inspection by the Divisional General, who inspected us at 2.30 p.m. In a short speech, he referred to the splendid work done by the D wing in the recent operations, and wished us best in the [future].	

Army Form C. 2118.

WAR DIARY
or
INTELLIGENCE SUMMARY.
(Erase heading not required.)

Instructions regarding War Diaries and Intelligence Summaries are contained in F. S. Regs., Part II. and the Staff Manual respectively. Title pages will be prepared in manuscript.

Place	Date	Hour	Summary of Events and Information	Remarks and references to Appendices
NINNEZEELE	10/8/17		Laying continued much Coy. arrangements. The draft met R.S.M. Patrol work was practiced after dark	
"	11/8/17		Laying much Coy. arrangements. The Res. Bombing N.C.O. took a class of 2 N.C.Os per Coy. Draft of memorandum from 29 I.B.I. includes 30 w N.C.Os. Good quality of men	
"	12/8/17		Sunday. Church Parades. Weather much improved. Draft of arrived. All old hands - 2nd, 4th, 7th Battn. One N.C.O. and 1 man of 10th returned.	
"	13/8/17		Laying much Coy. arrangements. Will interview again Commanding Officer in regard to Lewis Gun takers in the draft.	
"	14/8/17		Laying much Coy. arrangements. Rengaining of training was received to move to forward area on 16th inst.	
"	15/8/17		As far as possible refitting and reorganization were completed and preparations were made for the move tomorrow. An advance party has sent to take on Camp in Hesselroch 14-15.	

WAR DIARY or INTELLIGENCE SUMMARY

Army Form C. 2118.

Place	Date	Hour	Summary of Events and Information	Remarks and references to Appendices
NINNEZEELE	16/8/17		2d Battalion marched to Brigade camp at 14.15, to marched off at 8.30 a.m., having the Brigade starting point at ULES TROIS ROIS) at train & Rest Route and by STEENVOORDE to ABEELE. A halt of about half an hour for breakfast was made at ABEELE, entrainment station starting at 9.15 a.m. and moved off about 9.40 a.m. Train arrived at the ASYLUM, YPRES shortly after 11 a.m. and the Battalion marched to camp. Shelling was continued during the afternoon.	
YPRES	17/8/17		Shelling and all preparations for going up the line was hurried on, and the Battalion was practically completed only a number of No 24 bursts still being required. In the afternoon orders were received that we would take over the line on the 18th from our front, relieving the 9th Battalion, CONNAUGHT RANGERS. the Battalion moved off at 4.15 p.m. in motor by Vlamertinghe at 10.00 p.m. distance route was by YPRES and "H" TRACK. Lincoln was met at MILL COTTS. Battalion HQ was in SQUIRE FARM, and the front line followed roughly the C.T. line from D.25.a.4.0 to D.19.C.8.3. Coys. was disposed follows, D. Coy Right front, B Coy Centre, C Coy Left front, A Coy Support, A Coy being in between D.19.C.4.2 and D.25.a.37. Relief complete at 12.00 midnight.	

WAR DIARY or INTELLIGENCE SUMMARY

Army Form C. 2118.

Place	Date	Hour	Summary of Events and Information	Remarks and references to Appendices
SQUARE FARM.	18/9/17.		Touch was established with the 9 SeaForth on our right, but not with the Battalion on the left. FROST HOUSE and LOW FARM are in our hands, but BECK and BORRY are German. **AP**	
			A quiet day was passed. The line is almost neutral held in still holes what are being dished up when possible to channel. The walks in front, which great aids can into BORRY FARM and other strong points were kept by our heavens this afternoon during which any unofficial state of the line great difficulty has been experienced in getting early definite information as to the enemy's defences. It appears to later he has any strictly new shell holes relying on defended farms and emicali dug outs for his defence. A machine gun was located at BORRY FM. which fired occasionally by night. A scheme for a slight attack on BECK HOUSE was carried for and submitted, but not put into operation. There was some trench artillery firing also on our right, from LOW FM. to FROST HOUSE. CAMPBELL would carry out. **AP**	

A.S34 Wt. W4973/M697 750,000 8/16 D. D. & L. Ltd. Forms/C2118/13 N. 147.

WAR DIARY / INTELLIGENCE SUMMARY

Army Form C. 2118.

Place	Date	Hour	Summary of Events and Information	Remarks and references to Appendices
SQUARE FARM.	19/8/17		At 4.40am. our artillery carried out a Bombardment scheme, this included a creeping barrage di rah di (ground for hostile M.G.s) Shortly after the bombardment (about 6.20am.) a party of 2 men, one from BORRY to BECK HOUSE, and 3 men entered what appeared to be a dug-out about 50 yards N.E. of BECK HOUSE. They were fired on (but without success). The Battalion on our left (2/5 WORCESTERS) reported that a party of the enemy had been seen to leave the O.G. trench as a result between our left and their right. In consequence each Battalion sent out a strong patrol after dark the whole area between the two Battalions was thoroughly patrolled, but no traces of any enemy in large numbers could be found. A few hostile M.Gs. were established about D.19.c.8.6. Enemy artillery was rather active to-wards in PONTISAN and FREZIENBERG. Casualties:- Killed 1 wounded 8.	

Army Form C. 2118.

WAR DIARY
or
INTELLIGENCE SUMMARY.
(Erase heading not required.)

Instructions regarding War Diaries and Intelligence Summaries are contained in F. S. Regs., Part II. and the Staff Manual respectively. Title pages will be prepared in manuscript.

Place	Date	Hour	Summary of Events and Information	Remarks and references to Appendices
SQUARE FARM	20/9/17		A quiet day. No change in the situation. The Battalion was relieved by the 8th Seaforths and 11th Argylls. The Seaforths relieved our left – "C" Coy, half of "B" and 2 Platoons of "A". The rest of the Battalion was relieved by the Argylls. The relief was delayed but the two right platoons of "C" relieving unit being much delayed, the whole Relief was completed at 2.30 a.m. 21st. Casualties:– Killed – wounded.	
SQUARE FARM	21/9/17		The Battalion on relief marched to Camp at 14.15. A.O.9. Being and was unable to "turn in" in Camp at 6.30 a.m. The day was spent in resting, cleaning and refitting for serious future operations. On arriving which was issued by Brigade. E. Casualties:– Wounded 4. fighting was emptied by 8.30 p.m.	Chet 25.
YPRES	22/9/17		The Brigade is in Divisional Reserve for operations looming. At 9.30 a.m. the Battalion moved off to take up position in the ECOLE, but was not by a runner with an order to stand fast, located the return in 2 hrs when orders	

A5834 Wt.W4973/M687 730,000 8/16 D.D.&L. Ltd. Forms/C2118/13.

WAR DIARY or INTELLIGENCE SUMMARY

Army Form C. 2118.

Place	Date	Hour	Summary of Events and Information	Remarks and references to Appendices
			is now certain. At the same time news was received that while the attack on the left had been partly successful, on the left — Hill 35 having been reached — the night had not succeeded. The Battalion was in the ECOLE by 4.30pm and the C.O. went to MILL COTTS to get instructions from Brigade. At 5.5pm a verbal message from Brigade states that the situation had now improved, and that it was unlikely that the Battalion would be involved. There were no further developments.	
ECOLE YPRES	23/8/17		The situation remained unchanged. A midnight attack by the 40th and 45th Brigades was reported to have failed. At 4.0pm orders were received to march back to camp at H.19.c.0.8. Owing to a misunderstanding the Battalion went to the camp we had previously occupied (H.17.a.0.9.) Battalion was in camp by 10.0pm	

WAR DIARY or INTELLIGENCE SUMMARY

Army Form C. 2118.

Place	Date	Hour	Summary of Events and Information	Remarks and references to Appendices
H17a.0.9.	24/8/17		About mid-day the Bn. moved into the camp recently vacated about 1000 yds S.E. Accommodation but b to bad, bivouacs and shelters with Bn. HQ in Nissen huts. Arranged programme of training for the remainder of the day by Coy. by Coy. Training to comprise rehearsal for coming attack over new work and practising assembly of attack in lines of small groups of 3 and 4 O.R. each under their group commander.	
A.18.c.08.	25/8/17		Plans for training practised by an order received to prepare to the evening to the O.G. line and move to Reserve btls. 44th Bn. during their attack on GALLIPOLI at 11pm. Bn. moved off about 8pm and proceeded by the ASYLUM and the POTIZTE ROAD to O.G. 1 and 2. A and B Coys were accommodated in O.G. 1, C and D Coys in O.G. 2 and Reserve briefly near RUPRECHT FARM. Bn. MG at MILL COTS. The night was quiet — to Br. to our knew we were employed. Received the attack of the 9th Black Watch on GALLIPOLI was practically driven back from the farm buildings and they is now the Crest of HILL 35.	
O.G. Area	26/8/17		Orders received to relieve the 9th Black Watch to the left sector of the 44th Bn. front. Relief was complete at 2:50 am 27th inst. Bn. HQ at SQUARE FM. B and C Coys to front line to HILL 75. D Coy in support and A Coy in Reserve to POMMERN CASTLE line	

WAR DIARY or INTELLIGENCE SUMMARY

Army Form C. 2118.

Place	Date	Hour	Summary of Events and Information	Remarks and references to Appendices
POPERINGHE CASTLE	27/8/17		The front area was quiet so far as enemy shell fire was concerned, but PANNETT CASTLE and the heavily shelled area also For HQ. in SQUARE FM, shell appearance took refuge in the centre of the enemy's barrage line. A another tank believed in front and support lines we reported his approach and others were received that of the previous later so, the tank moved 300 yds N it is dawn opposite GALLIPOLI and we were further ???? Strong patrols together and took possession. As ??? we were taken to organise an attack for 1.55 p.m. in conjunction with the 6 W Queens on our left. We were ??? 2 platoons for the attack on the Northern side of the farm. The XVIII Corps on our left ??? also ??? barrage on ?? on the Northern barrage ??? and XIX Corps front barrage on the enemy's front, still the artillery along the barrage ??? ???. At 1.55 p.m. we attacked with 3 officers and 120 O.R. drawn from B and C Coys. The attacking party. assisted of picked men from both Companies, and as soon as they left our trenches they were met with very heavy machine gun and rifle fire and heavy Cannonade — one Cannon, a number gun and rifle fire N. 9 the farm buildings proved to be held Another Castle B.Lt. N. 9 the farm being was strongly held. of Lewis machine guns.	

WAR DIARY
or
INTELLIGENCE SUMMARY.
(Erase heading not required.)

Place	Date	Hour	Summary of Events and Information	Remarks and references to Appendices
			The attacking party attempted to advance to their groups by 2nd Lieut Sykes. Sons of snipers attacked. Made his with[er?] and did 2 hrs. afterwards the attack continued and went back to his original line. Meanwhile the Hun to his left, having before coming up to our left, and our afternoon became that the battalion on our left was back in their original line. From hence after this the attack commenced the enemy placed a heavy barrage along the FRERENBERG – ST JULIEN Road and to the valley between SQUARE Fm and POMMERN CASTLE. This continued almost without a break for seven hours. All communication between gun and Bn MQ. was practically untenable, the Hun Commanders very keen by Bn MQ. for Bn to the afternoon to westwards. Their stay rather unusual, but they prevented any the afternoon in walking their they were 2 hrs. spent in today from POMMERN CASTLE and into this attack from no Stood-hole travelled. After the attack the night was quiet, except for occasional bursts of heavy fire on SQUARE Fm. we had trepanum our Position in front by creating posts, and helping up the main line. Father was advised to bring down our 2 good and of Infantry was and the Casualties were MM and 74 O.R.	MM.

WAR DIARY or INTELLIGENCE SUMMARY

Army Form C. 2118.

Place	Date	Hour	Summary of Events and Information	Remarks and references to Appendices
POMMERN CASTLE	28/8/17		Weather conditions very bad. Men's clothes and boots wet through to skin and men. During the night A Coy relieved B Coy in the front line and B Coy went to POMMERN CASTLE. Men were C. to the 3rd line where D Reserve support. The day was again spent to find & fix a shelter for men. Covered in. SQUARE FM. the heavily barrage a bpmt. Decided to on right. Were to have carried on to attack on INGOLAN FM. but this was cancelled and they were relieved by half Co. 7/R.K.R. Sco Bnd.	A.M.
"	29/8/17		The work of taking equipment and baggage stout continued. At night we were relieved by the other half of 7/R.K.R. Sco Bnd, with the exception of B Coy which were left in Br. Reserve to there. POMMERN CASTLE live stores. Relief was complete at 11.20pm and the Bn. relieved filled O.C. and went to H.A. at MILL CRSS.	A.M.
O.G. rule	30/8/17		A quiet day spent in making the men to were relieved at night by the 8th Lanc Fusiliers and billeted in Camp at H.17 a.o.9. Amongst those who 2 am 3rd inst., Bn. L. led reserves.	A.M.

A5834 Wt. W4973/M657 750,000 8/16 D.D. & L. Ltd. Forms/C.2118/13.

WAR DIARY
INTELLIGENCE SUMMARY.
(Erase heading not required.)

Army Form C. 2118.

Place	Date	Hour	Summary of Events and Information	Remarks and references to Appendices
Camp at H17a 0.9.	31/8/17		Men have been relieved that we moved down at 4 p.m. near VLAMERTINGHE and marched to WEMAERS CAPEL W. of CASSEL. At about 3 p.m. we left Camp and proceeded by bus from VLAMERTINGHE to HARDIFORT where we marched from Arlichin arriving about 8 p.m. Battalion recommended to good billets and horses. I spent 4 last 4 not at the effort of the recent fighting the men were in good spirits and are the Tho: march well. MW	

R. Stokes.
Lieut. Colonel
Comdg. 14th Wyk. L.I.

28031 W3125/M2250 1000m 6/17 M.R.Co.,Ltd. (1367) Forms W3091

Army Form W.3091.

17.L.
10 sheets

Cover for Documents.

CONFIDENTIAL

Nature of Enclosures

WAR DIARY
FOR SEPT 1917

10/11 High. L. I.

Notes, or Letters written.

WAR DIARY
INTELLIGENCE SUMMARY
(Erase heading not required.)

Army Form C. 2118.

Place	Date	Hour	Summary of Events and Information	Remarks and references to Appendices
WEMAERS CAPPEL	1/9/17		The morning was spent in preparation for entraining. At 1:30 pm the Battalion paraded at the most southerly of the Church in WEMAERS CAPPEL and marched to CASSEL STATION. A misfortune befell in the arrangement was caused by the non-appearance of the lorries which were to convey officers valises and men's staff to the train. Nevertheless the necessary re-loading was 2 hour late while the train trotted leisurely and the strategy provision arrived first on time. trailed the train. The journey to ARRAS took about 5 hours and we arrived about 9 pm. Everything stored — Nearly, speed and quick unloading of the place by a posting of 2 officers and 100 O.R. in the Station Brs. Auty, in a brilliant party and the remainder marched to VERDUN CAMP AGNEZ LES DUISANS. The men were billeted after they ceased fighting and the purr was slow but no one fell out.	JMcK
AGNEZ LES DUISANS	2/9/17		Sunday. The forenoon was spent in resting the men and getting them cleaned up. Army to the humid move to be had been little opportunity of doing this before. Church Parade for Presbyterians in the evening in the Church Army Hut. AGNEZ.	JMcK
"	3/9/17		Major Dunn and Capt. Greenshields Chaves Commenced at 9am. At 11 am the Commanding Officer inspected the lines. his staff in full marching order. The morning of rifles commencement and Camp was allotted time in which to attend Revolvers and Lewis Gun. The following Lamb have announced Military Cross. Capt. J.A. M^cKINLAY. 2Lt. J.W. ELING-SMITH. In addition 8. O.R. have earned the Military Medal.	JMcK

Army Form C. 2118.

WAR DIARY
or
INTELLIGENCE SUMMARY.
(Erase heading not required.)

Instructions regarding War Diaries and Intelligence Summaries are contained in F.S. Regs., Part II. and the Staff Manual respectively. Title pages will be prepared in manuscript.

Place	Date	Hour	Summary of Events and Information	Remarks and references to Appendices
AGNEZ LES DUISANS.	4/9/17.		Guns Limbers and Squadron prepared for Inspection & Gen. Simpson and Prisons were selected to replace Casualties and training commenced. At 11.30 am there was a battalion parade when the R.S.M. took a loading of arms etc. All equipment was checked as sentried.	AM
"	5/9/17.		The forenoon was spent in specialist instructions. At 1.45 pm the Commanding Officer met the Missing Inter Allied Officers who had been nominated deputation to gallantry in the recent operations. Corps went to the AGNEZ baths in turn during the afternoon. Intimation has been received that the XVIIth Corps front has been broken in two between the 2nd Lancashire Fusiliers in the centre section of the ? of the night seen of the Devonshire front. A number of the Devonshire front. A number of Messin personal left subsection of the night seen of the Devonshire front. A number of Messin personal remained in the line, from about I.31.d.9.5. to run from ARRAS to FAMPOUX and remained the line, from about I.31.b.4.8. b. I.31.d. 9.5. (PELVES MAP) Preparations made for move following day to BLANGY PARK CAMP where we were taken in Mot. Rise Am places at R.H. Reys Pets.	AM
"	6/9/17.		About 10 am the battalion handed off from the Brad picket N. of CARLISET and proceeded by ARRAS and ST. NICHOLAS to the station. The day was extremely hot and during break were stricter to the west by the station. Both whole cay of the front and along truck for bathing.	AM

WAR DIARY
INTELLIGENCE SUMMARY

Place	Date	Hour	Summary of Events and Information	Remarks and references to Appendices
BLANGY	7/9/17		A number of officers upon returning the line 6th (later on) and advance parties were ordered to late on atrive etc. At 8.10 pm the first platoon thrown off. and the battalion proceeded to the Railway and via FEUCHY where guides from the 2nd Lancashire Fusiliers met us. Parti to the line taken by BATTERY VALLEY and thence by track to the relief front to H 35 d. The relief with B on D coys to front line, support in MUSKET RESERVE TRENCH and C Coy in RESERVE in LANCER LANE. Relief was complete about 12.30 p.m. Shells from both very quiet. There was occasional burst harassing of SCABBARD ALLEY, CURIO ALLEY and CURLY TRENCH, but practically no shelling out a moderate amount of rifle and M.G. fire. Ration came up by limber to the dump at H 35 d. Near the line was a water point for which water could be drawn at any hour day or night. Trenches were in good order but completely needed. There was practically continuous W. list very thick. Have breads and SAA reserves for Bn. And Coy dumps. The food nights were being quiet. Ration was carried by C. Coy. No arrangements to work to HAPPY VALLEY beside the water point, to the Bn. we had behind the last coys from stores and Timmy Cooker. And has no battalion workshop. 6/7th R.S.F. on left. 7/ P.K.O. Sea Forth on right.	Mn.

Army Form C. 2118.

WAR DIARY
or
INTELLIGENCE SUMMARY.
(Erase heading not required.)

Place	Date	Hour	Summary of Events and Information	Remarks and references to Appendices
PELVES Sector	8/9/17		Arranged with 73rd Field Co. R.E. to finish a Crutchman for us to place electric last night. The day we very quiet. In collection R.E. material and prepared by-laws work parties etc. C. Coy began carrying rations and A Coy supplied a working party to load Bar Dumps. Patrols sent out by Bomb. Coy. but nothing unusual was observed.	Appx
"	9/9/17.		Another quiet day. Work was carried out on the trenches during the forenoon. Revetting was At night. work for hay was conducted at I 31 b 4.1. Loop hole sapheads and sump pits were dug. Continued in CURB ALLEY. Wave X Sap was deepened. At 11pm a pl. T.D Coy and 1 NCO and 10 patrol N.Q.Y. Sap and formed Wimplin form the Lewy line. They initiated an ammo. & Lewes of the 38th Bn. when they limpet look to prisoner. Prisoner sent 19 yrs old had only been down a day to the trenches and was much surprised of a violent reception.	Appx.
"	10/9/17.		Unnecessary day. C. Coy. moved from LANCER LANE to Shellers & HAPPY VALLEY near JOHNSTON AVE in relocation of Bn. N. Boundary. C. Coy worked on dug outs and Shellers in WELFORD RESERVE Trench continued the private Coy at the relocation to the shelters from contrimas from on Yesterday. 6/7th R.S.F. as on left relieved by 11th A.+S. Highlrs.	Appx.

Army Form C. 2118.

WAR DIARY
or
INTELLIGENCE SUMMARY.
(Erase heading not required.)

Instructions regarding War Diaries and Intelligence Summaries are contained in F. S. Regs., Part II. and the Staff Manual respectively. Title pages will be prepared in manuscript.

Place	Date	Hour	Summary of Events and Information	Remarks and references to Appendices
PELVES Salli	11/9/17.		Quiet apart from some light shelling of RIFLE Support area about 2 p.m. Enemy trench mortar active, most of ammunition seems expended in front of our own HILL 70 and filled with Lewis Gun teams. Between a sapline at rear of Pelves had trenches as by end front. Coy.	A.M.
"	12/9/17.		Before very quiet. Several Trench Mortar shots from our left Coy front. During the day patrols in the hinterland were going away on shot L.G. and Rifle Grenade Craters. Two pioneer parties were employed for work under 73rd Tunnelling Co. R.E. and one for New Zealand Tunnelling Co. from on RIFLE SUPPORT, CURBS ALLEY, and WELFORD RESERVE continued.	A.M.
"	13/9/17.		Situation quiet. Seven 5.9's shells fell in region of CHAIN ALLEY about 12.30 p.m. At night our trench mortars arrived in front of the lines hill Gonnelieu. Other work continued.	A.M.
"	14/9/17.		Quiet. Lots of strafing to lines and SAA and bombs were arranged. Bombs stores were concentrated at the junction of saps with front line. Also a permanent store was made at T.31 A.6.B. being continued. 11th A.I.F. Infantry on our left relieved by 7th Canterbury Regt.	P.M.
"	15/9/17.		Work of mining stores for trench etc. continued. Bomb shot continued of LONE LANE near Bn. HQ. 11.20 p.m. Bn. returned to 12th Highland L.I. 11.20 p.m. Relieved by 12th Highland L.I. Bn. returned to SCOTS VALLEY CAMP. Casualties for tour 2 OR. slightly wounded. H 25.C 5.3. (Sheet 51B NW.)	A.M.

Army Form C. 2118.

WAR DIARY
or
INTELLIGENCE SUMMARY.
(Erase heading not required.)

Place	Date	Hour	Summary of Events and Information	Remarks and references to Appendices
SCOTS VALLEY	16/9/17		A working party of 200 O.R. was found for work on WILDERNESS CAMP. Otherwise the day was spent in making and cleaning up. A number of N.C.Os and O.Rs. made their way every day to Corps School at HAUTE AVESNES. Battalion & Bde. Reserve. Accommodation in billets huts and bivouacs.	am
"	17/9/17		Working party found as above. In addition a small permanent party was appointed for work under 73rd Pioneer Co. R.E. The Battalion was paid and Courses of Instruction for specialists were commenced.	am
"	18/9/12		Party of 103 O.R. chiefly from 1/6 (?) Batt L.I. received. Batts for A and B Coys at Dvl. Baths RUE DE LILLE ARRAS. Working party to WILDERNESS CAMP reduced to 160 O.R. W. in addition a party of 1 Officer and 65 O.R. was found for work under OTMO at ATHIES	am
"	19/9/17.		Baths for C and D Coys. Wiring and Revetting class commenced for N.C.Os and Senior men under 73rd R.E.	am
"	20/9/17		The same continued. Company Authorized Petrol patches Battn HQ certain having A Coy Red, B Coy Green, C Coy Yellow and "D" Black.	am
"	21/9/17.		Working parties and specialist training continued as above. No 19644 Pte F BEATON transferred Retaining Heart. Lt-Col R.F. Forbes DSO was on leave and Major R.P. Echlin assumed Command	am

A5834 Wt.W4973/   70,000 8.16 D D   Forms/C2118/13

Army Form C. 2118.

WAR DIARY
or
INTELLIGENCE SUMMARY.
(Erase heading not required.)

Place	Date	Hour	Summary of Events and Information	Remarks and references to Appendices
SCOTS VALLEY	22/9/17		Working parties and training continued as before. A lecture demonstration was held for officers at 5 pm under the officer of R.E.	Mm
"	23/9/17		Piano Giru lessin of "B" Coy deputation to ST POL station for Anti-aircraft work. Remainder was returned to SCOTS VALLEY CAMP at 11.45 am and by 11th A.rt. Inspection and batteries to BLANGY PARK in Div. Reserve. Party went for work under DTMO. Church Parade for Protestants was held at 5:30 pm to BLANGY PARK CAMP at 5:30 pm	Mm
BLANGY PARK	24/9/17		In view of the fact that so many men who had been in permanent fatigue reported had "Light Duty" on length spent in Chauncy. be issued 1 party of 100 O.R. for work buying paper at ARRAS STATION. The fatigue was as before till 27th inclusive. 6 cooks attended demonstration at III Army Cooking School ALBERT	Mm
"	25/9/17.		The Commanding Officer inspected burial and orthotic A Hygiene programme of training Commenced. Specialists were surprised at 11am. the inspected Messes. A Coy at musing and meeting, B Coy on a musketeer mange, C Coy practice attacked when wood and D Coy had the assault Course. The training area is situated near FRED'S WOOD and the railway embankment from an excellent site for a musketry range. Bicycles and Lewis Guns sent to D.A.D.O.S. to be overhauled.	Mm
"	26/9/17.		Training Continues as above. Party of 5 O.R. under an I.O. Officer appointed to Army Rest Camp at ST. VALERY.	Mm

Army Form C. 2118.

WAR DIARY
or
INTELLIGENCE SUMMARY.
(Erase heading not required.)

Place	Date	Hour	Summary of Events and Information	Remarks and references to Appendices
BLANGY PARK	27/9/17		The same continued. A boxing and wrestling class for NCOs proceed under R.E. from Divisional HQ in ARRAS hurst ranges.	Mn
"	28/9/17.		Training Continued. Battalion attended talks and drew clean clothing. Reprimands were scrutinized by Dept. Gen. NCOs. & member of Morris Committee this bt: Likewise am on 1st Oct from Pte Digwell Inspection.	Mn
"	29/9/17.		Today the men attention to musketry. A number of the Lewis Guns proceed at the BUTTE DE TIR range ARRAS and fired grouping practice at 100 x. Their were also 120, 8" groups.	Mn
"	30/9/17.		In the forenoon there were Church Parades for all denominations. Anglicans in Camp; Church of England at ST. NICHOLAS and Roman Catholics at FREDI WOOD. Men proceeded to lui. Men proceeded at 2pm for instructions in Physical Training under Sgt Instrs. Class of Men appeared in preparing for tackle fourneau. Remainder of day spent in preparing for tackle fourneau. During our stay at BLANGY PARK the men played several football matches against 7/8 K.O.S.C.Bn. having been taken advantage of the scavenging piece and phase has been issued from ARRAS.	Mn

R. Arrowsmith Major.
Cmdg. 10/a W/k. L.I.

Army Form W.3091.

Cover for Documents.

10/11 High. L.I.

Nature of Enclosures

WAR DIARY
FOR
OCTOBER 1917

CONFIDENTIAL

Notes, or Letters written.

WAR DIARY
or
INTELLIGENCE SUMMARY.

Army Form C. 2118.

Place	Date	Hour	Summary of Events and Information	Remarks and references to Appendices
BLANGY PARK.	1/10/17		In the afternoon the Commanding Officer inspected Companies in full marching order. Preparations were then made for the line. B and D Coys marched off at 2 p.m. and quided at FAMPOUX and were let into the LANCER LANE and R.E. and M. posts by 5 p.m. The remaining two Coys and Bn. HQ went by train about 10 p.m. from BLANGY to FAMPOUX. Relief was complete at 1.15 a.m. and the Bn. took over the Rt. Bn. area of the left Bde. sectn. of the Divisional front, from the 8th Seaforth Hghldrs. On our right were the 11th A. and S. Hghldrs and on our left the 7/8th K.O. Sco. Bord. Bn. disposition — 2 Coys in front line and supp. and SCABBARD SUPPORT, and 2 Coys to LANCER LANE. The right-support Coy in addition holding R.E. and M. posts & supports in GAVRELLE LAGOON. Bn. HQ T.25.c.3.9. (PELVES MAP.)	
Rt. Bn. ROEUX Sectn.	2/10/17		Situation very quiet. Morning spent in making arrangements for stores, trench stores, & supplies on the sectr. particularly in the trenches held. In property matters before the winter sets in. All the Duckboards & gangways lifting out swampy field day beneath. Also the trenches had been the scenes of hard trench when they have fallen in and broken up. Many men a few had fallen in — have been instructed to be on guard to widen LAGOON road for the trenches position by men of 1st. D. pioneers and.	
			Parties of 1/M. 1/60 (R. Supplies for 9th Division clearing apart trips to WELFORD RESERVE	

Army Form C. 2118.

WAR DIARY
or
INTELLIGENCE SUMMARY.
(Erase heading not required.)

Instructions regarding War Diaries and Intelligence Summaries are contained in F. S. Regs., Part II. and the Staff Manual respectively. Title pages will be prepared in manuscript.

Place	Date	Hour	Summary of Events and Information	Remarks and references to Appendices
Rt. Bn. Roeux Suln	3/10/17		Relieved in the sector came up by transport by road to CHINSTRAP LANE within easy reach of Camp. Italic's drawn from water point in HAPPY VALLEY. A good deal of work has been done today in repairing front steps and preparing front and support trenches for matting. MM	
			Our Artillery arranged a shoot on ARCHIE TRENCH I 25 b 30.05 from 10am – 11am. Stay very quiet until about 6 pm when on going I found 3 batches S.E. of MONERY Ave Ave Sap retaliation. Another burst of fire took place about 8 pm attempting to interest A.S. pts. Enemy put up green light apparently an S.O.S. Call and his guns with 10 minutes after. The reply to been fire & apparently a recurrence of red lights. Casualties slain here & yesterday. Our LAGOON Post has a depth of 4'6" as far as we covered to be dug. the two known it to front and to the flank. The night then was very quiet. MM	
"	4/10/17		Another very quiet day. A good deal of work was done on the lines during daytime and matting. The sap have been deepened to a depth of 6'. Patrols reconnoitred the front of the new tramway from T 25 c 70 90 to "ARCHIE TRENCH" at Wiear to I 25 d and the ground E. of Sap. No trace of the enemy has been seen. The new LAGOON POST has completed with shelter	

WAR DIARY
or
INTELLIGENCE SUMMARY.

Army Form C. 2118.

(Erase heading not required.)

Place	Date	Hour	Summary of Events and Information	Remarks and references to Appendices
Rlv. Bn. ROEUX Sector	5/10/17		And heard bombs. Our own post out in front and on the flank are the garrison for the withdrawn from the old post to develop the new. The night was quiet.	
	6/10/17		Another very quiet day. Report that if work was done on the trenches including wiring. 16 cwts of iron were put out in front of LAGOON post. Patrols reconnoitred. No hun's have been to view of the hun'ys wire. I have sent as to enemy patrols were met. The night was quiet. I have arranged interior housing.	
			A quiet night with 2 guns shelled off Rhu trench bearing about N.E. continuing from 11-25am to 5.15am and gave shells altogether. 17 shells put into NEW LAGOON POND (J 25 A 7.8) at about 5.10.	
	7/10/17		At 11.30am v/15. T.M. Bly bombarded M.G. emplacements at J 25. b 4.2. 3.5. 6th 12.30 p.m. 18 phos supplied curving fire, for the shoot. No had 6 from the left platoon section of our front line J 25/3 and conducted his rifles. At 9.15 pm. Shortly after commenced about midday.	

WAR DIARY
INTELLIGENCE SUMMARY
(Erase heading not required.)

Army Form C. 2118.

Place	Date	Hour	Summary of Events and Information	Remarks and references to Appendices
			We simulated an attack on ARCHIE TRENCH I.25.d.6.8 - I.25.d.3.8 in conjunction with a raid carried out by the 11th A.I.T. Regt on our right. We fired 1 drum from each Lewis Gun that was in use and 10 mins rapid fire from every rifle & machine to elicit 10 rounds each detailed burst of rapid fire from our snipers. Artillery (Canadian) retaliated. The remainder of the night was very quiet, and enemy answer of rifle on the trenches. The carriers and the 7/8th R. Oter. Borderers on our left took over the new LAGOON post situated at I.25.c.6.6. & on our left. Orientalia. In front the post and trenches to the battalion on our left.	NM.
Ri.Bn. ROEUX Sector.	8/10/17		A very uneventful day. Enemy quiet. Artillery disposing the day and harassing the route marching SCARPE SUPPORT. Patrols went out and reconnoitered ARCHIE TRENCH. Another party N.W. the point from I.25.c.95. B.5. between the tramway. No trace of enemy and at E Sap and returning to pivot Hawthorne. A standing patrol kept C Sap but no trace of enemy was seen. Touch with the 7/8 K.O. Sea Bord & LAGOON Post.	NM.

WAR DIARY
or
INTELLIGENCE SUMMARY

Army Form C. 2118.

Place	Date	Hour	Summary of Events and Information	Remarks and references to Appendices
Rt. Bn. ROEUX Sector	9/10/17		Situation quiet. Bn. in relieved by 12th Highf. L.I. and with drew to the Bde. Support area. HQ. and A and C. Coys to STIRLING CAMP on the ATHIES ST. NICHOLAS road N. of the Railway Trench, B and D Coys to the Railway cutting near FAMPOUX. Relief was complete at 10.15 p.m. Casualties for the two I.O.R. killed, 5 O.R. wounded.	p.m.
STIRLING CAMP H.13.d.8.7.	10/10/17		Training began, working parties to work in forward area, under 91st Tunnels R.E. 9th Gordon High. to hire New Zealand Tunnelling Co. have arrangements to carry on small Chinese a comp, numbers etc, been to training on a scale sent out to provide a larger available than the one taken for work	p.m.
"	11/10/17		The same as yesterday. In addition troops are found for men for Camps, schools & MONCHY TRENCH I 31 A.	p.m.

WAR DIARY
INTELLIGENCE SUMMARY.
(Erase heading not required.)

Army Form C. 2118.

Place	Date	Hour	Summary of Events and Information	Remarks and references to Appendices
STIRLING CAMP H.13.d.8.7.	12/10/17		Found three enemy parties on Yesterday with another established party for Staff Company to ARROW TRENCH O.2.6. Weather unsettled, very wet and parties did not return this morning. Church was held during the day for Canadian Men to Machinery, Regiment honored and buried. a.m.	
"	13/10/17.		The same continued. No additional parties found. Carries out a number of small improvements in Camp. p.m.	
"	14/10/17		Working parties continued. Additional parties found for transport under New Zealand Tunnelling Co. Church Parade was held in the presence of STIRLING CAMP, and at STN. Aud ow. H.23. c.4.6. in the afternoon for the presentation. p.m.	
"	15/10/17		The same work parties and classes of instruction continued. p.m.	

WAR DIARY
or
INTELLIGENCE SUMMARY

Army Form C. 2118.

Place	Date	Hour	Summary of Events and Information	Remarks and references to Appendices
STIRLING CAMP.	16/10/17.		Training working parties. Preparations made for the relief of the 7th Bn. Gordons	Mm
	17/10/17.		Found all the morning working parties. Battalion relieved in STIRLING CAMP and H 23 C by 11th A.& S. Highrs. Relief complete about 6 p.m. The Battalion took over to ARRAS, were accommodated in BAUDIMONT BARRACKS, ARRAS & Areas in town in the vicinity	Mm
ARRAS.	18/10/17.		A Coy. found several parties for work and the remainder of the battalion occupied themselves and their spare in billets. Preparations made to carry out a course of training during the following days.	Mm
	19/10/17.		A Coy. spent forenoon cleaning up. B. Coy found working parties. The C.O. inspected C and D Coys to full marching order at 9 a.m. These Coys. then cleaned their kits at billets and spent the rest the afternoon at G.H.Q. Specialist classes paraded for instruction under Specialist officers.	Mm
	20/10/17.		C and D. Coys. found working parties. Bn. H.Q. inspected in full marching order by C.O. at 9 a.m. A & B Coys. did musketing and bayonet fighting on RIFLE CAMP RANGE.	Mm

WAR DIARY
or
INTELLIGENCE SUMMARY.

(Erase heading not required.)

Army Form C. 2118.

Place	Date	Hour	Summary of Events and Information	Remarks and references to Appendices
ARRAS	21/10/17.		The Battalion attended baths during the forenoon. the GRANDE PLACE, St ANDREW'S CLUB, RUE PASTEUR. Protestant Church parade at 2.30 p.m. to St ANDREW'S CLUB, RUE PASTEUR. 3 Officers and 5 NCOs left for Corps School at HAUTE AVESNES.	Maj
	22/10/17.		The Commanding Officer inspected A & B Coys at full marching order in the BARRACK SQUARE at 9 am. Classes of instruction for specialists were held. Remainder did general training on ground at G.H.Q.	Maj
	23/10/17.		Application and Rapid fire practices were fired by the whole battalion on the BUTTE DE TIR RANGE. In the evening about 300 of the men were taken to a performance of the Divisional Troupe.	Maj
	24/10/17.		C & D Coys had RIFLE CAMP control course in the forenoon. A & B Coys had the training area to G.H.Q. MOAT RANGE. In the afternoon Lewis Gunners fired at the MOAT RANGE. A battalion concert was held in the evening at St ANDREW'S CLUB, RUE PASTEUR.	Maj
	25/10/17.		Preparation made for relieving 9th BLACK WATCH in left battalion area of PELVES sector. B and D Coys went by bus from same place to Brown Line at 6 p.m. Headquarters and the same and little was Remaining 2 Coys at 9.30 p.m. Relief was completed by series on 6/9/17. Night very quiet.	Maj

WAR DIARY
or
INTELLIGENCE SUMMARY.

Army Form C. 2118.

Place	Date	Hour	Summary of Events and Information	Remarks and references to Appendices
LEFT Bn. PLUG ST. Sector	26/10/17		Bn. frontage from I 31 b 5.8 to I 31 a 8.5 on the South. Schemin Hem Gravel: weather wet and cold. Practically whole garrison employed in keeping the trenches clear. Revetting parties manning firestep parties to keep the trenches in better state. From the two slops the front, enlivenment + prov. works started at throughout. Patrols used out and examined gaps in enemy's wire throughout to be keeping open by L.G. fire. Enemy flare when we were out heavy. Three Civilian + one Grenade Rifleman wounded.	P.M.
"	27/10/17		Schemin Grovel: weather rather better in the earlier part of the day, rain later. The same took two casualties and the batteries in Ontario and Anna. The burial parties continued and at kopering Hund the stores kept on. The Commanding Officer Capt. V.R. ROUVIN handed over to Major R.C. FIELD and on Capt. M.S. for his services to Casualties.	P.M.
"	28/10/17		Improvement and new materials. A lot of shelling on the Anzac line which targets have been started in rest places. Enemy artillery moderate.	P.M.

Instructions regarding War Diaries and Intelligence
Summaries are contained in F. S. Regs., Part II.
and the Staff Manual respectively. Title pages
will be prepared in manuscript.

WAR DIARY
or
INTELLIGENCE SUMMARY.
(Erase heading not required.)

Army Form C. 2118.

Place	Date	Hour	Summary of Events and Information	Remarks and references to Appendices
Left Bn PELVES Sector	29/10/17		Work continued on same lines as above. A great deal of revetting was done in front line, CURB ALLEY and CURB SWITCH N. A Coy relieved B Coy in right front, D Coy was relieved by C Coy in left front. Situation quiet. Major R. Nasmith M.C. wounded.	AM
	30/10/17		Another quiet day. During daylight revetting etc was carried on. At night we thickened the wire in places along the front and sent out patrols which examined gaps in enemy wire	AM
	31/10/17		Enemy artillery much more active. Intermittent T.M. fire continued almost until dark. One of our patrols sent out between 7 and 8 p.m. got close up to enemy wire at about I 31 6. 8. 8 and saw party of enemy coming across the open to their front line in full marching order as though carrying out a relief. Artillery was informed and our guns were active till about 10.30 p.m. Remainder of night was quiet.	AM

R. Mose
Lieut Colonel
Comdg 10th Regt. L.I.

10/11th (S) Bn. Highrs. L.I.

War Diary. Nov. 1917

James A. Fowler. Major
for Lt-Col Commdg.
10/11-H.L.I.

3/12/17

Army Form C. 2118.

WAR DIARY
or
INTELLIGENCE SUMMARY.
(Erase heading not required.)

Instructions regarding War Diaries and Intelligence Summaries are contained in F. S. Regs., Part II. and the Staff Manual respectively. Title pages will be prepared in manuscript.

Place	Date	Hour	Summary of Events and Information	Remarks and references to Appendices
Left Bn. PELVES SECTOR	1/11/17		Situation Quiet. Work continued as about posting SCABBARD SUPPORT and CURB ALLEY. Cleaned WELFORD RESERVE and deepening LONE LANE. Patrols went out three during the night on each Company front but had nothing unusual to report.	Ann
"	2/11/17		The Battalion was relieved in the line by the 12th Highland L.I. and returned to WILDERNESS CAMP leaving permanent work parties of H.Q. in HAPPY VALLEY for work near R.E. R.Bn was to FEUCHY CAVES on the FEUCHY CHAPEL ROAD from permanent parties for work under N.Z.E. Tunnelling Co. Relief by 12th H.L.I. was complete about 12.30 p.m. In WILDERNESS CAMP (H 31 A) the Battalion was accommodated in Nissen Huts and was to Bde. Reserve. Battalion principally employed in tidying up & painting as ready to the trenched area which improved permanently the little accommodation as usual to the Battalion remains in the area during Staylth. During the eight days that the Battalion remains in the trenches the weather was very variable and cold. Two days some within the trenches being camp found extremely helpful.	Ann
WILDERNESS CAMP.	3/11/17		Finding working parties and carrying out small improvements to the Camp. Also 8 pm there was a Concert held of C.G. B Co. Ann the present area. Wind East & light. Plenty H.Q. Bt. Strong F. GORDON CAMP H.Q. included to among under Q.M. Battn. (Present) 3. OR Wed. L.6 Div. L.F. School. The Battalion has just	Ann

19.L.
16 sheets

Army Form C. 2118.

WAR DIARY
or
INTELLIGENCE SUMMARY.
(Erase heading not required.)

Instructions regarding War Diaries and Intelligence Summaries are contained in F.S. Regs., Part II. and the Staff Manual respectively. Title pages will be prepared in manuscript.

Place	Date	Hour	Summary of Events and Information	Remarks and references to Appendices
WILDERNESS CAMP	4/11/17		Sunday. The usual working parties were found. There were Divine Service in the forenoon to Camp for Presbyterians and Church of England. Roman Catholic attended Service in 11th Field Ambulance in THIOY. L: ORR and L.S.R. went to Corps Schools at HAUTE AVENES.	Run
"	5/11/17		No.1 Platoon A Coy. went to WARLOY. Lieut D. STALKER reported for duty. Coy. baths at supper and in 9.30 a.m. A Army Musketry Camp. Sergeants Lectures.	Run
"	6/11/17		Working parties as above. Major G.A.C. M'NEILL returned from III Army Infantry School and took no command over part of A Coy.	Run
"	7/11/17		9.30 a.m. Physical Training	Run
"	8/11/17		As above. Working parties continued.	Run
"	9/11/17		As above.	Run

WAR DIARY
or
INTELLIGENCE SUMMARY.
(Erase heading not required.)

Army Form C. 2118.

Place	Date	Hour	Summary of Events and Information	Remarks and references to Appendices
WILDERNESS CAMP	10/11/17		The morning working parties were found by the Battalion and in the afternoon we were relieved in WILDERNESS CAMP by the 11th A.P.S. Infn. from 3.30 pm and will to-day move to ARRAS h.H. BAUDIMONT BARRACKS, Bn. HQ. k RUE BAUDIMONT. The four fields were occupied as & the lads occasion that the Bn. was in ARRAS. A working party of 50 O.R. will be found for to-days ammunition trainload for D.T.M.O.	
ARRAS.	11/11/17		Sunday. The Bn. paraded for Divine Service to include:— Presbyterians to ST ANDREWS CLUB RUE PASTEUR 2.15 pm Church of England PLACE DE LA MADELEINE 11 am Roman Catholics to Roman Catholic Club 9 am A number of officers and other ranks left for courses at Army Schools. AVRI LE CHATEAU. Accommodation in cellars in GRANDE PLACE reconnoitred for use in case of bombardment. A permanent party of 2 officers and 50 O.R. sent to INDIA CAVE CEYLON AVE ROEUX for work under 73rd Field Co. R.E.	
"	12/11/17		A fun army party of 2 officers and 115 O.R. went to FEUCHY CAVES for work under N.Z. G Tunnelling Co. 9 am. Lewis Gunners Signallers and Bombers paraded for instruction under their respective officers. A Bn. committee meeting was held at 2.15 pm at RUE PASTEUR to make arrangements for recreational training. Meeting attended by Major R.P. GAFFIKIN and CAPT. H.T. KINLOCH	

WAR DIARY
or
INTELLIGENCE SUMMARY.
(Erase heading not required.)

Army Form C. 2118.

Place	Date	Hour	Summary of Events and Information	Remarks and references to Appendices
ARRAS	13/11/17		Spent day training activities as per programme. Remainder of men available were employed in the battalion bath in the GRANDE PLACE. Arranged two new batches of 3 NCOs handling instructors and to attend lectures at Corps School. L/C HUGHES and 3 NCOs SOMERVILLE 376 Gnr Pvunll Arrim School by Major [illegible]	
"	14/11/17		Training continued as above. Arms of A Coy inspected by B.M. Ammunition Party of 2 Offrs & 210 OR. A Coy under 7.A. Smith M.C. commenced practising for a small mine [illegible] Carried out repeat & part of Lewis fuel film in the trenches. I 25 A Dump not having been taken B Coy for practice use Debuslin to the old No Mans Land N. of the CAMBRAI ROAD in G 30.	
"	15/11/17		Forenoon and Afternoon A B & C Coys have the BUTTE DE TIR Rifle Ranges employed on application and snap shooting practice. Rifle party Battalion then training. Arms of B Company were inspected by the Bde Ammunitions. [illegible] Musis received to Camp Runnif Wishes of attire to be taken in the event of the enemy retiring. (Copy attached). Arrangements were forwarded to publish known as General E of BLANGY.	

WAR DIARY or INTELLIGENCE SUMMARY

Army Form C. 2118.

Place	Date	Hour	Summary of Events and Information	Remarks and references to Appendices
ARRAS	16/11/17		The Battalion paraded E. of FRED'S WOOD (H19a) at 10 am and practised the advance to the Brown Line in A/234 under Ypres army. Practice showed need of more practice in the influencing of pushing by means of rifle grenadiers and a stiffening of the push-up of all ranks to improve themselves. Raiding party continued the same approach and also rehearsed the raid after dark on the new ground. The 3rd Battalion attended a meeting preparatory of the FROLICS pierrot party of the 61st Division at 2.15 pm to be the Theatre, arranged through the Kitchener of U. 61st Division. AA & QMG 61st Division. Lt.Col. A.T.C. SINGLETON DSO.	Amn
"	17/11/17		The day was known up to a General training and preparation in the relation to the line trenches. Reparation and Trench Relieve was inspected by the Rt. Hon. GOC VIII Corps.	An
"	18/11/17		The Battalion handed off the BAUDIMONT BARRACKS at 9am and marched to BLANGY PARK and FEUCHY INVERNESS AVE where Guides from 8th Seaforth had awaited the Relief. The Complete relief 12.30 pm. Battalion South Western from R. SCARPE (inclusive) to I 31.b 75.85 junction of SCABBARD ALLEY and front line. Relieve to the Scales line up to front to 6 point street H 24 d 25.25. At 3 pm South West discharged along the whole front by Private Thomson. Left Flank by 8th Seaforth. The hostile artillery was comparatively inactive	

WAR DIARY / INTELLIGENCE SUMMARY

Army Form C. 2118.

Place	Date	Hour	Summary of Events and Information	Remarks and references to Appendices
Right Sector R.36.a.7.4. ALBERT SECTOR	9/11/17		Bn. Frontages are front and support lines and communication trenches. HAPPY VALLEY is the boundary of Bn. HQ is at sunken shelter dugouts in the line B Coy Rt. front, D Coy Left front. A Coy Suppt in WELFORD RESERVE Support Bn HQ to JOHNSON AVE. C Coy in Reserve to LANCER AVE. On our Left were the 7/8 K.O. Sea Bns. and on our right the 6th Cameron Highlanders 45th Inf Bde. The night was fairly quiet. Patrols were out from both front - coys and from the line of the bumps to No Man's Land. The Rt. opposition to thoroughly reconnoitred and on patrol was succeeded in locating ARCHIE TRENCH, the bn. from Rt. to Emmenchnt known as ARCHIE SUPPORT, have also [reconnoitred] in the sector SCABBARD ALLEY and SCABBARD SUPPORT both regains chain and [routing]. WRIST and ELBOW regains deepening and [routing]. Connecting from Emmen 60 m will had the depths across for sonic under the R.E. to [revetting] and also constructing Nullahs and upon for the Suppliers for clearing Spoil under Gl Section Major (Pioneers). During the afternoon our artillery were active and spread harassment went carried on. The [Renewed] in attempting a good deal of work and patrols went out as upon the patrol line in front ARCHIE TRENCH from the Left Coy succeeded in killing its work and watch for some time in the hope of capturing a prisoner but did not succeed in doing so. The raiding	

WAR DIARY
INTELLIGENCE SUMMARY

Army Form C. 2118.

Place	Date	Hour	Summary of Events and Information	Remarks and references to Appendices
Regt. Battn. PRIEUX PELVES–SUBIN	22/11/17		In relief opened fire on our batteries and during attacking shelled our front and support line and our communications with considerable vigour. The shelled party relieved from kitchen about 6.10 a.m. Casualties 1 Officer and 5 O.R. wounded. During the day the enemy sent back quiet and throughout the night our continued aeroplane patrolling.	a.m.
			On the premises A Coy relieved B Coy in Regt. front and in the afternoon C Coy relieved D Coy in Left front. From about 1.45 p.m.–3 p.m. the enemy shelled our Sectors very heavily and a serious attempt was made to cut our forward line to night. Attempts to raid. The hostile Artillery and our own shelled our breastworks in Chaussure partially supporting our trenches and was considerably damaged by heavy shell fire.	p.m.
"	23/11/17	3 a.m.	Spurred by R.E. upon position for known as the CHALK PIT back lines to front and support trenches were made for 30 minutes. The enemy did but maintained heavy retire. The day was comparatively quiet. No the complete large aeroplane activity at times and a fair amount of hostility. Harassing work on the trenches and did a fair amount of hostility.	a.m.

WAR DIARY
INTELLIGENCE SUMMARY.

Army Form C. 2118.

Place	Date	Hour	Summary of Events and Information	Remarks and references to Appendices
Right In ROEUX Sector	24/11/17		Visibility good. Enemy aircraft movement. Enemy batteries in back areas the neighbourhood of ROEUX very active. At 11.40 a.m. R.F.C. reported that enemy batteries between ROEUX and MONCHY appeared to be slightly increased. The artillery opened fire and scattered the hostile working parties from about 12 new trenches and saps in front—these were our listed trenches and rifle and machine gun action on the front line and east of positions. Enemy retaliated with nothing abnormal shelling. During the night—to east and our patrols encountered numerous new put-up enemy targets. No movement. The enemy appeared to have withdrawn from advance. Shots of aircraft on our small reference were heard in the vicinity of the gun posts T.25.d. 7.9	a.m.
"	25/11/17		Situation normal. Repair and of work on dug outs broken shelters improving. Anything during the night we had work in front of the front line trenches along front of DIRK ALLEY. Troops were opposed opening up new trench ready for handing over.	a.m.
"	26/11/17		Battalion was relieved about 4 a.m. by 12th Infantry L.I. and withdrew to Bde support. Disposition: Bn. H.Q. A.M. Coy to a near RAILWAY CUTTING H23 c. B Coy to STIRLING CAMP (H13 d) other to LANCER AVE and K.L.M. Posts. Chandelier for bn. to be two amendered broadcasts 30.	p.m.

WAR DIARY or INTELLIGENCE SUMMARY

Army Form C. 2118.

Place	Date	Hour	Summary of Events and Information	Remarks and references to Appendices
H.23.C.	27/11/17		In Bde Support. Bn found numerous working parties mostly for the 73rd E & R.E. Active worked at night opening CHINSTRAP LANE and digging new support line N. of the SCARPE at J.20.a. Parties which were provided the 15th Division Bn. acting up Rifle Bn. had to be Division and billeting in the front of the 61st Division to be in readiness to move (two Coys in LANCER AVE) & H.16.b and d and occupy the GAVRELLE SWITCH & Bn in Bde Reserve with 7/8th K.O.S.B.s in trenches up from RIFLE CAMP and last on the trenches system immediately N. of the recently won by Canadians.	Bn.
"	28/11/17		Trenches parties as above. At about 16 pm Bn received (Bn. orders) to H.16.b and d. to return to Bde Reserve to other work and the Right Bn. sector to the 15th Division front. The 2/5 K.O. Bns. taking over from ARRAS and last month 3rd cooks to our Lft. Bn. Hd sector and H.16 & 70.65 on the 24/17. Head of the Camp. Coys to new left trenches B.A.C.	Bn.
"	29/11/17		Officers reconnoitred tuition front taken over by K.O.S.B. Yesterday which will be taken over by us on night 3/4th prox. 100 O.R. supplies as support to Canadians 4" Battn. work for Special Coy. R.E.	Bn.

WAR DIARY
or
INTELLIGENCE SUMMARY.

(Erase heading not required.)

Army Form C. 2118.

Place	Date	Hour	Summary of Events and Information	Remarks and references to Appendices
Bryges Reserve Hill 6.	30/1/17		Friday took station to opened on R.E. Reconnaissance 1 hus Continued. Enemy shells area just W. of the Estate for about 30 minutes from 9.30 am — 10 am. Situation normal.	

A Combe Lieut Colonel
Comdg. 17/a Hghs. L.I.

SECRET.
Ref. Trench Map A.
(attached) A
21 B. N.W.

WARNING ORDER.   Copy No. 1
                 10/11th High. L.I.
                 A/334.
                 15.11.1917.

1. (a) In the event of the enemy withdrawing, he must not be allowed to carry out the operation unmolested.
   (b) The advance of the XVll Corps will be carried out on the following principles.
      (i) Strong patrols acting as advanced guards will be pushed out to keep touch with the enemy.
      (ii) These patrols will be supported by larger bodies who will make good all ground gained, the objectives of each bound being secured before the advanced guards move forward to the next one.

2. The objectives and boundaries of the Division and Brigades will be in accordance with the attached tracing A.

3. (a) On any signs of weakening on the front, patrols followed by advanced guards will be pushed forward to gain touch with the enemy. Full use must be made of Lewis and Machine Guns, and patrols must be handled with dash and resolution, retaining touch with the enemy.
   (b) The advanced guards will seize each successive objective and hold it until the main body moves up and consolidates it. The advanced guards will then push forward to the next objective.
   (c) The main body will not move forward from any line until its flanks are secure, but any points of tactical importance, in advance of the actual line, will be seized at once.
   (d) The present front line will remain the main line of resistance until the NEW line is consolidated and communications secured.
   (e) The greatest care must be taken to keep in touch with Units on the flanks.
   (f) In the event of hostile M.Gs. being encountered, Lewis Guns and M.Gs. will be employed to give covering for the Infantry, pushing on, dislodging M.G. by outflanking and the use of Stokes Mortar and Rifle Grenades.

4. Should this withdrawal take place, the Battalion will be in one of the five positions detailed below at the time it occurs.
   (a) Left Front Battn. Right Brigade.
   (b) Reserve Battn. (WILDERNESS CAMP). Right Brigade.
   (c) Right Battn. Left Brigade.
   (d) Support Battn. Left Brigade.
   (e) "C" Battalion. Brigade in Reserve.
   A course of action to be taken is detailed below for each of these positions.

5. (a) Should the Battalion be holding the left Bn. front of the Right Brigade, it will take part in the pursuit.
   Boundaries between the Battn. and the Battns. on its flanks are shown on tracing A. attached. Action will be taken by the two front Coys. in accordance with para. 3. on receipt of orders from Bn. H.Q. and as soon as they move forward, the support and reserve Coys. will occupy the trenches vacated by them.
   The Left front Coy. will form a defensive flank round S. and S.E. of PELVES facing N. This flank guard will not be withdrawn until PELVES has been reported free of the enemy.
   The consolidation of each objective will be by means of Strong Points. Detailed instructions will be issued before the Battn. occupies this sector.

   (b) Should the Battn. be in Reserve to Right Brigade, it will be prepared to move up on receipt of orders and occupy the trenches vacated by Left Front Bn. Right Brigade on moving forward.

   (c) Should the Battn. be holding the Right Battn. front of the Left Brigade, detailed action will be as follows:-
   The left front Coy. will push forward patrols to secure the following

/following

        Cross roads I.25.d.7.9.
        Cross roads I.26.a.70.30.
        PELVES and ground to North of it.

The Right Front Coy. will push forward patrols to secure the following.
        High Ground I.26.c.10.10.
        CHALK PIT I.26.c.70.80.
        BIT LANE (Northern End.)

Patrols should consist of one or two sections and will be preceded by Coy. snipers and observers who will be employed as ground scouts. The Patrol will move in small groups which will be able to deal with isolated obstacles while the main advance goes on. In rear of these groups will come the remainder of the platoon in extended order and accompanied by 1 Lewis Gun. When the front Coys. go forward their place will be taken by the support and reserve Coys.

Half sections 46th Machine Gun Coy. will be at the disposal of each of the front Coys. and 1 gun 46th T.M. Batty.

O.C. Support Coy. will detail a party of 1 Officer and 8 other ranks to examine undestroyed German dugouts etc. with a view to discovering traps. This party will be accompanied by 2 experienced sappers.

(d) Should the Battalion be in Support to the Left Brigade, on receipt of orders, the 2 Coys. in Railway Cutting H.23.c. will be prepared to occupy positions vacated by the support and reserve Coys. of the Left Battn. The remaining 2 Coys. will occupy CORDITE RESERVE and CRUMP TRENCH. Bn. H.Q. will be in CRUMP TRENCH.

(e) Should the Battn. be in Divisional Reserve in ARRAS, it will be prepared to move to LANCER AVE. between H.24.b.7.9. and Railway H.23.b.30.10. Battn. H.Q. to H.30.b.5.9. Route ARRAS - CAMBRAI ROAD.

                    Marshall
                                Capt.
             Adj. 10/11th (S) Battn. High. L.I.

Copy No. 1. War Diary.
        2. File.
        3. "A" Coy.
        4. "B" Coy.
        5. "C" Coy.
        6. "D" Coy.
        7. Transport Officer.
        8. Quartermaster.
        9. Signalling Officer.
      10. Lewis Gun Officer.

SECRET.
Ref. 51 B. N.W.

10/11th (S) Battn. Highland Light Infantry. Copy No. 1.

10/11th High. L.I.
A/234 (1)

ADDENDUM No. 1 to A/234 of 15.11.17.

1. Ref. para 5 (c) the following will be the formation to be adopted in sending out patrols.

        O   O   Ground Scouts.

        Section.

  OOO   OOO
half section half section

    O   O--------- leaders of half sections

      O Section leader.

_____ Remainder of platoon in extended order with Lewis Gun.

Where points such as the CHALK PIT are encountered and have to be secured, a party with Lewis Gun will be left to garrison them while the main body moves on.

2. Inter Coy. boundaries for the advance will be as follows:-
Junction WRIST ALLEY and front Line, I.35.d.6.7., thence along Light Railway to I.36.b.2.8., then along road through PELVES Village to road junction I.31.c.4.1. thence E. to Brigade boundary.
Both front Coys. will therefore share in the clearing of PELVES and para 5 (c) will be amended accordingly.

                          Marshall
                              Capt.
           Adj. 10/11th (S) Battn. High. L.I.

Distribution as for A/234.

CONFIDENTIAL

Army Form W. 3091.

Cover for Documents.

WAR DIARY

Nature of Enclosures.

10/11th High L.I.

DECEMBER
1917

Notes, or Letters written.

WAR DIARY or INTELLIGENCE SUMMARY

Army Form C. 2118.

Place	Date	Hour	Summary of Events and Information	Remarks and references to Appendices
Reserve Right Sub-Sector				
A16.B.7.6.	1/10/17		Situation quiet. General working parties formed and cleaning up trenches. During the absence of O. Col. R.F Forbes D.S.O also proceeded to Army to take over command of 146th Inf Bde during the absence on leave of the Brigadier the temporary command of the Battalion devolved upon Major R.P. Easton.	
	2/10/17		Working parties as before and arrangements made to relieve 7/8th N'th K.O.S-Bord. in the Left Section of Right Sub-sector tomorrow.	
	3/10/17		Situation quiet - Battalion moved forward and relieved 7/8th A&K.O S.o Bord in Left Section of Right Sub-sector (B'n HQ at H.24.d.8.8) Relief complete 6.30 p.m. Disposition of Coys - B. Coy right front, D. Coy left front. C. Coy supports, A. Coy Reserve.	
Left Section - Right Sub-sector	4/10/17		Situation quiet - Patrols in front line were active and despatched. Patrols moved out and reconnoitred no mans land but no trace of the enemy seen again. Our wire was also patrolled and carefully inspected along the front line and found to be rather patchy. Front condition asking grounds have for evening and day firing.	
Hq A&B.	5/10/17		Situation normal - Patrol mine again out during the night but no signs were seen of enemy patrols though sounds of hacking were heard in front line. Enemy was out all night wiring without line in front of CORONA and also from front loop. No. of a gun shell bombardment on enemy wiring opposite our allies front.	

WAR DIARY
or
INTELLIGENCE SUMMARY.

Army Form C. 2118.

Place	Date	Hour	Summary of Events and Information	Remarks and references to Appendices
	6/12/17		Our night and rear flight goes over inferenced in CRETE TRENCH and Bn. H.Q. Situation work continues where support line in front of CORONA from strong hand B. Towards CORFU. Patrols were out on no mans land throughout the night but no trace was seen of any enemy patrol. At 9.30 a.m a small red German air telling balloon came down somewhere near Guyana at SINGLE ARCH and was not hit by Bde H.Q. Front to-day was his same.	
	7/12/17		Situation again quiet. Strongpoint A & B have been improved by deepening and extending new fire steps also by defensive of CHEMICAL TRENCH. Close cropped hair has been sent to left of double apron were complete from the Railway on its north to junction of CORONA and CORFU. A rifle grenade area field into our lines then afternoon with a message written in German what were passed to 46th Inf Bde H.Q. The single Kandelabra of the enemy was "Merry Christmas — marks peace!" Major R Harwell M.C. which return from leave resumed command of the Battalion.	
In Reserve Billets	8/12/17		Situation unchanged. Hand work was carried on throughout the night and day. Patrols which reconnoitred to mans land not with no enemy movement. Bn. were relieved today by 11th Bn. A.I.F. Night Relief complete 10.10 pm. and Bn. withdrew to reserve billets in ARRAS.	
Bn. H.Q. at 18 Rue BAUDIMONT ARRAS	9/12/17		Battalion in BAUDIMONT BARRACKS ARRAS. Divine Service and cleaning up. Party of 1 Officer and 64 O.R. carrying service for Bde. Winning trades in front line area.	

WAR DIARY or INTELLIGENCE SUMMARY

Army Form C. 2118.

Place	Date	Hour	Summary of Events and Information	Remarks and references to Appendices
	10/10/17		Battalion stood to arms at 6 a.m. being ready to move at half hour notice and stood down at 9 a.m. Training - class instruction - box respirator drill and inspection - musketry instruction - Lewis Gunners and section and platoon. Sunday fatigue to yesterday carrying parties. Permanent party made up of 1 officer and 22 O.R. still with Bttn. morning party at railway cutting H23c and 20 O.R. and 1 officer with N.Z.E. digging at FEUCHY CAVE.	
	11/10/17		Battalion stood to arms again this morning. Battalion is 8'r on duck to-day, time of duck being from midnight 10/11 and to midnight 11/12 and during which time is to work however at 2 hours notice. Training as yesterday also bathes for 1 Coy at Duisans Baths.	
	12/10/17		Again stood to arms at 6 a.m. Training - Musketry practice all coys on BUTTE de T.R. rifle range. Usual working parties.	
	13/10/17		Battalion stood to arms from 6 a.m. to 6.30 a.m. Inspection of all rifles by Armourer Off/Sergt. Bates for 3 Coys and Bt. H.Q. Same working parties as before.	
	14/10/17		Stood to arms as same period as yesterday. Inspection of trained rifle Grenadiers by Divisional bombing officer at BALMORAL CAMP.	
	15/10/17		Battalion on fatigues from midnight 14/15 was to midnight 15/16 was. Battalion stood to arms as yesterday. Training - slow and extended order drive. Inspection of air bags around Bt. H.Q. by Communication Officer. Wire carrying party.	

WAR DIARY
or
INTELLIGENCE SUMMARY.

(Erase heading not required.)

Place	Date	Hour	Summary of Events and Information	Remarks and references to Appendices
	16/12/17		Battalion about to move in mind. Divine service. Reconnaissance of line to be taken over. Tomorrow from 8th A. & S. Seaforth.	
	17/12/17		Stand to moved here until 8.45 a.m. Battalion proceeded from billets and relieved 8th Seaforth in the left section of the Left Sub Sect'n. Bn H.Q. at M.6.b.3.3. Slight snow. onwith followed by frost. Disposition of Coy. A Co. right front. C. Coy left front. D. coy supported B Coy. Reserve.	

Army Form C. 2118.

WAR DIARY
or
INTELLIGENCE SUMMARY.
(Erase heading not required.)

Place	Date	Hour	Summary of Events and Information	Remarks and references to Appendices
Left Subsector W. Div. XVII Corps. Bn. HQ. H.6.6.3.3.	18/12/17		Situation quiet. Have had working parties digging different trench extensions. CONRAD TRENCH, CAB ALLEY and CURZE SUPPORT, CAB and CURZE C.T. have been put in to places during the first and the intanglement generally strengthened. No hostile Patrols are out but transmitters were heard in front although sounds of work could be heard from his trenches.	A.m.
"	19/12/17		Situation normal. Enemy kept hostile CONRAD and CAB at intervals from 10 a.m. to 1 p.m. Enemy artillery not active. Work continued as above.	P.m.
"	20/12/17		Situation normal. Hun put out in front of CONRAD TRENCH. New L.G. position constructed at I.1.a.20.70, for the defence of the left flank. Enemy working on his trenches. No enemy patrols encountered.	P.m.
"	21/12/17		Situation quiet. Normal hun activity. Both authors patrols. Hostile post still looking, interpreters not active and intermittent and lively in postern. I have been to there in places for enemy purposes.	P.m.
"	22/12/17		Situation quiet. During the afternoon and evening hostility felt activity occurred on the front of Batt.y brigade. This has been due to a relief of	

WAR DIARY
or
INTELLIGENCE SUMMARY.

Army Form C. 2118.

Place	Date	Hour	Summary of Events and Information	Remarks and references to Appendices
	22nd (cont)		keeping a sharp look out was kept all night and nothing unusual occurred to be seen or heard. During the night there was an observed burst of fire from enemy T.M.S. lasting about 6 min. Enemy 2 times.	Phm
"	23/12/17		Forenoon Quiet. From about 1.45pm to 3pm enemy shelled CORSE SUPPORT CURSE SUPPORT, CONRAD and CALEDONIAN AVE. Patrols kept in touch. 4.2s and 5.9s. Also trench trench mortars, no squeal. 7th Battalion was relieved by the 7/8th K.O. Sco. Bord, and withdrew to the Bde. support position. Relief completed 7.15 p.m.	Phm
In Support. H.11.C.	24/12/17		Disposition of Bde. Support. Bn. H.Q. NORTHUMBERLAND LANE H.11.C 68.92. 3 Coys at HUDSON and HUZZAR trenches and 1 Coy at LEMON. In the position the battalion found working parties amounting to about 150 men. Ranks on the open. Battn. Front. Patrols were transmitted and arrangements made between 10th Sco. Rifs in the Centre sub Section in the following day.	Phm
"	25/12/17		Working parties found as above. The Battalion moved Tomorrow and relieves the 10th Sco. Rif. in the Centre subsection (Bn. HQ. H.6.A.05.00). Relief completed 7.8 pm. Disposition B Coy Right Front, D Coy Left Front, C Coy in Support. And A Coy in Reserve. Evidence has been. Apparently for the first time in the section Yuletide's, there has been no followed by frost, and the trench bricks are frozen.	Phm

Place	Date	Hour	Summary of Events and Information	Remarks and references to Appendices
Trench Sub-sector	26/9/17		Batn. Code returns up to NORTHUMBERLAND LANE, but having 8/R have intercepted enemy messages referring up to our position of heavy T.M. ammunition etc. The higher HQrs for action providing an holding posts were fwd established. Nothing unusual occurred. Patrols attempting to enemy on hill having was compelled to retire to account of the higher knowledge which made to push their movement at a surprising distance.	
	27/9/17		Situation Quiet. A good deal of snow fell during the day and SAA and Bomb stores had all been kept clean considerably under the threat of knowing the ammunition empty... The Bn. find a 8th Hampshires tomorrow. Arrangements for the reorganisation to be traded a line between posts. Arrangements for the reorganisation have ned 7/8th K.O.Sco Bord on left and 12th Hamps L.I. on right. After Very Quiet. Made had tot handed to enemy which the hostiles to any worn them to the open. Shows up so thickly from these... Trench braids were trapped, shows kept clear of snow and weapons kept upon carried out. The Hampshires referred Lewis... carried about to form. B Coy on the right area which to - on of 10 K.Pa Regt. the was her prime of relieving 12th Hamps L.I. We took on the first line on our left from the 7/8th K.O Sco Bord. A Coy two 1 platoon moved up and took up the Many posts. E.F.G and 1st were then disposed B supported O'Court C left and in support. On eng. 7/8th K. o Sco Bord A Coy in Support	

WAR DIARY
or
INTELLIGENCE SUMMARY.
(Erase heading not required.)

Army Form C. 2118.

Place	Date	Hour	Summary of Events and Information	Remarks and references to Appendices
Left Subsector Bn. HQ. H.6.d.0.0.	28/12/17		Remained in CHICKEN RESERVE to assist in the battalion. Bn. HQ. did not move out to CHICK AVE between the head quarters of what had now become the left subsector of the divisional front. Move complete 7.30 p.m. P.m. Situation quiet. Work was done on improving posts along the front line by night. An officers' patrol went out to establish where our reconnoitred No trace of the enemy could be seen but screams of work could be heard from his trenches. P.m.	
"	29/12/17		Situation quiet. The Battalion was relieved by the 7/8th K.O. Sco. Bord. and battalion to left. Relief Bn. position. Relief complete 7 p.m. Disposition as Reserve. Bn. HQ. HARRY TRENCH H.6.C.16. 3 Coys to GAVRELLE SWITCH B. A. Coy to CHICKEN RESERVE in Reserve to 7/8th K.O. Sco. Bord. P.m.	
Reserve H.6.C.16.	30/12/17		Finding working parties. Ammunition salvaged 120 mm. Generally cleaning the area and forming a Bn. stove at H.6 a. 3.0. for bombs and S.A.A. P.m.	
"	31/12/17.		The same continued. Preparation made for handing over to the Welsh Guards tomorrow. P.m.	

R. Brooke
Lieut. Colonel
Commdr. 10th K.R.R.L.

28031 W3125/M2250 1000m 6/17 M.R.Co.,Ltd. (1367) Forms W3091.   Army Form W. 3091.

Cover for Documents.

10/11th (S) Bn. High. L.I.

Nature of Enclosures.

WAR DIARY

FOR

JANUARY 1918

To 120th Bde 1.2.18

Notes, or Letters written.

Army Form C. 2118.

WAR DIARY
or
INTELLIGENCE SUMMARY.
(Erase heading not required.)

Instructions regarding War Diaries and Intelligence Summaries are contained in F. S. Regs., Part II. and the Staff Manual respectively. Title pages will be prepared in manuscript.

Place	Date	Hour	Summary of Events and Information	Remarks and references to Appendices
Hqr Suppt Bn Left B Coy Left Ahu XVII Corps GAIRELLE SWITCH	Janry 1st 1918.		The Battalion was relieved by the 1st Welsh Guards. Relief complete about 6 p.m.; Battalion billeted in BAUDIMONT BARRACKS ARRAS (Bn HQ No 18 RUE BAUDIMONT) now moved to Corps Reserve in BERNEVILLE on the following day by march route.	M.M.
ARRAS	2/1/18.		Baggage was sent ahead by train from ARRAS and preceded by ARCN S - BEAUMETZ road. The Battalion marched out of ARRAS at 2 p.m. and proceeded on account of heavy frost to BERNEVILLE, arriving about 3.30 p.m. Route very difficult on account of heavy frost after snow. Battalion accommodated in Nissen hut Camp; HQ, RUE DE SIMENCOURT. Huts all double-Nissen, hard work required for some to minimum roof etc. and hard hard tasks all round the lead.	M.M.
BERNEVILLE	3rd & 4th Janry.		There has been some spirit activity in cleaning cleaning up and all equipments taken over and scrubbed. Clothing and boots were repaired, and all deficiencies in equipment clothes and hose great.	M.M.

Place	Date	Hour	Summary of Events and Information	Remarks and references to Appendices
BERNEVILLE.	5-15/1/18		Platoon training. Platoon Commanders took in hand the training of their platoons. Section were Reorganised and placed under Section Commanders. Training consisted of steady drill, open order drill arm swing drill and small platoon Schemes. Platoon attacks on strong points were practised also advancing to Schemes. The training area N and E of WAILLY artillery formation, bivouac bits were also used in the practice. in readiness for field training, and the sticky mud was also on the practice ground by the camp to BERNEVILLE. Specialist training was carried out daily for an hour and the camps to have was allotted the use of "D" Rifle Range at SIMENCOURT. and the short range to have been the Lewis platoon. BERNEVILLE VILLAGE and the ARRAS - DOULLENS road. Training was greatly hampered throughout the period by the very bad weather which made the ground impassable for tactical training. On these days that this mainly was carried out, and lectures were held in bivouac areas On such days have been on Anti-Gas lectures, and Lewis Gun Drivers and Rifle Grenadiers were instructed in specialists, and recruits have been selected. In the meantime of their weapons. W.O. have held a week Lectures on Lectures for Officers and NCOs in the course held BERNEVILLE with Divisional arrangements. Afternoon has devoted to Recreational Training. Football matches have been arranged between platoons and companies, and tug of war and boxing contests take place	

A.5831 Wt.W4973/M687 750,000 8/16 D.D.&L.Ltd. Forms/C.2118/13.

WAR DIARY
or
INTELLIGENCE SUMMARY.

Army Form C. 2118.

Place	Date	Hour	Summary of Events and Information	Remarks and references to Appendices
BERNEVILLE	16-22/1/18		Company training was carried out on the same lines as specified last week. Coupled with field work. By attack Schemes were practised on the WAILLY area. Musketry, Lectures and recreational training continued as above. On 21/1/18 the Battalion was inspected in marching order by the G.O.C. 15th (Scottish) Division. The Inspection was held before taking place on the RUE SIMENCOURT approved by a renewal of the men who had rallied and Coys. presence and inclusive of a speaker of an hour.	[signature]
do.	23-30/1/18		Battalion training Attack Schemes were practised chiefly on the WAILLY area principally on R.S. and H. on two occasions Coopers were taken out and ammunition taken on the ground. Different attack formations were experimented with by Specially the troops were made up of half sections in the march and attacks are made on a two-company front all. Lewis Gunners and Rifle Grenadiers in the second line of waves. On Jan 26th the Battalion acted as Enemy for 46th Inf. Bde. Scheme and took up a position near the PICHEUX - MERCATEL and BLACK Communication trenches.	

Army Form C. 2118.

WAR DIARY
or
INTELLIGENCE SUMMARY.
(Erase heading not required.)

Place	Date	Hour	Summary of Events and Information	Remarks and references to Appendices
BERNEVILLE	30/1/18		On Jany 29th the Battalion took part in Support Battalion to a Brig. attack Scheme. Attack was S.E. from BERNEVILLE and the front system lies the WAILLY - ARRAS road. Information received that the battalion is to be transferred to the 40th Division and will proceed there on Feb. 1st.	
"	31/1/18		Preparation for departure. Battalion to be proceed tomorrow by route-march to billeting area. Ration strength about 9 offrs, ERVILLERS. About 50 O.R. 900.	

A. Stobie Lt. Col.
Comdg. 19th Wpts. L.I.

WAR DIARY or INTELLIGENCE SUMMARY

Army Form C. 2118

February 1918

Place	Date	Hour	Summary of Events and Information	Remarks and references to Appendices
BERNEVILLE	1/2/18		The Battalion marched out of BERNEVILLE at 9 am and proceeded to MAILLY and BLAIRVILLE to a point near BOISLEUX AU MONT where we were met by BCaps & guides and then entrained by HAMELINCOURT to ERVILLERS where the Battalion debussed. The Bn then marched via the ERVILLERS – HAMELINCOURT road to the 119th Inf. Bde. Two Coys accommodated in huts in the MORY NORTH CAMP and two Coys and Bn HQ in MORY NORTH CAMP.	M.M.
MORY	2/2/18 – 6/2/18		During this period the Battalion supplied working parties to the 2 Coys of the ERVILLERS – HAMELINCOURT road under the 119th Bn. the Battalion relieved the 2 Coys of the CAMP. Working parties then formed up north of the spinbrunn north of the huts and were marched away by guides from the Battalion commander. Immediately N. of BULLECOURT in the left subsector of the 40th Div. front: On 4/2/18 men were received that the Battalion were relieved the 1/2 South Wales Borderers in the Right Subsector of the Bn front on the 6th/7th.	M.M.
Right Subsector Left Subsector 40th Divison Bn HQ Nail. 3/6 SW V 25 6 8.1	6/2/18 – 11/2/18		The Bn left MORY NORTH CAMP at 5 pm and proceeded to the Lincoln Relay was completed by 5TH N.W. (B17a) at 5.30 pm. C Coy left front; A Coy Rt Support and B Coy Rgt Front. C Coy left front; On our left was 18th Welsh Regt. and on our right the 12/13 Dn. 9.30 pm. Arrangements. On our left were to rail to LOCUST (GUINNESS DUMP) AT Coy Left Support. Ration was brought up by Rly. and left Coys respectively. PELICAN and PORTER DUMPS for R. and left Coy respectively and held up to Crux CIRCUS U 25 a 5 6 and then also from trench Carts kept up the Hot area.	

WAR DIARY
or
INTELLIGENCE SUMMARY.

(Erase heading not required.)

Army Form C. 2118.

February 1918

2.   /Bruit Vlg V.

Place	Date	Hour	Summary of Events and Information	Remarks and references to Appendices

From ST. LEGER. Standing patrols were out nightly about 150 yds to front of our line and active patrols pushed forward and reconnoitred the Enemy's advanced positions in the vicinity of DOG TRENCH. A great deal of work was done towards this line in the way of consolidation. The relief by the 59th Division did not take place and a move to Divisional Reserve was made to look up the front line of posts about 11/2/18 in addition upon which TRIDENT on the right and TRIVIAL on the left and TRIDENT on the right and almost behind VULCAN on the left and TRIDENT on the right were placed. The Battalion was relieved. In addition the coot on RAVINE VALLEY complete when the Battalion was relieved. In addition the front line positions along the frontier front and a considerable amount of work was done on VALLEY this line of posts.

TRENCH the times the line was very improved. On 8/2/18 about 6.20 A.M. the S.O.S. signal front of the line to the 3rd Division front was reported at a moment along the line to the front. Casualties were normal except for the heavy shelling of VALLEY hrs in our front. A.E. M. Doughall and two O.R. were TRENCH for a period of about 30 minutes. Considerable movement behind the Enemy's line towards amount the Counter-Attack. Communication was through parades that to move to Bn reported therefore the 8th am and one Corougt parade that to move to anticipating an attack. Special orders on trenches being the movements of the 8th/9th and a precautionary Covering the Post-Avon by our artillery as were on 9/2/18. Everything Remained normal.
In the morning of 10/2/18 about 6 am a patrol consisting of 1 Lieut R.W.
Leonor and 3. O.R. proceeded up TRIDENT T ALLEY and reconnoitred the approach to

WAR DIARY or INTELLIGENCE SUMMARY

Army Form C. 2118.

February 1918

3   10/11th K.R.S.

Place	Date	Hour	Summary of Events and Information	Remarks and references to Appendices
ERVILLERS			DOG TRENCH. About 60 yds short of the Trench they encountered a portion of TRIDENT ALLEY in what the enemy has apparently been recently working. They had uncovered a sunken stairs, cupper cut which appeared to lead for some distance. Labour, pumps and trench cleaning apparatus had been brought forward as though they were intending to reopen the spot with a view to utilising Minenwerfer army, or possibly as a sniping point at night. Plans and arrangements were made to destroy spot with a view to hindering enemy's work. The parties withdrew the bomb stores into the shelter and for several hours and although a party of the enemy r/d A Hun returned not to come near their position.	
	11/2/18	About 9.15 pm a Coy patrol ex returning to 2 Coys r/s 4 Skirmisher William and ENNIKILLEN CAMP met ERVILLERS.		Mn.
	12/2/18 – 16/2/18	At 11 am the Battalion marched out of ENNIKILLEN CAMP and proceeded to YORK LINES MERCATEL to Corps Reserve. For four days we were employed on Camp: Splendid weather made but were carrying potato picks over day and special improvements were carried out; numbers and pleton having been transported to the On 15/2/18 when were relieved that the battalion had been posted to 120th Inf Bde and was now proceed to join the Brigade at BLAIRVILLE on the following day.	Mn.

On 13/2/18, 2 Officers and 93 O.R. joined on transfer from 17th H.L.I. 17th.

WAR DIARY
or
INTELLIGENCE SUMMARY.

Army Form C. 2118.

February 1918

4.

Place	Date	Hour	Summary of Events and Information	Remarks and references to Appendices
BLAIRVILLE	15/2/18 - 21/2/18		About 1.30 pm on 15/2/18 the Battalion marched off from YORK LINES via MERCATEL - HENDECOURT and went into No 3 Camp. HENDECOURT, where it relieved the 13th East Surrey Regt which was holding the 120th Inf Bde. On the way the Battalion passed the 119th Inf Bde in YORK LINES. Moving from Camp movement and platoon training was continued. During the next few days movement and platoon training was continued. Inspection was carried out in the valley west of BLAIRVILLE and part shooting on the slope north in the afternoon. The movement of the Battalion involves chiefly of Skirmishers and Bayonet fighting and rapid trenching. On 18/2/18 the Battalion the Bde was inspected by the G.O.C. 40th Div. at the former between the Camp and HENDECOURT VILLAGE. On 17/2/18 the Coys less from ST. LEGER & WARCOURT relieved as reminders by Major Commander Companies	
YORK LINES MERCATEL 21/2/18 - 28/2/18			About 10.30 am on 21/2/18 the Battalion marched from No 3 Camp HENDECOURT and proceeded to YORK LINES MERCATEL. Lt. Col R.F. FORBES. D.S.O LEINSTER REGT proceeded on leave Major A. H. SEAGRIM took over temporary command of the Battalion. From 22/2/18 to 24/2/18 limited working parties 600 men with Officers were employed on the Battle Zone of the Corps Line 3rd System digging and wiring parties left Camp 4.30 pm returning about 2. am. During this period training was confined to Coy Drill	

WAR DIARY or INTELLIGENCE SUMMARY.

Army Form C. 2118.

February 1918

19th H.L.I.

Place	Date	Hour	Summary of Events and Information	Remarks and references to Appendices
YORK LINES MERCATEL 21/2/18 - 28/2/18			On 22/2/18 a draft of 19 O.R. joined from 3rd Infy Battn. From 22/2/18 to 27/2/18 the Battalion was exercised in Open order training and steady drill. Improvements were effected in the Cookhouses & Splendid Walks round the Huts were provided with. On the 25/2/18 a draft of 42 O.R. arrived from 32nd Battalion About 10.40 a.m. on the 28/2/18 the Battalion marched from YORK LINES MERCATEL to Billets at BERLES AU BOIS	79h

M. Dalgin
Major
Comdg. 19th H.L.I.

40th Division.
120th Infantry Brigade.

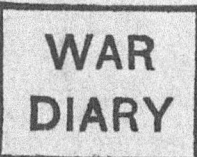

10th/11th BATTALION

HIGHLAND LIGHT INFANTRY

MARCH 1 9 1 8

MARCH 1918
27th M.V.

WAR DIARY
or
INTELLIGENCE SUMMARY.

Army Form C. 2118.

Place	Date	Hour	Summary of Events and Information	Remarks and references to Appendices
BERLES AU BOIS	1/3/18		Today was spent in settling down to billets and cleaning up after yesterdays march from MERCATEL. Reconnoitring parties were appointed and arrangements made for continuing Battalion training. Conference of Commanding Officers was held at Bn. HQ POMMIER in the afternoon.	Am
"	2/3/18		Training commenced on ground N.W. of BERLES — MONCHY AU BOIS. Show, but a more wintry day, but a route march carried out and in the afternoon Senior Officers attended a lecture on "The Front Wooden at Home" in the Y.M.C.A. Hut at BEHAGNIES.	Am
"	3/3/18		Sunday. Church Parade for men of all denominations who wish to be present. No training was done.	Am
"	4/3/18 — 5/3/18		Companies carried out Physical Training, Company Drill, Musketry Exercises. Testing Rifles and Handling of Ammn on ground in W 16 and 17 (Sheet 51c).	Am

WAR DIARY or INTELLIGENCE SUMMARY

Army Form C. 2118.

Place	Date	Hour	Summary of Events and Information	Remarks and references to Appendices
BERLES AU BOIS	6/3/18		The Battalion carried out a practice counter-attack on the 6th Brigade line running through W.17. The scheme was to advance from BERLES to Column of route along the BERLES-RANSART road as far as point 147. Thence in artillery formation and then extend to the attack. 9 hostile aeroplanes on Sunday 8th that will curtail aeroplane observation.	
"	7/3/18		The C.O. and Company Commanders reconnoitred the area S.W. of MONCHY LE PREUX to discuss the attacking and picketing the Second System in the neighbourhood of a more successful enemy attack should he force BEUGNATRE not a mere military position N. and S. of LAGNICOURT. The Battalion area practised the same relief spur in W.16 and W.17. Scheme was yesterday to ground in W.16 and 17, Intention is to ensure that the Battalion could be supported by the Corps Commander with following day, as preparation commenced yesterday, in view of the opposition to tactical practice attack moved up for tomorrow was postponed.	
"	8/3/18		At 10 am the Commanding Officer held a preliminary inspection of the Battalion in fighting order. The Corps Commander's inspection took place first and the attack POMMIER and in a of the POMMIER - BERLES AU BOIS road and General Holden examined the Bde. and spoke of the fighting qualities of Scottish troops. He informed the Senior Officers and expressed to Companies the Bugle formed is to be used when the feet is a counter attack.	

A5834 Wt. W4973/M657. 750,000 8/16 D. D. & L. Ltd. Forms/C.2118/13.

WAR DIARY
or
INTELLIGENCE SUMMARY.

(Erase heading not required.)

Army Form C. 2118.

Place	Date	Hour	Summary of Events and Information	Remarks and references to Appendices
BERLES AU BOIS	9/3/18		B/Ln the brigade & engineers held a Bn HQ PUMMIER and emergency firm moves to enemy out & tactical scheme on the following day.	am
			Bn called orders. Heads of the Brigade have to practice Counter Attack in many positions in the system of ESSARTS and the FERME DU BOIS DU QUESNAY. The Battalion detailed with its HANNESCAMPS Bn Hd Ats Huptuin in Bde Reserve. Tactics were 1st Hp to move up in supt & as the H.H. ATS Huptuin to become not available & proceeded by two convoys sheltered and accompanied by two men Hying aeroplanes flew over the troops had a pink convey a suspect plg his Hying aeroplane on HANNESCAMPS al this point convey from emplacing positions. Divnes what etc. at HANNESCAMPS al this point from emplacing positions. Drivers who marched back to billets on Horseback of the scheme an the Battalion then marched from there and took over Command of the battalion Lt Col. R.F. Forbes D.S.O. relieved from leave and took over Command of the battalion	am
"	10/3/18		Church Parade was held in the morning. No training other than Regm PW. Inf. ATO R Lines Reg. joined the battalion	am
"	11/3/18		Training was carried out under Company arrangements to ground to W.16 and 17. Water from Maintain Reserve in the following day to ERVILLERS	am

WAR DIARY or INTELLIGENCE SUMMARY

Army Form C. 2118.

Place	Date	Hour	Summary of Events and Information	Remarks and references to Appendices
BERLES AU. BOIS	12/3/18		The day was spent in preparation for the move. A dump of old Snyders rifles and ammunition had accumulated & a fatigue was formed in the QM Stores and ammunition held 8.30 SS/35. paraded left at 4 o'clock to accompany. At 6.45 p.m. the Battalion marched out of BERLES and proceeded by BIENVILLERS, MONCHY AU BOIS, AYETTE, COURCELLES au BOMECOURT to ERVILLERS which was reached about 1 hour before the intended accommodation in BELFAST CAMP. On reaching Ervillers the Batt. became SOS supply were issued out to all the Battalion. Signals were promptly in the bivouacs when I was thought forward and the troops kept hard at work dismantled.	
ERVILLERS	13/3/18 – 20/3/18		During this period the Battalion remained in BELFAST CAMP for 3 hours hitter 12 hour duties and 12 hour nights at night. Training was carried on in the area near the camp in the direction of GOMIECOURT and HAMELINCOURT. Lt & Quar. Med. Mr. Littlechild Beverley was also evacuated on 15/3/18 & Col. R.F. from DSO, M.C. took over Command of the B.N. (England) 2nd Batt. and remainder of the Batt were taken on triangle Cab by Major P.W. Jupp D.S.O, working parties were found for burying Cab between MORY and ECOUST & 600 OR on 17th inst. 300 OR on 19th and 20th inst. The parties under Officers were good and although troops had been under a practice for the opening of the enemy offensive no attack developed.	

Army Form C. 2118.

WAR DIARY
or
INTELLIGENCE SUMMARY.
(Erase heading not required.)

Instructions regarding War Diaries and Intelligence Summaries are contained in F.S. Regs., Part II. and the Staff Manual respectively. Title pages will be prepared in manuscript.

Place	Date	Hour	Summary of Events and Information	Remarks and references to Appendices
	21/3/18 – 26/3/18		Arr at the 20th knol: a learning place for Material Unit - the knol take over from of the 3rd Armoured four on 22nd and then transferred one type control over on 21/3/18. In action. See Appendix A attached.	An An
ADINFER	27/3/18	1.30 am	the battalion about 136 strong marched off from the position that had been occupied in the SW corner of ADINFER WOOD and passed the 15th Column at RANSART. The Bn proceeded by road route to WARLUZEL via RIVIERE, GOUY EN ARTOIS and BARLY arriving about 7.30 pm. There were long halts at GOUY EN ARTOIS and just outside SIMENCOURT on account of GOUY EN ARTOIS, The remainder of the day was spent in settling down in huts.	An
WARLUZEL	28/3/18		Day was spent in resting and cleaning up kits, which opened by mail from HENU and Stephen baggage was collected from BERLES AU BOIS. Orders were received to march on following day to MONCHY BRETON area	An

Army Form C. 2118.

WAR DIARY
or
INTELLIGENCE SUMMARY.
(Erase heading not required.)

Instructions regarding War Diaries and Intelligence Summaries are contained in F. S. Regs., Part II. and the Staff Manual respectively. Title pages will be prepared in manuscript.

Place	Date	Hour	Summary of Events and Information	Remarks and references to Appendices
WARLUZEL	29/3/18	7.30 a.m.	The Battalion paraded and if WARLUZEL and proceeded by GRAND RULLECOURT and AMBRINES to AVERDOINGT where a halt was made for dinner. Battalion then proceeded to billets in MAGNICOURT EN COMTÉ where billeted this present.	
MAGNICOURT EN COMTÉ	30/3/18	5 a.m.	Sam: warning order received that the 40th Division was being transferred to the XV Corps. Will a view to returning to the 57th Division on the following day. At Conference of the day was given to leave in the course of the day. A.10 a.m. main Battalion started at 10.40 am for DIEVAL and proceeded via SAILLY SUR LA LYS area. Baggage or heavies BRUCES an extra party followed by 1st Bn transport and the transition halted at DIEVAL by HOUVELIN and BATUS and proceeded by lorries ESTAIRES in Battalions to NOUVEAU MONDE where ESTAIRES and Battalion recommended to billets in NOUVEAU MONDE.	
			SAILLY 9 p.m. During War news that the 172nd Inf Bde was to take up the line tonight. 31/3/18	
NOUVEAU MONDE	31/3/18		Battalion left billets about 2.30 p.m. and relieved 2/5th South Lancs Regt in Reserve Right Bde FLEURBAIX Sector. Relief complete 6.45 p.m. Bn HQ at [illegible] H.31.c.7.7. Trench Strength about 350 O.R.	

signed [signature] Major
Comdg. 19th HLI

A 5834 Wt.W4973/M687 750,000 8/16 D.D. & L. Ltd. Forms/C.2118/13.

Appendix A

10/11th (S) Battn. Highland Light Infantry.

Ref. Sheets
51 b S.W.1/20,000.   Report on Operations 21.3.18 to 27.3.18.
& 57 d 1/40,000.

At 5 am. on morning of 21st the Battalion was in camp at ERVILLERS. Several shells entered the camp causing casualties so it was decided to move the Battn. into the open towards GOMIECOURT.

At 1-45 pm. orders were received to proceed to VRAUCOURT to occupy the Corps line.

At 2-45 pm the Battn. moved from ERVILLERS and at 4-45 pm Battn. H.Q. were established at C.19.c.00.50. Battn. disposed as follows:- 2 Coys. between B.17.b.4.3. to B.24.b.4.7. 1 Coy. C.19.a.1.9. to C.19.a.8.1. 1 Coy. about B.24.b.1.1. The night of 21.3.18 was quiet. Battn. on left 4th Lincolns. on right 14th A. & S.H.

22nd About 12-30 pm on 22.3.18. information was received from Right Front Coy. that the enemy were attacking and the 14th A. & S.H. had fallen back, leaving his Right flank in the air. O.C. 14th A. & S.H. was informed and asked to rally and reinforce his left. The enemy was temporarily checked, but at about 2 pm. further attacks were launched by him and the troops on our Right gave way. We continued to hold out until orders were received to form a defensive flank along ECOUST - BEUGNATRE road. Great difficulty was experienced in withdrawing as the enemy was pressing heavily in large numbers.

At about 5-45 pm. the enemy was found to be in VRAUCOURT in large numbers and as the ECOUST - BEUGNATRE road was being enfiladed by heavy rifle and M.G. fire from the direction of ECOUST, it was decided to withdraw to the Army line. This was done about 6-30 pm. In the meantime, Units had become considerably scattered and the men were inclined to break in disorder, and it was only owing to the rallying of the men by individual officers that order was restored.

No news had been received from Coys. for some time, but they could be seen putting up a very stout resistance about B.18 and C.13.

At about 7 pm. the situation at the Army Line was well in hand and the front was held as follows:- 14th A. & S.H. in Right, 10/11th High. L.I. Centre, 14th High. L.I. in Left.

The night of 22.3.18. was quiet. Our artillery periodically shelled the roads leading from VRAUCOURT to LORY and our patrols were active in front of our own wire.

23rd At daylight, the enemy on morning of 23rd., the enemy could be seen in large numbers on the high ground to N.E. of LORY, making good targets for our artillery. He also tried to bring up Field Guns, these however, came under our Lewis Gun fire and were forced to withdraw. The enemy appeared to make repeated efforts to mass for an attack, but on coming under our artillery and M.G. fire withdrew. In the meantime, our line was persistently shelled by 4.2., 5.9., and .77 guns. Trench Mortars were also used against us.

During 23rd. Battn. H.Q. were at B.29.a.2.2. About midnight 23/24th, orders were received to move Battn. H.Q. to a position at about B.28.a.00.00. On reconnoitring this position, it was found to be unsuitable for Battn. H.Q. and a position at H.4.a.3.2. was considered more suitable.

24th At about 11 am on 24th, the Sgt. Major of "C" Coy. rejoined the Battn. They had become detached during the fighting on 22nd. and had been with a Battn. of 59th Division.

About 3 pm. heavy shelling was heard on the Right and it was evident that the enemy was trying to work round our Right Flank. The attack, however, did not develop.

About 4 pm. orders were received to move Battn. H.Q. more to the right, so a position was taken up at H.10.a.2.8. At about 6 pm. the enemy again attacked heavily on our right and appeared to be working well round our flank towards BAPAUME. The Army line, therefore, became untenable, and the garrison started evacuating in disorder. All stragglers, however, were rallied around Battn. H.Q. and a strong post formed with the ultimate idea as the troops withdrew from the Army line to form a defensive line running through H.3. central - H.9. central towards GREVILLERS. In the meantime, orders had been received that the Battn. was to be relieved by a Battn. of 125th Bde. At midnight (24/25) 24/25th, the new line was held as follows:- 14th A.&S.H. on Right. 10/11th H.L.I. centre, 14th H.L.I. Left. Battn. H.Q. moved to BEHAGNIES. At dawn on 25th, the enemy again attacked heavily from 25th the direction of FAVREUIL, pressing in the Right flank of the Brigade which fell back on BEHAGNIES until becoming much split up. By 8 am, enemy snipers and a few M.G.s were in SAPIGNIES and from personal reconnaissance it was evident that our Right flank was again in danger. All stragglers were therefore collected and formed into parties irrespective of the Units to which they belonged and an outpost line formed on the Right flank of the village of BEHAGNIES. In the meantime the village itself was subject to heavy shelling and rifle and M.G. fire, which seemed to come from three sides and casualties were heavy. In addition to the hostile fire our own guns started shelling the vicinity of the old Divisional H.Q., the shells apparently coming from the direction of TRIANGLE COPSE. The position now looked serious, the enemy having worked well round our right flank was pressing heavily from the direction of BIHUCOURT and by 3 pm. it was decided to evacuate the village and withdraw towards GOMIECOURT. The Battn. strength was now reduced to 90 all ranks and a position was taken up at A.30.c.2.9. with Battn. H.Q. in the Chateau at GOMIECOURT. In the meantime as the relief ordered for the night of 24th had not taken place, orders were received to the effect that the Battn. was to be relieved by 5th East Lancs. and that at dusk we were to withdraw to DOUCHY. This move was started at 8 pm. DOUCHY being reached at midnight.

About 11 am on 26th, information was received that the enemy 26" had broken through in the vicinity of HEBUTERNE, that the 120th Bde. would form a defensive flank in the neighbourhood of ADINFER WOOD. The Battn. being detailed to take up a position in Reserve During the night 25/26th. numerous stragglers had come in, and these together with a certain number of men who had rejoined from Details, brought the strength of 135 other ranks with 6 officers. Two Coys. were therefore formed and an outpost line established in F.1.c. with Battn. H.Q. at F.1.c.6.6.

At about 10 pm., orders were received for the Battn. to withdraw at 1-30 am on 27th to a Brigade rendezvous at HANSART, prior to marching to WARLUZEL. This latter place was reached at about 1-30 pm.

During the operation the total casualties were 16 officers and 343 other ranks.

Major.

5.4.1918. Comndg. 10/11th (S) Battn. High. L. I.

40th Division.
120th Infantry Brigade.

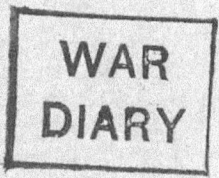

10th/11th BATTALION

THE HIGHLAND LIGHT INFANTRY

APRIL 1 9 1 8

WAR DIARY
or
INTELLIGENCE SUMMARY

Army Form C. 2118.

Place	Date	Hour	Summary of Events and Information	Remarks and references to Appendices
ROUGE DE BOUT H.31.a.75.60 36 N.W.	1/4/18		Battalion in Angale Reserve. Quiet day with occasional bursts of enemy shelling mostly in the vicinity of CROIX BLANCHE. Maintenance and repairs carried out. No unusual enemy activity.	
	2/4/18		As above - Still quiet with no increase of shell fire. Work carried on same as yesterday.	
	3/4/18		Another quiet day. At 2 p.m. orders received to relieve the Right Battalion (1st A.&S.H.) Tonight and overhire by 21st Middlesex. These orders were cancelled at 6.30 p.m. and relief did not take place.	
	4/4/18		From 6.30 to 6.45 a.m. heavy shelling by 4.2 and 5.9 rounds recently of H31.c.1.9 but no casualties or damage caused. Shell shelling of CROIX BLANCHE at intervals throughout the day. Relieved 14th A.&S. Hughrs right 8th of Right Bde in the line - H.Q. at KILLAY HALL No a. 30.30. Relief complete 11.55 p.m. Our position at ROUGE DE BOUT taken over by 21st Middlesex.	
KILLAY HALL N2 d. 30.30	5/4/18		Right Bn. with line very quiet. Work on repair and upkeep of bunkers. Disposition - C Coy Right front - D Coy left front - B Coy support and A Coy Reserve. Patrol from each of front coys report no man's land in very bad and waterlogged condition but saw no signs of enemy.	
	6/4/18		As above - Our patrol again active but no sign except of enemy. Day forward quickly. Hand went tonite on Relieve by 18th Mdd. Regt. - Relief complete 11 p.m. and Battalion withdrew to ESTAIRES - Camp at L.23.b.	

WAR DIARY or INTELLIGENCE SUMMARY

Army Form C. 2118.

Place	Date	Hour	Summary of Events and Information	Remarks and references to Appendices
ESTAIRES Camp at L.22.b.	7/4/18		In Divisional Reserve. Cleaning up equipment and Divine Service.	
	8/4/18		Whole Reserve. Orders to hand over camp to 5th Bn. D.L.I. standing to mount. their arrival. Handed over 2.30 p.m. and Battalion moved to NOUVEAU MONDE with Bn. H.Q. at G.33.a.10.95. Working parties of Officers and 50 O.R. supplied to work under R.E.	Appendix "A"
In action 9/4/18 – 11/4/18			See Appendix "A"	Appendix "A"
STRAZEELE	12/4/18		In Corps Reserve. Allies arrived in STRAZEELE the previous evening. Spent in watching the area. Shortly after our arrival information was received that the Enemy had stopped between the 119th and 121st Bde. Commenced to dig in to the South and East of the WOOD of STRAZEELE and the 120th Bde. took up a rearward position along the North Easterly E and W. to hill N. of the D le PRADELLES (R of HAZEBROUCK 5A 1/100,000). The Remainder of the day passed uneventfully. Patrols were sent out at nightfall. Bombs FLETRE and the CAESTRE – METEREN road but nothing unusual.	

WAR DIARY
or
INTELLIGENCE SUMMARY

Army Form C. 2118.

Place	Date	Hour	Summary of Events and Information	Remarks and references to Appendices
PRADELLES	13/4/18		2 Coys Reserve. Nothing very material [...] 11 am Enemy trench mortars and a [...] to shelling of his morning. South of PRADELLES and BORRE and patrols but [...] 1.30 pm when information was received that the troops were to evacuate [...] about [...] 1.30 pm when information was received that the transport lines were withdrawn on short notice and [...] were ordered to the transport lines were HONDEGHEM. The movement of the troops left PRADELLES shortly after 4 pm and reached the transport lines about 6 pm. Men were then shown their line [...] to ZUYTPEENE which were reached about midnight. So difficulty was experienced in billeting in the dark as the battalion was much scattered. BM	
ZUYTPEENE	14/4/18		9am The Battalion marches out of ZUYTPEENE and proceeded by the COIN PERDU to CLAIRMARAIS where a halt was made for dinner. March was continued at 2pm by ST OMER to TATINGHEM where accommodation was found to billet. The battalion about 340 strong was billeted in farms and houses in the village and Bn HQ in the TATINGHEM - LONGUENESSE Road. BM	
TATINGHEM	14/4/18 — 22/4/18		The Battalion remained at TATINGHEM for a week and during this period the work of refitting and resting was carried out. On 16/4/18 and 17/4/18 reinforcements amounting to about 160 O.R. were received into the Bn. Officers [...] came later on 15th [...] L.t. The officers reinforcements, Capt J.K. BAKER and [...]	

WAR DIARY or INTELLIGENCE SUMMARY

Army Form C. 2118.

Place	Date	Hour	Summary of Events and Information	Remarks and references to Appendices
VAL D'ACQUIN	21/4/18 – 30/4/18		Lieut W.S. HAMILTON joined the Battalion & Commenced at once the training of his two Scouts and the training as Reporters by instructors from the 4th Army Musketry Camp at NORTBECOURT. Front was done in the 2nd Army Range near QUELMES. In addition a physical trained Instructor from the Army Staff has attached to the Battalion and Carried on a Course of training. No further Reinforcement arrived and at present Battalion cannot be to be employed in training troops or to Appear further than 20/4/18 Orders were received to move on the following day to VAL D'ACQUIN.	A.M.
		At 2.30 p.m. 21/4/18 the Battalion left TATINGHEM and proceeded by LEULINGHEM and QUELMES to ACQUIN. Battalion was accommodated in VAL D'ACQUIN in —farms to the unwrap and Bn HQ in the Battalion hut (the village). In the VAL D'ACQUIN training was Continued on the Same lines as at TATINGHEM and nothing definite was received but report to On further Movements until on 23/4/18 when were received for the formation of a Composite Battalion Consisting of 1 Bn HQ and 2 Coys for 4th Mysty Coy and 2 Coys 10th/11th Kings Lish. This Battalion was to proceed to CASSEL and Standing there would leave on 24/4/18 and be employed on the Construction of	

WAR DIARY
or
INTELLIGENCE SUMMARY

Army Form C. 2118.

Place	Date	Hour	Summary of Events and Information	Remarks and references to Appendices
			Reference Map. The instructions to the Battalion which were forwarded into 2 Corps and set off at 11.15 from VAL D'ACQUIN, the orders being cancelled almost immediately afterwards at (L) 2 Corps returned to billets. Instructions for the reduction of the Battalion to a training staff and movement which were prepared of those to be returned on the staff and those to be sent to the Base to amplify on 27/4/18. These preparations were suspended and orders were received for the Corporals Battalion Reserve detailed to proceed forward on the 28th. The Battalion was afterwards relieved by and so went into place until the 30th when the 2 Corporals Corps left the Battalion at 6.15 am to proceed to the ST. MOMELIN area from to a further hour forward. Details of Bn. HQ still remaining handed to SENINGHEM on its absence. On 30/4/18 are been accommodated there in farms. Ap.	

Signed Captain
Comdg. 10th Bn. L.I.

Appendix "A"

SECRET.   10/11th (S) Bn. Highland Light Infantry.
Ref. CROIX DU BAC
  Sheet 1/20000.
HAZEBROUCK 5a.   Report on Operations 9/4/18 - 12/4/18.
  1/100000.

At midnight 8/9th April the Battalion was the right Battalion of the Brigade in Divisional Reserve and was accommodated in billets in LE NOUVEAU MONDE with Bn.H.Q in a house at G.27 C 3.0.

At 4-20 a.m. 9/4/18 a very heavy enemy bombardment of both front and back areas commenced and LE NOUVEAU MONDE and ESTAIRES were shelled with heavy guns. The morning was very misty and it was impossible to form any accurate estimate of the extent of the bombardment or see any lights which may have been put up. At 4-25 a.m. our orders were received to "stand to" and await orders. The bombardment continued without cessation but no definite information of what was happening could be obtained. At 4-50 a.m. the S.O.S was reported from the Right Battalion of the Right Brigade in the line. Arrangements were made to get up transport with mobile reserve of S.A.A. and to despatch personel detailed to be left out of action. In the event of a move forward it was decided to send a carrying party of 20 O.R. to Brigade H.Q. to be used for bringing up ammunition and rations.

At 6-20 a.m. the Battalion was ordered to move to an assembly position in G.33b and there await orders for a further advance. By 7 a.m. Companies were in positions as ordered and Bn. H.Q. remained in the assembly positions subjected to fairly heavy shell fire and at 8-30 a.m. orders were received to hold the line COCKSHY HOUSE POST (exclusive) to LAVENTIE EPOST (INclusive) in depth with 151st Brigade on Right and 14th H.L.I on Left. "D"Coy., plus 2 platoons of "B"Coy., was sent to occupy the front line COCKSHY HOUSE POST (exclusive) to LAVENTIE E POST (inclusive); "C"Coy., plus "B"Coy., (less 2 platoons) was allotted line from MUDDY LANE POST to LAVENTIE N POST; "A"Coy., took up Reserve position in G.27.d.   Bn.H.Q. moved to the Factory at G.27. C N.I.   By 10-40 a.m. all Coys., had reported in position with the exception of "D"Coy., together with 2 platoons of "B"Coy.   Nothing was heard of these 6 platoons from the time they moved off and several attempts to gain touch with them all met with failure. As the Support Company shortly afterwards reported touch with the enemy it can only be concluded that on moving forward the first Coy., on arrival found the enemy established in the line they were to have taken up and were killed or captured to a man as up to the time of writing no one has returned to give any information.

For some time the situation remained very obscure. The enemy appeared to have broken through on the Portuguese front and to have got in behind the front Battalions of the Right Bde. in the line. At 12-20 p.m. the 14th H.L.I. reported that their Left Coy. was being heavily attacked. At this point repeated efforts were made to get in touch with the 14th H.L.I. in the line of LAVENTIE N.POST but without success as the enemy advance was becoming rapid and the attention of all concerned was fully taken up with beating him off on their immediate front. At 12-50 p.m. a message was received from "C"Coy., to the effect that the whole line from MUDDY LANE POST to LAVENTIE N POST was being subjected to very heavy shell and M.G. fire and that the enemy was advancing in thick waves towards the latter post.

[margin note: A.& B.Coy C.S.O. For about 1¼ hours the Battalion remained]

At 1-5 p.m. a message was received from Bde. to the effect that the 2nd R.S.F. were in touch with Middlesex on Left but not in touch with anyone on their Right and that the enemy appeared to be working round on that flank. Meanwhile one platoon of "A"Coy., had been sent to MUDDY LANE POST to reinforce "B"Coy., there and one platoon to LAVENTIE N POST to reinforce "C"Coy., The two remaining platoons of "A"Coy., were now sent at 1-12 p.m. to prolong "C"Coy's. line to the left from LAVENTIE N POST and establish touch with 14th H.L.I.

At 1-50 p.m. O/C. 14th H.L.I. reported that touch had not yet been established and the enemy appeared to be within 500 yds., of his immediate front. Meanwhile the 2 platoons of "A"Coy., sent forward to get in touch, found it impossible to make their way along the road running through G.28 d and 34 a. to LAVENTIE N POST because of the incessant hostile M.G. fire brought to bear on the road and took up a position astride it in G.28.d. where at 1-40 p.m. they reported that they were holding on and that the enemy were pressing towards NOUVEAU MONDE. At 2-10 p.m. Bn.H.Q. was established at G.20.C.7.5. Between 3 p.m and 3.30 pm what remained of the two platoons of "A" Coy astride the road in G 28 d, fought a rearguard action and crossed the temporary bridge at NOUVEAU MONDE which was blown up at 3.40 p.m. Meanwhile troops of the 50th DIV. had been passing up to hold the line of the river and the remnants of "A" Coy attached themselves to the Batt. of Yorks holding the line N. of LE NOUVEAU MONDE. Personnel Bn.H.Q. dug themselves in along the line passing through Bn.H.Q. which was established in a shell hole at G.20.C.7.5. Here the remainder of the afternoon was fairly quiet with the exception of about one and a quarter hours comparatively heavy shelling with 4.2 and 77 mm Guns.

At dusk, in accordance with instructions the Bn., withdrew along with the remainder of the DIV. to a point of concentration at LE Pt MORTIER and the night was passed there with Bn.H.Q. at the Estaminet at the road junction G.3.b 7.5. About 4 a.m. orders were received for the Bde., now formed into a composite Bn., under O/C 14th H.L.I., to take up a position before dawn in A.27.C and d. A defensive position was taken up in the area indicated with details of 10/11th H.L.I. and 2nd. R.S.F. on the east of the road running through 27. b and d., and 14th H.L.I. west of the same road. Bn.H.Q. of 10/11th H.L.I. and 14th H.L.I. was established in the farm at A.27.b.5.1., the forenoon was quiet.

At 11-25a.m. 10/4/18 instructions were received that the Bde., in CROIX DU BAC was being heavily counter attacked and the composite Bn., was ordered forward to occupy the STEENWERCK SWITCH on the Left of the 119th Bde. At 11-45 a.m. the Bn. moved up and occupied the line with 10/11th H.L.I. on Right in touch on its Right with E. Surreys and on Left with combined force of 2nd R.S.F. and 14th H.L.I. At 1-20 p.m. a message was received from the right section of our line to the effect that the enemy appeared to be coming through on the Right and that considerable movement could be seen in that area. Meanwhile our line was being subjected to fire from Aerial darts.

At 1-50 p.m. an officer sent out from Bn.H.Q. to reconnoitre returned with the following information with regard to the situation; "At 3-10 p.m. a message was received "The enemy occupied G.10 central and "had probably crossed the STILBECQUE river at above G.10.b. and d. The "STEENWERCK SWITCH was held by troops of 40th DIV. as far south as G.10.b. "4.8 and 119th Bde. were trying to extend southwards." At 3-10 p.m. a message was received stating that the enemy appeared to be considerably closer and heavy Rifle and M.G. fire had developed to Right and Left of our line but no attack had as yet developed on our immediate front. Troops of 25th DIV. retired from their advanced position in the area of LE SEQUEMEAU and fell back and the line of the STILBECQUE river. Immediately afterwards a message was received that the Loyal N.Lancs. and Lanc. Fus. were being rapidly forced back and the enemy could be seen advancing in deep waves on our immediate front and left. At 3-30 p.m. we were in touch with the enemy now about 400 yds. away and they appeared to be attempting to cross the river on the front of the E.Surreys on our Right.

Bn.H.Q. moved to A.21.c.1.5. and at 4-8 p.m. all available men from Bn.H.Q. were collected and sent forward to reinforce the line. At 4-30 p.m. a message was received from the line stating that there appeared to be no troops on our Left and that on the Right the SWITCH was partially vacated so that in consequence it seemed likely that we might soon have to conform to the movement. Instructions to hold on at all costs were issued to Coys., which were at the same time informed of a counter attack to be carried out by 29th DIV. and starting from the NEUF BERQUIN - ESTAIRES road in the direction of STEENWERCK. Bn.H.Q. moved to A.20.c.1.7. At 6-25 p.m. information was received that the enemy advance had been temporarily checked and our troops had moved forward for about 200 yds. in A.27.b. in the direction of the SWITCH LINE from which they had been forced to withdraw. Touch was established with 119th Bde., on our Right. The situation on our Left remained obscured and we were unsuccessful in discovering any troops on that flank beyond the remainder of the L.N.Lancs. 25th DIV. who held above as far as the B of LE GD. BEAUMART. No further enemy Infantry action developed and at 8-40 p.m. the situation was found to be as follows; 88th Inf. Bde., 29th Div., were holding a line facing S. and S.E. through A.12 central A.10 central and A.15.a central and between this point and our left at the B in BEAUMART there was a complete gap. which we were unable to fill. A party of about 200 Sappers and Pioneers was collected and sent up to dig in on a line forming our Left with the Right of the 88th Bde. and so the situation remained throughout the night of the 10/11th which was comparatively quiet and uneventful apart from small encounters between opposing patrols. Information was received that the 29th Divisional counter attack had been postponed till dawn.

No counter attack developed on our front but early after dawn on the 11th inst. it became apparent that the enemy was bringing pressure to bear on our Right. He could be seen massing in the region of LA BOUDRELLE and step by step the troops on our Right were forced back until finally we were compelled to conform to the movement and withdraw our line slightly in a Northwesterly direction by FROID NID FARM towards the CHIEN BLANC where a stand was made along the line of the thence swung round in defence of LE VERRIER towards the FERME DU BOIS. BY 12 noon this line was established and echeloned back to afford protection against attack on either flank. Bn.H.Q. moved to a house about 800 yds. west of the cross roads W. of LE VERRIER on the LE VERRIER - VIEUX BERQUIN road. The situation remained practically unchanged throughout the day. On the left of our line forward of the FERME DU BOIS we were temporarily compelled to withdraw slightly but the situation was restored by sending forward a small local reinforcement.

By 2-30 p.m. the 92nd Bde. 31st DIV. had come up and commenced digging themselves in astride the VIEUX BERQUIN - LE VERRIER road near the cross roads W. of LE VERRIER and our troops acted as a screen to cover this operation. At 4-30 p.m. a warning order was received to be prepared to come out of the line about 9 p.m. Detailed orders followed to the effect that a Bde. of 31st DIV. would counter attack at 7 p.m. starting from a line running roughly from BAILLEUL STATION to the cross roads W. of LE VERRIER. On this attack passing through us and our positions being taken over by Another Bde. of the same DIV. the details of the 40th DIV. were to withdraw to their Transport lines. At 7 p.m. the counter attack took place and appeared to be successful. Batches of prisoners were passed back through our hands and the remainder of the night was quiet. The relief promised for the preceding night took place about 6 a.m. 12/4/18 when the Battalion withdrew to STRAZEELE. Casualties during the operation amounted to 14 officers and 410 O.R.

LIST OF OFFICER CASUALTIES.

Operations 9th to 13th April 1918.

KILLED.

Capt. W.G.D.G. Rorison.   Killed in Action 9.4.1918.

WOUNDED.

Major P.W. Jupe., D.S.O.   Wounded 11.4.1918.
Lieut. A.A. Bowman.   "   9.4.1918.
2/Lt. S. Duncan.   "   9.4.1918.
  "   R. Aitken.   "   10.4.1918.
  "   A.M. Russell.   "   9.4.1918.

WOUNDED AND MISSING.

2/Lieut. A.I. King.   9.4.1918.

MISSING.

Capt. T. Christie.   Missing. 9.4.1918.
Lieut. G.W. Wotherspoon.   "   "
  "   R.A. Cuthbertson.   "   "
  "   J.D. Cousin.   "   "
  "   D. Stalker.   "   "
2/Lt. J. Ellis.   "   "
  "   P. Hughes.   "   "

H

LETTER FROM
　　MAJOR P.W. JUPE
　　　　10/11 H.L.I.
　　　　　　[40 DIV]

See also diary 6/7 R.Sc. Fus [Pi]
　　　　　　[59 DIV]

COPY.

Sheet 51.b.S.W. 1/20,000.
      57.d.   1/40,000.

To Lt.-Col. Forbes, D.S.O.

              10/11th Battn. H.L.I.

    The following is a brief account of the work of the Battalion since the morning of 21/3/18 for your information.

    At 5 a.m. on morning of 21st the Battalion was in camp at ERVILLERS. Several shells entered the camp causing casualties so it was decided to move the Battalion into the open towards GOMIECOURT.

    At 1.45 p.m. orders were received to proceed to VRAUCOURT to occupy the Corps line.

    At 2.45 p.m. the Battalion moved from ERVILLERS and at 4.45 p.m. Battalion H.Q. established at C.19.c.00.50, Battalion disposed as follows:-

    2 coys between B.17.b.4.3 to B.24.b.4.7.
    1 coy C.19.a.1.9 to C.19.a.8.1.
    1 coy about B.24.b.1.1.

    The night of 21st/22nd was quiet. Battalion on Left - 4th Lincolns - on Right - 14th A & S.H.

    About 12.30 p.m. on 22/3/18 information received from RIGHT FRONT Coy that enemy were attacking and that 14th A & S.H. had fallen back leaving his RIGHT FLANK in the air. O.C. 14th A & S.H. informed and asked to rally and reinforce his LEFT.

    The enemy temporarily checked but at about 2 p.m. further attacks were launched by him and the troops on our RIGHT gave way. We continued to hold on until orders received to form a defensive flank along ECOUST - BEUGNATRE road. Great difficulty was experienced in withdrawing as the enemy was pressing heavily in large numbers.

    At about 5.45 p.m. the enemy were found to be in VRAUCOURT in large numbers and as the ECOUST - BEUGNATRE road was being enfiladed by heavy rifle and machine-gun fire from the direction of ECOUST it was decided to withdraw to the ARMY LINE. This was done about 6.30 p.m. In the meantime units had become considerably scattered and the men were inclined to break in disorder and it was only owing to the rallying of the men by individual officers that order was restored.

    No news had been received from Coys for some time but they could be seen putting up a very stout resistance about B.18 and C.13.

    At about 7 p.m. the situation at the ARMY LINE was well in hand and the front was held as follows:-

    14th A & S.H. on Right; 10th/11th H.L.I. centre; 14th H.L.I. on Left.

    The night of 22nd/23rd was quiet. Our artillery periodically shelled the roads leading from VRAUCOURT to MORY and our patrols were active in front of our own wire.

At daylight on morning of 23rd the enemy could be seen in large numbers on the high ground to N.E. of MORY making good targets for our artillery. He also tried to bring up Field Guns. These however came under our L.G. fire and were forced to withdraw. The enemy appeared to make repeated efforts to mass for an attack but on coming under our artillery and machine-gun fire withdrew. In the meantime our line was persistently shelled by 4.2, 5.9, and .77 guns, T.M's were also used against us.

During 23rd Battalion H.Q. were at B.29.a.2.2.

About midnight 23rd/24th orders were received to move Battalion H.Q. to a position at about B.28.a.00.00. On reconnoitring this position it was found to be unsatisfactory for Battn. H.Q. and a position at H.4.a.3.2 was considered more suitable.

About 11 a.m. on 24th the Sergt.-Major of C Coy rejoined the Battalion - they had become detached during the fighting on 22nd and had been with a battalion of 59th Division.

About 3 p.m. heavy shelling was heard on the RIGHT and it was evident that the enemy was trying to work round our RIGHT FLANK. The attack however did not develop.

About 4 p.m. orders received to move Battn. H.Q. more to the right so a position was taken up at H.10.a.2.8.

At about 6 p.m. the enemy again attacked heavily in on our RIGHT and appeared to be working well round our flank towards BAPAUME. The ARMY LINE therefore became untenable and the garrison started evacuating in disorder. All stragglers however were rallied around Battn. H.Q. and a strong post formed with the ultimate idea as the troops withdrew from the ARMY LINE to form a defensive line running through H.3 central, H.9 central towards GREVILLERS. In the meantime orders had been received that this Battalion was to be relieved by a battalion of 125th Brigade. At midnight 24th/25th the new line was held as follows:-

14th A & S.H. on Right; 10th/11th H.L.I. Centre; 14th H.L.I. Left. Battn. H.Q. moved to BEHAGNIES.

At dawn on 25th the enemy again attacked heavily from the direction of FAVREUIL pressing in the right flank of the Brigade which fell back on BEHAGNIES units becoming much split up. By 8 a.m. enemy snipers and a few machine guns were in SAPIGNIES and from a personal reconnaissance it was evident that our RIGHT FLANK was again in danger. All stragglers were therefore collected and formed into parties - irrespective of the units to which they belonged - and an outpost line, as strong as possible, was formed on the RIGHT FLANK of the village of BEHAGNIES. In the meantime the village itself was subject to heavy shelling and rifle and machine-gun fire which seemed to come from three sides and casualties were heavy. In addition to the hostile fire our own guns started shelling the vicinity of the old Divisional H.Q. the shells apparently coming from the direction of TRIANGLE COPSE. The position now looked serious, the enemy having worked well round our RIGHT flank, was pressing heavily from the direction of BIHUCOURT and by 3 p.m. it was decided to evacuate the village and withdraw towards GOMIECOURT. The Battalion strength was now reduced to about 30 all ranks and a position was taken up at A.30.c.2.9 with Battn. H.Q. in the Chateau at GOMIECOURT.

In the meantime, as the relief ordered for the night of 24th had not taken place, orders were received to the effect that the Battn. was to be relieved by the 5th East Lancs, and that at dusk we were to withdraw to DOUCHY.

This move was started at 8 p.m. DOUCHY being reached at midnight.

About 11 a.m. on 26th information was received that the enemy had broken through in the vicinity of HEBUTERNE, that 120th Bde would form a defensive flank in the neighbourhood of ADINFER WOOD, the Battalion being detailed to take up a position in reserve.

During the night 25th/26th numerous stragglers had come in and these, together with a certain number of men who had rejoined from "details" brought the strength to "135 other ranks with six officers". Two companies were therefore formed and an outpost line established in F.1.c with Battn. H.Q. at F.1.c.6.6.

At about 10 p.m. orders were received for the Battalion to withdraw at 1.30 a.m. on 27th to a Brigade rendezvous at RANSART prior to marching to WARLUZEL. This latter place was reached at about 1.30 p.m.

During the operations the total casualties were 16 officers and 343 other ranks.

       P.W. JUPE,

        Major,

     Commanding 10th/11th H.L.I.

April 2nd 1918.

COPY.

                                        Windwhistle,
                                                Freshfield,
                                                      Lancashire.
                                  8th November, 1926.

The Secretary,
    Historical Section (Military Branch),
        London, E.C.4.

Sir,

    With further reference to your 1918/M/33 dated 18th January 1926, when going through some old papers yesterday I came across the enclosed and thinking same may be of interest to you in connection with your letter quoted above I venture to send it to you, and shall be greatly obliged if you will kindly return after perusal.

                            Yours faithfully,
                                P.W. JUPE,
                                    Major,
                                (late H.L.I.)

18th January, 1926.

Ref. 1918/M/33.

Major P.W. Jupe, D.S.O.,
    Windwhistle,
        FRESHFIELD, Lancs.

Dear Sir,

      I should be very much obliged if you can help me in working out the positions of the units in the 120th Brigade on the morning of 22nd March 1918 and their movements during the day.

      The position of the 10/11 H.L.I., shown on enclosed sketch (which please return) is taken from an entry in the battalion diary, timed 4.45 p.m. 21st. The diary also says "the night 21/22 was quiet. Battalion on left 4 Lincolns, on "right 14 A. & S. Hldrs." The next entry is timed 12.30 p.m. 22nd March, and says the 14 A. & S. H. had retired and left the flank of your right front company in the air.

      Later the Brigade diary says: "at 1.30 p.m. it was "reported that the enemy had forced back the left of the 6th "Div. The 10/11 H.L.I. refused their flank towards Vraucourt "Sugar Factory and 14 H.L.I. were ordered to extend this flank "along the Vraucourt - Beugnatre Rd. to the Army Line.......... "The right of the A. & S.H. was in the air......and about 6 p.m. "they were forced to withdraw to the defensive flank along the "Beugnatre Rd."

      Later: "battalions were forced back to the Army Line which "was finally occupied about 7 p.m. 14 A. & S.H. on right; 10/11 "H.L.I. in centre; 14 H.L.I. on left; and the brigade was in "touch with 6th Division on right."

      Finally: "at 11.10 p.m. orders were given for 10/11 H.L.I "to come out into reserve and for the other 2 battalions to "hold the Army Line."

      The questions I should like to put to you are:

(1)   Did the 10/11 H.L.I. stay in the positions as sketch, during the night 21/22; or did they get up to front line of 3rd system, on the left of the 14 A. & S.H. ?

(2)   When the 10/11 H.L.I. refused their flank, on which side of them did the 14 H.L.I. come; and where, later on, did the 14 A. & S. H. come ?

(3)   Was the final order of the 120th Bde on the night 22nd/23rd, in the Green (Army) Line14 A. & S. H. on right;

over

10/11 H.L.I. centre; 14 H.L.I. on left ?

(4) Did the 10/11 H.L.I. come out into reserve on night 22nd/23rd; and if so

(5) Did 6/7 R. Sc. Fus. take their place ?

(6) Was touch ever gained with the unit next on the left of the brigade during the night 22nd/23rd ?

I should be very grateful if, in addition to these questions, you can give me any other information as to what took place on this bit of the front, on the 22nd and 23rd March.

I am, Sir,

Yours faithfully,

COPY.

          Windwhistle,
            Freshfield,
              Lancashire.

          15th April 1926.

The Secretary,
 Historical Section (Military Branch),
  Audit House, E.C.4.

Sir,

  Reference your 1918/M/33 dated 18th January 1926. I find it very difficult to remember exactly what took place on the dates named by you - but so far as I can recollect my answers to your questions are as follows:-

1. The 10/11th H.L.I. remained in the position indicated on sketch on the night 21st/22nd March.

2. I cannot remember any details regarding this question.

3. So far as I remember the position of the three Battalions was as stated.

4. No. The 10/11th H.L.I. remained in position in the Army Line on the night 22nd/23rd.

5. No.

6. Yes, but I cannot remember the unit. I fancy a Welsh one.

  My recollection of the whole affair is rather vague, but perhaps the following entries made in my private note-book at the time may be of some guide to you.

<u>March 21st.</u> At Ervillers. Bosch "push" started 5.30 a.m. Ordered to Vraucourt - 3rd system.

<u>March 22nd.</u> Battle of Vraucourt - retired noon. Took up position Army Line.

<u>March 23rd.</u> Army Line held. Moved Battn H.Q. to Moray.

<u>March 24th.</u> Battle of Army Line - retired to Behagnes during night.

<u>March 25th.</u> Battle of Behagnes - retired to Gommecourt. To Douchy for the night.

<u>March 26th.</u> Moved to Adinfer.

<u>March 27th.</u> Left Adinfer 1 a.m. Marched to Warluzel.

  I am sorry I have been so long replying to your letter, but it has taken me some time to get my facts together.

  If I can be of any further service to you kindly let me know.

      I am, Sir,
       Yours faithfully,
        P.W. Jupe,
         Major (late H.L.I.)

CONFIDENTIAL

10/11th HIGHLAND LIGHT INFANTRY

WAR DIARY
FOR
MAY 1918

SECRET

Army Form C. 2118.

10/11th Batt L/ of
WAR DIARY
or
INTELLIGENCE SUMMARY.
(Erase heading not required.)

Reference BELGIUM HAZEBROUCK 5A

Place	Date	Hour	Summary of Events and Information	Remarks and references to Appendices
SENINGHEM	1/5/18 2/5/18 3/5/18		Battalion H.Q at SENINGHEM resting. Remainder of battalion found cookhouse and staff attached to and forming composite battalion with 11th A.P.C.	JMK
WATTEN	4/5/18		Proceeded from SENINGHEM by march route and were joined at WATTEN by remnants of battalion. Battalion accommodated hastily in huts formerly on billets. Lt Col A H SEAGRIM proceeded to hospital. temp command 10/11th taken by Capt J JOHNSTON	JMK
	5/5/18		Divine Service parade with R.I.R.B Rev Cummins parade & presentation of medals won by G.O.C. 40th Division	JMK
	6/5/18		All personnel surplus to establishment of training battalion staff proceeded by train to day under 2/Lt Mackenzie to G.H.Q. needed to ST OMER and onward then on CALAIS	JMK
	7/5/18 8/5/18 9/5/18		Battalion Training Staff and augmented transferred in huts and camp.	JMK
ESQUELBECQ	10/5/18		Training Staff preceded by March route from WATTEN when Battalion transport now left under orders of 40th Division to proceed to here. Battalion assembled new farm billets and took to N.E end of ESQUELBECQ	JMK
	14/5/18		Parade weekly R.S.M and reconnaissance of area by available officers.	JMK

Army Form C. 2118.

WAR DIARY
INTELLIGENCE SUMMARY
(Erase heading not required.)

Instructions regarding War Diaries and Intelligence Summaries are contained in F. S. Regs., Part II. and the Staff Manual respectively. Title pages will be prepared in manuscript.

Place	Date	Hour	Summary of Events and Information	Remarks and references to Appendices
ESQUELBECQ	12/5/18 to 14/5/18		Same as for 11/5/18.	
	15/5/18 to 24/5/18		Reference Sheet 27 1/40000. Runners sent to defence position in course of preparation between HERZEELE and OUDEZEELE will continue to organizing same as an area to be held and defended by one Brigade. Brigades, Battalion boundaries and forward positions available for Battalion and Coy HQ. Machine Gun emplacements and strongpoints have also suitable ground and available water supply for transport lines & gun camps for Brigade and Battalion in reserve, and forward road reconnaissance will appointed improvements to broken and new roads necessary. Lt. Col. A.H. Seagrim reported sick on 20/5/18 and took over command of the Battalion. R.S.M. tasked to take over all Claims and ordering works.	
	25/5/18 to 31/5/18			

[Signatures]
Lieut Colonel
Comdg 1st Bn H.L.I.

www.ingramcontent.com/pod-product-compliance
Lightning Source LLC
Chambersburg PA
CBHW080911230426
43667CB00015B/2655